*Esquire*

The

# BIGGEST
# BLACK
# BOOK
# EVER

*Esquire*

The
# BIGGEST BLACK BOOK EVER

A **MAN'S ULTIMATE GUIDE** TO **LIFE** AND **STYLE**

HEARST BOOKS
New York

# CONTENTS

......................

**STOP ME IF YOU'VE HEARD THIS ONE:**

Long time ago, at breakfast with Lyle Lovett and his significant other, Lyle's SigOt got up from the table. Lyle stood. Another guest at the table asked Lyle: Why do you do that—get up when a woman leaves the table? And he replied: When you look like me, you need all the help you can get.

Now, Lyle is a compelling-looking man and this was him being typically modest. But I would posit that we are all, metaphorically, Lyle Lovett, and that we can all use all the help we can get, even if we are hesitant to ask for it.

In 2006, when we published the first edition of *Esquire's Big Black Book*, this was one of its stated missions: One of the keys to managing life gracefully is a certain level of competence. We've always believed that men should have a sense of what to do in any situation, whether that situation is a sudden stain on your perfect white dress shirt, ordering a drink for your date, manscaping, buying just the right gift, leaving a dull party gracefully or navigating the intricacies of any kind of social event. And, being men ourselves, we know that no man is actually the master of every possible scenario. But we know people who know.

In each issue of the 13 Big Black Books we've published, we include three sections that we call The Information. They've contained suggestions for maximizing nearly all the elements of a man's life: work, women, fitness, home, eating and drinking, suits, watches, shirts and shoes. After all these years, it dawned on us that, were we to take all the wisdom that had accumulated and combine it into a single volume, it would add up to something like a guide to life.

What's contained here is not instruction. It's more like suggestions. And the thing that became clear as I read through all the pages is that they don't wear out. Years back, I met Steven Soderbergh, the former film director, at a function and when he heard the word "Esquire," he immediately began talking about the Big Black Book. He told me that he removed the Information pages from each issue and stored them in a loose-leaf binder for future reference. In an era where everything is disposable and advice is just a Google search away, our guiding ethos has been to produce something that endures.

Special thanks to Nick Sullivan and Rich Dorment, who have been the guiding lights behind the Big Black Book. And a small shout out to Matt Goulet, to whom it fell to organize all this material and compile it for Mr. Soderbergh, for you and for the ages.

David Granger
Editor-in-Chief

**A STORY FOR YOU:** An editor at *Esquire* magazine, one who shall remain nameless, has a big meeting at the office one day. A meeting important enough for him to put on his go-to suit as he heads out the door that morning. But just hours before the meeting, he gets up from his desk and the seat of his suit trousers split up the back.

The editor does not panic. He does not flee the office to go waste his money on an emergency replacement. Instead, he remembers what he had just read in the Fall 2013 edition of *Esquire's Big Black Book*: Track down a couple safety pins and some regular tape, and stick close to the walls (see page 109). The meeting and the editor go on without a hitch.

It's with the same resourcefulness we hope you use this book. Peruse it and retain some wisdom. Or hunt down a definitive ruling when you're in a bind. We've organized it, loosely, into two parts. The life (Work, Women, Travel). And the style (Suits, Shirts, Watches). The two are not mutually exclusive, and one can inform the other. If you're reading the Work chapter, spend a few minutes in the Suit chapter, because how you dress for the office is an important part of how you should act in the office.

We've also included three of our favorite essays from the Big Black Book. Consider each a thoughtful respite from all the information surrounding them. Each encapsulates some of the most timeless ideas on dressing, be they for inspiration, for fit or for occasion.

In the end, we all want to achieve big things. Having a grip on the consistent little things—i.e., a working knowledge of how a suit should fit (page 105) or how to pack a cooler (page 81) or how to get through a 3PM office meeting (page 12)—frees us up to focus on the important stuff. Or at the very least, you should be able to save yourself from being caught with a split in your pants.

# CHAPTER ONE

# Work

NOTHING OCCUPIES A MAN'S TIME AND DEFINES WHO HE IS MORE THAN HIS WORK.

IT'S WHERE HE GENERATES HIS SELF-WORTH AS MUCH AS HIS MONETARY WORTH.

HEREIN, YOUR ROAD MAP TO SUPERLATIVE PROFESSIONAL STYLE, SARTORIAL AND OTHERWISE.

# Three o'Clock *in the* Conference Room

BASIC RULES FOR NAVIGATING AN OFFICE MEETING

FIG. D · FIG. F · FIG. B · FIG. E · FIG. A · FIG. B · FIG. C

Be the second or third person to a meeting. Never first and never last.

And then, choose your seat as if you were choosing a urinal, being aware of proximity to others.

Every once in a while, be the guy who sits next to the boss.

What you need for every meeting: something to write on, something to write with [FIG. A].

What you do not need: a drink, your cell phone, your assistant [FIG. B].

ALWAYS: Take notes on paper.
SOMETIMES: Take notes on an iPad [FIG. C].
NEVER: Take notes on an envelope, index card, or other strange object you're convinced makes you look creative.

Can you see what your colleague has written on his notepad? Good for you. Stop reading it [FIG. D].

Only the boss gets to put his phone on the table [FIG. E].

Which is to say, only the boss can check e-mail and texts.

No one can check his Twitter feed. No raising your hand [FIG. F].

Always stick up for yourself, but remember, you rarely benefit from blaming others.

On a conference call, you can push the mute button only once to make fun of another participant on the call. After that, it's just annoying.

Everybody knows you tried to deflect that question by asking another. Still, sometimes it's all you've got.

The lowest-ranking person in the room always takes the most notes. That said, interact with your coworkers as if you all had the same title.

If you're making a presentation, you are more than welcome to simply read the text from the slides. Especially if you don't expect people to pay attention.

THE RULES
OF BEHAVIOR

### For the Bar, After Work

1. **NEVER GET DRUNK** before your boss does.
2. **NEVER GET DRUNK** before your assistant does.
3. **ASSURE THIS** by keeping the level of your drink higher than everyone else's. Or apply this simple rule: one glass of water for every drink.
4. **NOTHING CHANGES** your relationship with your employees faster than letting them hear your singing voice. So don't.
5. **NO TOUCHING.**

### For Office Meetings

1. **INTERCEDE, DON'T INTERRUPT.** If you need to make a contradictory point, wait until the current speaker is finished. You'll be better heard. More important, you'll be listened to.
2. **JOKES ARE TOOLS, NOT TOYS.** Use them sparingly and strategically, to lighten a tense mood or defuse a gathering conflict.
3. **YES, YOU SAW THE BALL GAME.** You didn't, however, watch any political or religious programming. In fact, you are not—and have never been—either political or religious.
4. **NO TOUCHING.**

# HOW TO BUY A BUSINESS SUIT

## {1}
## Prioritize.

The basic unit of workplace style is the navy-blue suit. It should be your first purchase. After that comes solid charcoal gray, then striped and checked versions of these two fundamental shades. The black suit is tempting but should be resisted: Hit men and undertakers are not the businessman's role models.

## {2}
## Spend. Wisely.

The right $1,200 suit, fitted by a tailor, is better than two $800 suits off the rack.

## {3}
## Mitigate headaches.

Sure, the weightless vicuña blends and the fine-as-silk Super 180's look good. But they're also a pain to take care of. All-season midweight cloths feel good summer through winter, and resilient weaves like hopsack and gabardine won't wrinkle on a red-eye.

## {4}
## Maximize utility.

Chosen wisely, the three basic suits—one navy, one gray, and a pattern—can constitute an entire wardrobe. A dozen shirts and ties, in different colors and fabrics, turn them into a limitless backdrop for creativity.

AN ILLUSTRATED GUIDE TO

# SHAKING HANDS

**The Basic**
*Good for:*
First meeting.

**The Hand Grab**
*Good for:*
A warm introduction.

**The Summit**
*Good for:*
International détente.

**The Shoulder Touch**
*Good for:*
Heart-to-heart.

**The Neck Grab**
*Good for:*
Menacing send-off.

# INTERNATIONAL GREETINGS

**Brazil:** Handshakes last two to three seconds longer than in the United States, and Brazilians stand closer, approximately seven to eight inches apart. They aren't shy about hugging. If you have a close relationship, you might get kisses on the cheeks—two for tradition, and a third (for luck) if you're single.

**France:** You'll get the once-over, blatant or not. The French handshake is lightly gripped and one quick stroke. Social kissing, or *les bises*, are common, but not necessarily on the first meeting. Let women initiate this type of greeting. Touch cheeks, but kiss the air.

**Germany:** Give a strong, brisk handshake, then get down to business.

**Italy:** A cordial but firm handshake. Italians are extremely fashion-conscious and dress smartly but conservatively. Your counterpart will discreetly note a fine watch or shoe, but ostentatious jewelry is considered gauche.

**Saudi Arabia:** Be ready for a soft yet lingering handshake, without any up-and-down motion. Saudis of different genders will not shake hands.

**China:** Bow from the shoulders like you're giving a slight nod. Expect a lengthy, gently gripped handshake.

**Japan:** Bow from the waist with arms at the sides. Subordinates should bow lower and longer to show respect. If you're the higher-up, keep it brief. (As in China, expect a long, soft handshake.)

**India:** Put hands together in a prayer position, bow slightly, and say, *"Namaste."* They'll likely extend a hand to Westerners but will appreciate the gesture.

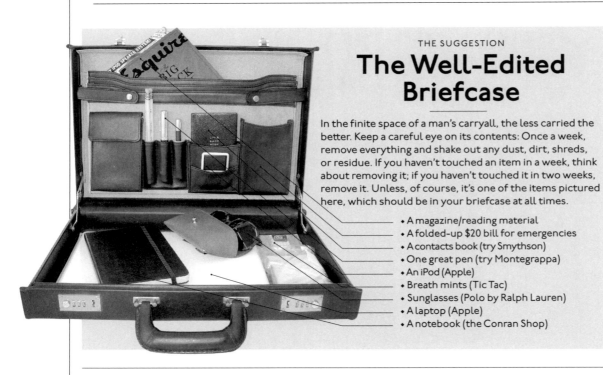

# The Well-Edited Briefcase

In the finite space of a man's carryall, the less carried the better. Keep a careful eye on its contents: Once a week, remove everything and shake out any dust, dirt, shreds, or residue. If you haven't touched an item in a week, think about removing it; if you haven't touched it in two weeks, remove it. Unless, of course, it's one of the items pictured here, which should be in your briefcase at all times.

- A magazine/reading material
- A folded-up $20 bill for emergencies
- A contacts book (try Smythson)
- One great pen (try Montegrappa)
- An iPod (Apple)
- Breath mints (Tic Tac)
- Sunglasses (Polo by Ralph Lauren)
- A laptop (Apple)
- A notebook (the Conran Shop)

## THE EVER-READY OFFICE CLOSET

FOR THAT FIVE-MINUTE WARNING BEFORE AN UNEXPECTED LUNCH, COCKTAIL, OR DATE WITH THE BOSS

1. A pristine, laundered white shirt. **2.** A pair of plain steel oval cuff links: They go with anything. **3.** Fresh socks and underwear to give you an unparalleled sense of well-being. (Trust us.) **4.** A plain navy tie, free of stains and creases. **5.** A home-grade steamer to spruce up your suit in no time. **6.** An umbrella. Because rain is the ruin of many a good jacket, and even a few promising careers.

## THE *RELAXED* MAN

What is acceptable—and what is not—when getting comfortable at the office

[MOST ACCEPTABLE]

Removing jacket

Rolling up sleeves

Loosening tie

Removing shoes

Unbuckling belt

Removing socks

Removing pants

[MOST UNACCEPTABLE]

# The Zoology of Office Politics

### THE BOSS

**Natural habitat:**
The corner office.

**Often heard saying:**
"No."

**Rules of engagement:**
Let him (or her) establish how formal or friendly things will be— if he asks after your kids or golf game, ask after his. If he doesn't, don't.

### THE BUSYBODY

**Natural habitat:**
The watercooler.

**Often heard saying:**
"Whatcha doin'?"

**Rules of engagement:**
Acknowledge presence and answer questions politely, but never open a new line of conversation.

### THE WHINER

**Natural habitat:**
In other people's offices, complaining.

**Often heard saying:**
"I have so much work to do."

**Rules of engagement:**
Never ask him for help; he'll only complain about it to others.

### THE FLIRT

**Natural habitat:**
Happy hour.

**Often heard saying:**
"That's a great color on you."

**Rules of engagement:**
Keep banter playful and intoxication moderate. No touching.

# Create Your Own *Business Card*

**Font:** Adobe Garamond. **Paper color:** off-white. **For the rest:** See below.

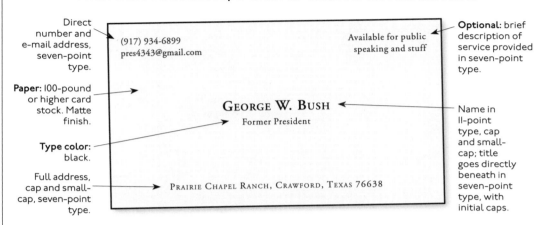

**Direct number and e-mail address, seven-point type.**

**Paper:** 100-pound or higher card stock. Matte finish.

**Type color:** black.

**Full address, cap and small-cap, seven-point type.**

(917) 934-6899
pres4343@gmail.com

Available for public speaking and stuff

GEORGE W. BUSH
Former President

PRAIRIE CHAPEL RANCH, CRAWFORD, TEXAS 76638

**Optional:** brief description of service provided in seven-point type.

**Name in 11-point type, cap and small-cap; title goes directly beneath in seven-point type, with initial caps.**

---

THE BUSINESS-CARD GUIDE

## "American Psycho" Edition

▸ Off-white backgrounds are a sign of good taste. Bone is good. Eggshell is better. Pale nimbus* is best.
▸ Serifs are a classic sign of good taste; sans serif is more modern and therefore suspicious. Preferred fonts include Romalian and Silian Rail.
▸ Opt for a tasteful thickness in paper stock; if your card is flimsy, people will think you're flimsy.
▸ Raised lettering: tasteful.
▸ Watermarks: whenever possible.

*This color doesn't really exist, but it's a slightly lighter white than eggshell.

---

### THE UNTOUCHABLE

**Natural habitat:** Somewhere else. Always somewhere else.

**Often heard saying:** "That was Rumsfeld's decision—I wasn't even here."

**Rules of engagement:** Never trust and never rely on, lest he blame something on you.

### THE HERO

**Natural habitat:** In the office.

**Often heard saying:** "Whatever I can do to help."

**Rules of engagement:** Give credit whenever it's due and offer to buy him a drink sometime.

### THE BACKSTABBER

**Natural habitat:** Hallways and dark corners, lurking.

**Often heard saying:** "Looks like *someone* had a rough night."

**Rules of engagement:** Keep interactions short and civil, and never say anything you wouldn't want broadcast on CNN.

---

## Ten Rules of 21st-Century Business Casual

**1)** Thou shalt not wear a polo shirt to work, especially an orange one.

**2)** Thou shalt reduce the number of pleats in your khakis to one on each side. But only if your thighs need them.

**3)** Thou shalt covet a well-cut blazer. And a well-cut blazer really needs shirt cuffs sticking out the sleeves.

**4)** While you're nice and comfortable in your khakis, the hungry-looking kid in the lean suit is getting the promotion.

**5)** We have nothing against short-sleeved shirts in the workplace, per se. Just make sure you wear the matching hat while salting the fries.

**6)** If you're wearing sneakers to work, no number of big deals or killer saves will make up for the fact that you are, in fact, wearing sneakers.

**7)** No logos, no mantras, and no ironic slogans. Your coworkers and clients do not need to know your team allegiances, your thoughts on the president, or your plan to drink till she's cute.

**8)** Dress every morning as if you're going to get promoted or fired. You'll want to look your best.

**9)** No one is going to trust you to take care of their money if you can't even take care of yourself.

**10)** You can dress like you're retired only when you're actually retired. For now, you're getting dressed for work, sonny.

# A BRIEF HISTORY OF THE BUSINESS LUNCH

## ▶ 1980s

**Your order:**
Three pieces of tuna sashimi and seaweed salad.

**Drinks consumed:**
Three Tabs, a shot of espresso, and plenty of Perrier.

**Duration of meal:**
26 minutes.

**Hot topic:**
The junk-bond mess.

## 2000s

**Your order:**
Chilean sea bass in wine-reduction sauce.

**Drinks consumed:**
One glass of white wine.

**Duration of meal:**
90 minutes.

**Hot topic:**
The subprime mess. ▼

## ▲ 1960s

**Your order:**
Sirloin steak (rare) with creamed spinach and a baked potato.

**Drinks consumed:**
Three martinis.

**Duration of meal:**
Three hours.

**Hot topic:** Plastics.

## ◀ 1940s

**Your order:**
Chicken potpie.

**Drinks consumed:**
Two cups of coffee, black.

**Duration of meal:**
Two hours.

**Hot topic:**
Those rumors about Mrs. Roosevelt.

---

> I don't want to achieve immortality through my work. I want to achieve it through not dying.
> —*Woody Allen*

## Lessons of the Movie Business Meal

### WHAT YOU CAN LEARN FROM THE MOVIES

**WALL STREET**
**Lesson:** Order off-menu to impress others.

**OFFICE SPACE**
**Lesson:** Be kind to your server—people respect good manners.

**THE GODFATHER**
**Lesson:** Excuse yourself before heading to the restroom.

**SWEET SMELL OF SUCCESS**
**Lesson:** Never dine with hacks. They'll stitch you up.

---

## THE GUIDE TO OFFICE FLIRTATION

{1} Make sure you're friendly before you even think of flirting. Attractions and relationships grow out of sitting next to each other, working in a group together, talking in the break room. In other words, flirting with the cleaning woman is off-limits, unless you are the cleaning man.

{2} Sarcastic banter: yes. Frequent touching, eye batting, and inappropriate hand gestures: not unless you want to meet with HR.

{3} If she's flirting with you and you're not interested, be polite but do not engage or encourage her. If she doesn't get the hint, avoid her.

{4} If you're interested in taking it further, take it outside. Go to the park, go to a bar, go to Starbucks. Don't initiate anything in the office.

{5} If it goes anywhere, tell your boss before rumors start going around. The point is to keep this thing professional. You don't want your boss finding out by a wink and a nudge in the elevator.

# The 5 Shirts, 4 Ties, 3 Suits, 2 Shoes, and 1 Overcoat You Need to
# Build a Working Wardrobe

These are the building blocks of a solid working wardrobe.
Once you've got them covered, you can experiment with more color and pattern.
But start out with these essentials and you'll always be ready for the office.

## 5 Shirts

*The shirt should have a supporting role in one's outfit. It's a backdrop—utility is paramount. Keep the color simple and it will go with everything.*

- 1 plain white French-cuff
- 1 plain blue French-cuff
- 1 dark-and-light-blue Bengal-stripe French-cuff
- 1 blue button-down oxford button-cuff
- 1 white button-down oxford button-cuff

## 4 Ties

*Simple always looks sharpest.*

- 1 plain navy (killer on a white shirt)
- 1 plain black (for funerals and cocktail parties)
- 1 regimental stripe (bold but refined)
- 1 subdued paisley or pattern (for variety)

## 3 Suits

*Because you should never wear the same suit two days in a row.*

- 1 navy two- or three-button wool suit. Your most flexible investment, good for post-work and fine for the boardroom, too.
- 1 charcoal flannel suit, single-breasted, two- or three-button
- 1 mid-gray glenurquhart (see "Four Uncommon Weaves," page 107) or pinstripe, in a lightweight wool

## 2 Pairs of Shoes

*Because shoes need a day off, just like suits.*

- 1 pair plain black cap-toe oxford lace-ups, in calfskin. To get you through the day and well into the night.
- 1 pair chestnut-brown, fine-cut wing tips. They go with everything except a black suit—which you don't need, anyway.

## 1 Overcoat

*Well chosen, it's an investment that will last for years.*

- 1 navy or black wool or cashmere fly-front overcoat, knee-length and close fitting

---

HOW TO
# USE A NAME IN BUSINESS

·

**Use a person's name the same way you would a good piece of punctuation—**
to accelerate expression, to pause in the middle of a thought, to reconnect to the subject of the conversation.
Its position in the sentence matters.

·

**A name should be used as an invitation,** a means of pulling someone into the conversation.
Only a mother is allowed to use a name as a rebuke.

·

**Don't put a person's name at the end of the sentence by rote.**
That's just an old salesman's trick, and it sounds like one. It may help you remember more names,
but keep in mind that your name is not Willy Loman.

·

**Greet people by their names whenever you can.** It's polite, for one thing.
But this habit is like a muscle; it gets stronger every time you do it.
Soon you will remember more names and be able to use them better.

·

**When you start a sentence with someone's name, mean what you say.**
Make that name part of a larger compact between you.

·

**Forgive a person when he forgets your name,** but use his name when you do.

# CHAPTER TWO

# Travel

GETTING FROM HERE TO THERE, WHETHER FOR BUSINESS OR PLEASURE, IS NEVER AS EASY AS

IT SHOULD BE, WITH SO MANY FACTORS BEYOND YOUR CONTROL FROM FLIGHT DELAYS TO WEATHER.

LEARNING, THEN, TO PLAN AND PACK LIKE AN EXPERT ENSURES YOU WILL EVENTUALLY

BE EATING LIKE A LOCAL AND ENJOYING YOURSELF LIKE YOU DESERVE.

# The Jettiquette *of Airplanes*

### THE RULES OF CIVIL BEHAVIOR AND DISCOURSE AT 35,000 FEET

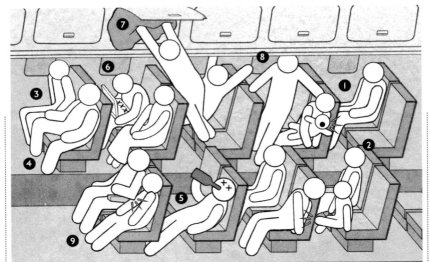

**1. You're sitting near a screaming baby:** Not much you can do. Try earplugs or headphones to drown out the noise.

**2. You're sitting near a screaming/kicking child:** If he's ruining your flight, ask the parents if they can tell their child to stop whatever it is he's doing. Say please and thank you when asking, and if that doesn't work, inform the flight attendants. They will take it from there.

**3. You want to spread your legs:** Draw an imaginary line from your armrests to the armrests of the seats in front of you. Don't let your knees cross those lines, and don't let anyone else's, either.

**4. Your neighbor wants to spread his legs:** If he looks like a leg spreader, mark your territory by positioning your knees just inside the imaginary lines you've drawn. If your neighbor's knees knock against your knees, do not cede an inch. It should take only a few moments of touching knees to sufficiently shame him back into his own space.

**5. You're having a cocktail:** Drink enough to relax, and keep your voice low.

**6. You're watching a movie on your computer:** If it involves "adult situations," position your player's screen at an angle so that you alone can see it.

**7. You've got a carry-on:** Don't wheel your bag behind you down the aisle—instead, carry it in front of you until you get to your seat. Try to stow it in an overhead bin in the general vicinity of your seat. (One row forward and one row back is fair game.) Wheels in first, handle out.

**8. You've got a window seat and you need to use the bathroom:** Exit facing the front, with your back to your neighbors.

**9. You want the armrest:** If you're sitting in a window or aisle seat, you already have one armrest all to yourself. When it comes to the middle armrest, the elderly, women, and children get first dibs. If, however, none of those apply or you're sitting in the middle seat, it's first come, first served. If one or both armrests are already taken, try reclining your seat all the way back and positioning your elbow behind your neighbor's.

---

### *The Unlikely Essentials*

"Due to a deathly fear of traveling without music, I pack my iPod and a backup iPod—other essentials are a passport and my [on-air] earpiece. I'm always one flight away from being on the air."—*Brian Williams*

### The Essential Airplane Accessories

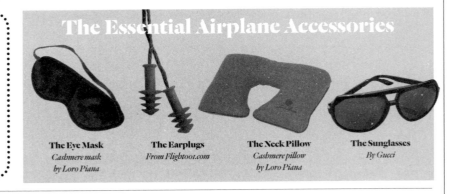

**The Eye Mask**
*Cashmere mask by Loro Piana*

**The Earplugs**
*From Flightoot.com*

**The Neck Pillow**
*Cashmere pillow by Loro Piana*

**The Sunglasses**
*By Gucci*

---

## THE VISUAL ARGUMENT

*The 1960s was the golden era of flight attendants*

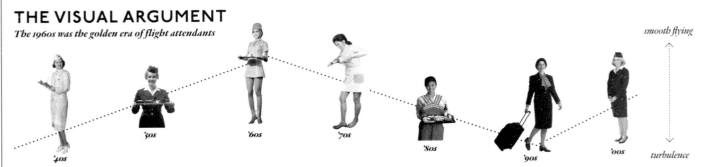

smooth flying

turbulence

'40s  '50s  '60s  '70s  '80s  '90s  '00s

# A GUIDE TO **TRAVEL GUIDES**

**LET'S GO**
**The good:** It offers great money-saving ideas for budget-conscious travelers.
**The bad:** A lot of the information is useless unless you're obsessed with the bottom line, and the whole book—including maps—is in black and white.

**TIME OUT**
**The good:** It's punchy and informed, with the sort of cultural recommendations and independent spirit you would expect from a company that makes local magazines, too.

**The bad:** Just like local magazines, it's full of ads. (When you're strolling Paris, do you really want to go to an Irish pub called O'Sullivan's?)

**FROMMER'S**
**The good:** It's specific where other guides are vague, suggesting down-to-the-minute itineraries for the varying amounts of time you might have.
**The bad:** It's sometimes too specific, and the amount of information can be just as exhausting as it is exhaustive. Also: thick and heavy.

**WALLPAPER**
**The good:** Up-to-the-minute advice on the cool bars, restaurants, and shops frequented by in-the-know locals.
**The bad:** A too-cool-for-school attitude gives short shrift to intellectual and historical landmarks.

**HG2 (THE HEDONIST'S GUIDE TO…)**
**The good:** User-friendly and no-nonsense, with well-informed chapters like Sleep, Eat, Snack, Party.
**The bad:** It's so chic, it's missing some of the stuff you would expect—and sometimes need—in a traditional travel guide. Like a few foreign phrases to get you by.

## *The Well-Timed* **Vacation**
### WHERE TO GO—AND WHEN

| JANUARY | FEBRUARY | MARCH | APRIL |
|---|---|---|---|
| *Margaret River, Australia* Temperatures in the mid-80s, beaches on the Indian Ocean, and hundreds of local vineyards. | *The Maldives* There's no such thing as out of season on these balmy Indian Ocean islands, but February is the driest time of year. | *San Pedro Town, Belize* Timing a trip to Belize is tricky because of the rain and the heat. March offers temperatures in the low 80s and the least rain. | *South Island, New Zealand* Autumn on South Island brings good weather and great opportunities for all manner of adventure. |

| MAY | JUNE | JULY | AUGUST |
|---|---|---|---|
| *Corfu, Greece* Beat the summer hordes by a month and check out the Greek island just as the wildflowers are blooming. | *Cape Town, Ghana* Take in a little bit of everything: beautiful beaches, rich culture, African wildlife, and not too many tourists. | *Reykjavík, Iceland* The sun barely sets from July through August, making it your destination for round-the-clock revelry. | *Santiago, Chile* Hit the slopes during the peak of Chile's ski season. The capital is an hour's drive from some of the Andes' snowiest peaks. |

| SEPTEMBER | OCTOBER | NOVEMBER | DECEMBER |
|---|---|---|---|
| *Zanzibar, Tanzania* The best weather and the calmest seas allow for the best diving and sightseeing conditions of the year. | *Northern Manitoba Coast, Canada* The best time to view arctic polar bears in their natural habitat. (Enjoy it while it lasts.) | *Phuket, Thailand* The least humid and oppressively hot time of the year, with superb kayaking through the region's limestone caves. | *Tallinn, Estonia* Nobody celebrates Christmas like the Estonians. Check out Europe's best Christmas market at Raekoja Square. |

### SLAY THY ENEMY:
## JET LAG

**Before you take off:** Set your watch to the local time of your destination and try to sleep and eat accordingly. The quicker your body starts getting used to your new time zone, the better.

**In the middle of the flight:** If it's nighttime where you're going, try to sleep, but don't knock yourself out with drugs or booze. When it's morning in your destination time zone, expose yourself to light (natural or artificial) to begin resetting your internal clock.

**Once you've landed:** Avoid napping. Some sleep debt may help you adjust to your new time zone.

**Exercise every morning:** A few push-ups help alleviate any jet lag-caused sleepiness.

## THE NE'ER-DO-WELL'S **GUIDE TO TRAVEL**

### You've Been Hurt

**DON'T PANIC:** Assuming you have any control over your situation—i.e., you haven't been hit by a bus or need immediate attention—do not head to the nearest hospital. (They may not provide adequate care.)
**DO YOUR RESEARCH:** Return to your hotel and ask the concierge for a good, reputable hospital in the area. If you don't trust your concierge, call your embassy.
**RECONSIDER YOUR PLANS:** If your injury requires a second opinion or follow-up, think about cutting your vacation short.

### You've Been Arrested

**SIGN NOTHING:** Even if it's in English, you might not be fully aware of the paperwork's implications.
**SAY AS LITTLE AS POSSIBLE:** Especially if there's a language barrier. Whatever you say probably won't help your cause, because, well, you've already been arrested.
**GET HELP:** Ask politely but firmly to speak to a representative from the nearest U.S. embassy or consulate, who can get you a lawyer and explain exactly what's going on. And until that person arrives, again, say nothing.

### You've Lost Your Passport

**GET ORGANIZED:** Assemble any alternate evidence of your identity: driver's license, credit cards with your name, photocopies of your passport.
**HEAD TO THE EMBASSY:** And if you've got a friend who can vouch for you (and who still has a passport), bring him along. He may be able to expedite the process.
**DRESS UP:** Embassies are constantly suspicious of U.S. citizens selling their passports for quick cash, so you might have an easier time if you don't look like a bum.

# THE RULES OF PACKING

## FOR SMALL SUITCASES

Store your miscellaneous gadgets in an old Dopp kit. It will protect them as well as keep them all in one place.

Save space and save your tie's integrity by rolling it up and placing it safely inside one of your shoes.

Sweaters, especially cashmere, should be folded and laid to the width of the suitcase to prevent bunching and wrinkling.

## FOR MEDIUM-SIZED BAGS

Place your lightest pair of shoes at the bottom of your bag. Wear your heaviest; it'll leave your bag lighter.

Your Dopp kit should be slim and shallow and contain travel-sized toothpaste.

Roll small items such as under-wear and T-shirts tightly, then use them to hold everything else in your bag in place.

## FOR LARGE SUITCASES

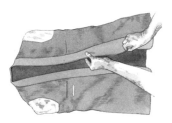

Turn your suit jacket inside out. The inner lining, now on the outside, will protect it from wrinkling.

Fold the jacket in on itself along the center of its back, then once more, until you've folded it into quarters.

Wrap the suit in dry-cleaning plastic at the bottom of the suitcase, so it will not move around and crease.

## HOW DO YOU SAY "RELIEF"?

WHEN TRAVELING FOR BUSINESS AND IN A BAD WAY, LOOK FOR THESE BRANDS:

| Shanghai | Milan | London | Cape Town | Moscow |
|---|---|---|---|---|
| For pain: | For pain: | For pain: | For pain: | For pain: |
| Bufferin Plus | Moment, Ketodol | Anadin, Nurofen | Myprodol or Adcodol | Citramon |
| For sleep: | For sleep: | For sleep: | For sleep: | For sleep: |
| Prescription only | Nottem | Nytol or Kalms | Tranquilyt or Biral | Glicin |

# THE PERFECTLY PACKED BAG

WHAT TO BRING IF YOU'RE TRAVELING FOR BUSINESS

### 24 HOURS

*What:* 1 suit (gray or blue, folded inside out to resist wrinkling), 2 dress shirts (folded), 2 ties (rolled up inside shoes), 1 sweater, 1 pair jeans, 1 pair dress shoes (unless you plan to wear them on the plane, in which case, leave out), socks, underwear. *How:* Arrange items horizontally across the width of the bag.

### 72 HOURS

*What:* 1 suit (gray or blue, folded inside out), 4 dress shirts (folded), 3 ties (rolled up inside shoes), 1 sweater, 1 pair jeans, 1 pair dress shoes (unless you plan to wear them on the plane), 1 pair sneakers, socks, underwear. *How:* Fold and stack from most casual (jeans) on bottom to least (suits) on top.

### 7 DAYS

*What:* 2 suits (gray and blue, folded inside out), 8 dress shirts (folded), 5 ties (rolled up inside shoes), 1 sweater, 1 pair jeans, 2 pairs dress shoes (but only 1 pair if you're already wearing dress shoes on the plane), 1 pair sneakers, socks, underwear, workout gear as needed. *How:* See: 72 Hours.

## THE RESTRICTIONS: Airline Carry-ons

| AIRLINE | WEIGHT LIMIT | SIZE LIMIT |
|---|---|---|
| AA | none | 45" (l+w+h) |
| Delta | none | 45" (l+w+h) |
| jetBlue AIRWAYS | none | 26" x 18" x 12" (Airbus) 24" x 16" x 10" (Embraer) |
| SOUTHWEST AIRLINES | none | 50" (l+w+h) |
| United | none | 45" (l+w+h) |
| Virgin | 22 lbs | 45" (l+w+h) |
| BRITISH AIRWAYS | none | 50" (l+w+h) |
| QANTAS | 15 lbs | 41" (l+w+h) for bag 73" (l+w+h) for garment bag |

## THE BACK-FRIENDLY GUIDE TO CARRY-ON BAGS
*by Steven McMahon, chiropractor*

**Start with good posture:** It's critical, no matter what bag you carry. Stand tall and walk tall.

**Be smart about your carry-on:** A centered backpack with its weight evenly distributed is the most back-friendly carry-on. Messenger bags, or any shoulder bag that unevenly distributes weight across the back, are the worst: They tend to stress the neck and shoulder on one side and rotate the hip and midback on the opposite side. Briefcase weight, meanwhile, should be relative to the arm strength of the person carrying it. If your shoulder is pulling down or you have to switch hands continually, it's too heavy.

**Consider the wheelie:** Wheelie bags with adjustable handles are excellent. You want your arm to be fully extended when you're pulling the bag, because if it's not, you'll strain your shoulder or hip.

**Listen to your body:** Don't ignore pain when it occurs. If you're carrying, lifting, or pulling a suitcase, backpack, or briefcase and you experience any kind of pain, stop and redistribute the weight more evenly.

*For more information, visit mcmahonchiropractic.com.*

"No matter where I go, I always carry a blazer. It is the male version of a Chanel suit. Always appropriate, and in an emergency, when worn with a tie, it can almost pass as a suit." —*Tom Ford*

# BEFORE YOU GO...

FLORENCE IS GREAT FOR ART, BUT WHAT ABOUT PILLOWCASES?
LESSER-KNOWN SPECIALTIES OF A FEW OF THE WORLD'S BETTER-KNOWN CITIES.

## Florence

### BRUNO FALUGI
*Bruno Falugi makes beautiful bedsheets, pillowcases, hand towels, and even lace window blinds.*
51/R VIA PORTA ROSSA;
011-39-055-214-957

### PINEIDER
*For beautiful, classic stationery and leather goods, head to the legendary Pineider. Its business cards are as unique as they are beautiful.*
4/7/R PIAZZA DE' RUCELLAI; 011-39-055-284-656

### CERI VINTAGE
*When you say you bought '70s clothing from Ceri Vintage, there's as good a chance you mean the 1870s as the 1970s.*
26/R VIA DE' SERRAGLI; 011-39-335-839-0356

### ANTIQUE MARKET
*If you like antiquing (and who doesn't?!), head to the sprawling Antique Market at Piazza dei Ciompi on the last Sunday of the month.*
PIAZZA DEI CIOMPI

### SANTA MARIA NOVELLA
*One of the world's oldest pharmacies, Santa Maria Novella was* started by Dominican friars in 1221 and opened to the public in 1612. *Even if you don't need toiletries or candles, you won't get many other chances to shop in a 17th-century store.*
16 VIA DELLA SCALA;
011-39-055-216-276

## MILAN

### G. LORENZI
*From horn-handled bottle openers to Japanese knives to briar-wood pipes, you'll find everything here that you would at the home of a highly sophisticated, slightly esoteric bachelor.*
9 VIA MONTENAPOLEONE;
011-39-02-760-22848

### MASSIMO ALBA
*Alba is not yet a big name on the fashion scene, but he soon will be. His quiet, relaxed store belies the detail and the passion he puts into every piece of his gentlemanly, lived-in clothing. Look for garment-dyed blazers and big tweed coats with a retro feel.*
8 VIA BRERA;
011-39-02-720-93420

### ASPESI
*Alberto Aspesi is an unsung hero of Italian men's wear, specializing in a supremely wearable* mix of functional and classic. *Look out for crunchy, unlined tweed jackets, military-influenced topcoats, and a range of excellent knits and shirts.*
13 VIA MONTENAPOLEONE;
011-39-02-760-22478

### 10 CORSO COMO
*When it opened back in 1991, Corso Como set the standard for the modern mini department store. You'll find clothes next to books next to scented candles. Fun.*
10 CORSO COMO;
011-39-02-290-02674

### AL BAZAR
*Thanks to his flamboyantly Italian take on personal style, Lino Ieluzzi has become something of a pinup of late for men's fashion. It's not for everyone, but if you're bold, stock up on his selection of luxurious yet idiosyncratic men's wear from a raft of both big and lesser-known names.*
9 VIA A. SCARPA;
011-39-02-433-470

## Paris

### ANNICK GOUTAL
*If you can't find a particular classic* woman's fragrance in the U.S., you'll find it here.
14 RUE DE CASTIGLIONE;
011-33-1-4260-5282

### MERCI
*Every bit of Merci's profits—on items like clothing, housewares, books, and music— goes to charity. If you value your sanity (and personal space), don't even think about going on the weekend.*
111 BOULEVARD BEAUMARCHAIS;
011-33-1-4277-0033

### DIPTYQUE
*You can get Diptyque candles in the U.S., but there's nothing like buying them at the legendary candlemaker's original boutique.*
34 BOULEVARD ST. GERMAIN;
011-33-1-4326-7744

### PORTE DE VANVES FLEA MARKET
*Smaller and more focused than its more famous cousin on the other side of Paris, Porte de Clignancourt, Vanves is a destination for serious sniffers of junk and curios. It's not cheap. And it's not uncrowded. Get there early.*
AVENUE GEORGES LAFENESTRE;
011-33-6-8689-9996

### The Renting of the Car
If you used a credit card, you likely don't need the collision-damage waiver, as most cards provide similar coverage. If you have decent health and car insurance, you don't really need the liability or personal-accident insurance, either. Besides, most car-rental coverage of those two varieties is supplemental, paying out only if you cannot fully collect from your primary insurer.

### The Insuring of the General Travel: *Health*
If you are traveling internationally, especially to a poorer country, most domestic health-insurance coverage is not substantial enough for comfort. You can usually get another $50,000 of coverage—including enough to be airlifted to a country with medical equipment that uses electricity—for a few hundred dollars.

### The Insuring of the General Travel: *Cancellation*
Over the last couple of years, everyone from airlines to Amtrak offers you trip-interruption or cancellation insurance. Which can be nice, if you or a family member is sick enough to preclude travel. But how many times has that really happened? If you're spending a lot of money on a trip, consider it. Otherwise, take your chances.

*With thanks to Ed Perkins at SmarterTravel.com.*

## The Visual Argument: A Gesture's Worth at Least Two Words
Simple ways to express your displeasure, no matter your location

**WHEN IN FRANCE:**
Raise your hand in front of you as you bring your thumb and fingers together.

**WHEN IN PORTUGAL:**
With your palm facing outward, extend your index and pinkie fingers while holding down the others with your thumb.

**WHEN IN PAKISTAN OR GREECE:**
Hold an open palm with fingers splayed toward your victim, as if you were a mime.

**WHEN IN THE MIDDLE EAST OR WEST AFRICA:**
Thumbs-up. Not as encouraging over there.

**WHEN IN INDIA OR KOREA:**
Point your index finger and straddle it with the index and middle fingers of your other hand.

**ANYWHERE ELSE:**
Draw your finger across your throat. Shake your head slowly if you are feeling particularly nefarious.

*With thanks to* Rude Hand Gestures of the World.

# FOUR WAYS TO GET AROUND

### Bicycle
*Benefits:* Eco-friendly, good exercise.
*Dress code:* Form-fitting pants. If riding at night, a reflective vest.
*Helmet?* Yes.
*Words of caution:* Always ride with traffic and not against it; lock it up between uses.

### Motorcycle
*Benefits:* Adrenaline rush and thrill of the open road.
*Dress code:* Motorcycle boots, Levi's jeans, leather jacket.
*Helmet?* Yes.
*Hazards:* Hells Angels.

### RV
*Benefits:* Instant access to bathroom and bed. No exercise whatsoever.
*Dress code:* Pants, shirt.
*Helmet?* No.
*Hazards:* Gas prices, parking, the frequent urge to take a nap.

### Kayak-Sailboat
*Benefits:* Works arms, lats, and back muscles.
*Dress code:* Polo shirt and seersucker shorts—this is a no-stress kind of boat.
*Helmet?* Not in a thousand years.
*Hazards:* Rapids, hippos, death by drowning.

---

HOW TO NAVIGATE

# THE AIRPORT BAR

BECAUSE A LAYOVER SHOULD NEVER END IN A HANGOVER

*That frozen-margarita machine churning away on the back counter?* You may wonder about its contents, but never sample them.

*You're ordering a beer, maybe a Scotch, neat.* Airport bartenders are not mixologists. They're barely bartenders.

*If you are engaged in conversation, be cordial.* And brief. And subtle when you turn your gaze back to ESPN.

*The bartender does not want to charge your phone for you,* even if you're "low on juice."

*Your jacket goes on the back of your chair.* Your bag goes under it. Neither goes on the chair beside you.

*There will be no* ordering of poppers, jalapeño or otherwise.

*There's no need to ask for her number*—unless you are romantic and misguided. (One exception: You both currently live in the same city.) Like airport seafood, airport romance is better left to people who don't know better.

*Never ask a stranger to watch your bag.* It's not that you don't trust him. He just has better things to do, like being free to leave whenever the spirit—or boarding announcement—moves him.

*Always pay cash.* You may not have time to wait for that credit-card slip.

---

## TRAVELING MISTAKES A MAN SHOULD NEVER MAKE

- **WEARING** a neck pillow at any moment you are not attempting to sleep.
- **SITTING** in the aisle seat of a train to deter someone from sitting next to you.
- **TRAIPSING** to the plane's bathroom in your socks. You've seen those floors.
- **RECLINING** your seat farther than you truly need to be comfortable.
- **ATTEMPTING** to prevent the person in front of you from fully reclining his seat. Yes, you're tall. Not his problem.
- **CONCERNING** yourself with whether or not liquids are out of your carry-on and in a separate plastic bag for security. No one does this anymore.

# Where to go?

FIND THE TYPE OF PERSON MOST LIKE YOU TO DISCOVER YOUR NEXT VACATION

## THE Relaxer

*You could go a whole day without seeing another person. (Except for your lovely wife, of course.) You are not stressed without a schedule. You prefer a good view to a TV, a beer to a cocktail, and a beach to a city. You are not uncomfortable with the idea of being assigned a personal vacation assistant.*

**YOUR DESTINATION: IXTAPA, MEXICO**
**YOUR BUDGET: $5,000**

A small town on Mexico's southwestern coast, Ixtapa has the beauty of Mexico's better-known destinations but fewer crowds. Stay at the lush and secluded Capella Ixtapa, a cliffside resort and spa that offers horseback riding and deep-sea fishing. Every room features a large balcony and an infinity plunge pool overlooking the Pacific. Hop on a hotel bike for a short ride to the beach. Just be sure to be back in time for the daily guac and beer that's delivered to your room.

## THE Athlete

*You'd prefer that every moment of your day be filled with adrenaline. Bungee jumping and hang gliding sound like good ways to relax. You enjoy riding in a boat, but would much rather be skiing behind it. While you have never said YOLO in earnest, you do believe in the general principle.*

**YOUR DESTINATION: QUEENSTOWN, NEW ZEALAND**
**YOUR BUDGET: $12,000**

New Zealand is home to some of the Southern Hemisphere's best ski resorts, and the Matakauri Lodge in Queenstown is within 35 miles of six of them. When you've worn yourself out, head back to the lodge, where deluxe suites have mountain and lake views, balconies, and your very own fireplace—in case a Scotch isn't quite enough to thaw you out.

## THE Tourist

*You've taken a lot of photos, including one in which you "held up" the Leaning Tower of Pisa. You don't mind crowds. You need an activity to stay entertained. If given the choice, you would never eat at the same restaurant more than once. You like Italian food. And Italians.*

**YOUR DESTINATION: CAPRI, ITALY**
**YOUR BUDGET: $10,000**

The island of Capri may have huge crowds, but it also has some of the best food, shopping, and vistas anywhere in the world. Stay in one of the Sea View suites at the Hotel Caesar Augustus, the mansion of a former Russian prince, for a view of Mount Vesuvius and the stunning Bay of Naples, with water so blue you'll wonder how it's real. When you tire of the tourists, pack a day bag (and plenty of water) and take off on one of the island's many backcountry trails. Just stay away from the ledges.

## THE Off-Peaker

*You love urban life. When you're not in New York City, it's because you went to dinner in Brooklyn. You enjoy shopping, the theater, and walking around without a plan. You occasionally comment on the beauty of architecture. You don't mind seeing a place without its usual bustle. In fact, you prefer it, because you can get restaurant reservations more easily.*

**YOUR DESTINATION: BUENOS AIRES, ARGENTINA**
**YOUR BUDGET: $6,000**

Northern Hemisphere cities like New York, London, and Paris can be miserable in the summer—hot, humid, and reeking of smells you don't want to identify. In Buenos Aires, the average high in July is just under 60 degrees. You get all the great dining, art, and exploring the city has to offer, but with a pleasant temperature and smaller crowds. Stay at the Palacio Duhau Park Hyatt, a spectacular classic hotel with modern finishes. Ditch the car and borrow one of the hotel's bikes for a ride around the city. Or maybe stay back and learn to tango.

# A VACATION FROM...

### CARS

Venice, Italy; *Mdina, Malta;* Fez, Morocco; *Hydra, Saronic Gulf Islands, Greece;* Cinque Terre, Italy; *Princes' Islands, Istanbul, Turkey;* Mackinac Island, Michigan; *Fire Island, New York.*

### CLOTHES

Cap d'Agde, France; *Platja d'Es Cavallet, Ibiza, Spain;* Saline Beach, St. Barts; *Plage de Tahiti, St.-Tropez, France;* Little Beach, Maui, Hawaii; *and, oh, yeah, Gunnison Beach, New Jersey.*

### FRESH AIR

Ski Dubai, an indoor ski resort; *CityCenter, the multi-structure, 67-acre indoor complex in Las Vegas;* a Virgin Galactic shuttle, outer space; *the honeymoon suite at the hotel nearest you.*

---

## The Lazy Consumer's Guide to Exchange Rates*

*You're shopping in the countries below and the price tag reads 100. Here's what it means for your wallet.*

| | |
|---|---:|
| European Union | 100 euros = $135 |
| Great Britain | 100 pounds = $159 |
| Hong Kong | 100 hk dollars = $13 |
| Japan | 100 yen = $1.20 |
| China | 100 yuan = $15 |
| India | 100 rupees = $2.20 |

\* Subject to change. But then you knew that.

---

## THE GREAT SHOPPING DESTINATIONS OF THE WORLD

### HIGH END

Savile Row, London
Madison Avenue, New York
Rue du Faubourg St.-Honoré, Paris
Via Montenapoleone, Milan
Via Condotti, Rome
Nanjing Road, Shanghai
Bahnhofstrasse, Zurich
Tretyakovsky Proyezd, Moscow

### LOW END

The Grand Bazaar, Istanbul
The souks, Marrakech
Naschmarkt, Vienna
El Rastro, Madrid
Porte de Clignancourt, Paris
Chatuchak Weekend Market, Bangkok
Stanley Market, Hong Kong

---

## OTHER PLACES *To Crash*

### THE PROS AND CONS OF ALTERNATIVES TO HOTELS

### B&B

PROS: Well, there's a bed. And breakfast! (Often served communally.) Plus: maid service, wake-up calls, easy to get a taxi to the airport.

CONS: *Did we mention the breakfast, i.e., early-morning meals that are often taken in the company of fellow B&Bers? Also, could be awkward should you have nighttime visitors.*

### Rental

PROS: Save money by cooking at home; more privacy for decadence (or peace and quiet); a sense of independence; you can throw dinner parties; multiple rooms.

CONS: *Strangers' creepy personal belongings (photos, half-used condiments); cleaning up after yourself; no towel, maid, or room service; the place is never as big as it looks on Craigslist; if there's a problem with air-conditioning, you can't change rooms; friends wanting to crash for free.*

### Time-Share

PROS: The peace of mind of knowing it's out there; no worries about footing the mortgage solo.

CONS: *Having a specific window for when you can go to your own vacation home; maintaining civility with time-sharing partners; everyone wants to use it for holidays.*

### A Second Home

PROS: Stock it with vacation clothes, so no need to bring tons of luggage; feeling like you've made it by owning a second home; if you separate from your spouse, you always have a place to go.

CONS: *Property value could go down; a slew of monthly bills (mortgage, water, gas, cleaning, lawn service); feeling guilty, as if you're cheating if you ever go somewhere else for vacation.*

---

## *Taxis Round the World*

### London
Tip: Round up to the whole pound, or 10 percent.
*Exit cab and pay outside. For an unmetered minicab, ask for fare beforehand.*

### Moscow
Tip: 10 percent.
*Price negotiated with driver or set beforehand; no meters. It's highly recommended that you not take a gypsy cab, and either find a taxi in front of a hotel or phone one up.*

### Oslo
Tip: No tipping required.
*But taxi drivers expect a small tip if they handle heavy luggage. Everything costs a lot because the service is built in.*

### New York
Tip: 10 to 15 percent.
*For unmetered livery cabs, ask for fare beforehand. For yellow cabs, the center light on means available; the center light off means taken; and if the two lights flanking the center light are illuminated, it's off duty.*

### Paris
Tip: Not usually given.
*But for outstanding service, a euro or two is fine. Cars occasionally stop when hailed, but mostly you have to queue at a stand.*

### Cairo
Tip: 5 to 10 percent.
*Solo men sit in front with drivers, solo women in back. Black-and-white cabs are unmetered hoopties. Yellow cabs are metered—and air-conditioned—but hard to track down on the street. Try to book by phone.*

### Milan
Tip: Round up to the nearest euro.
*Usually found at a taxi stand, rarely hailed on streets, but they might stop if empty.*

### DIVE IN SAFELY
The far edge of the deep end is safest, but as long as you're careful and you've checked that the depth is greater than nine feet, you're okay diving off the sides. And save the backflips for the diving board, Louganis.

### CHECK OUT WOMEN WITHOUT GETTING CAUGHT
Sunglasses with dark (i.e., non-gradient) lenses, for starters—and reserve said checking out for women who are near something else you could feasibly be observing. A plant, maybe. Or a menacing bird.

### REDUCE YOUR SPLASH
Raise your arms above your head, but rather than pointing your fingers, flatten your palms and join them together to create a kind of hand shield. Dive in, hands first, and your palms will help break the surface tension of the water, minimizing splash.

### SMOKE A CIGARETTE CONSIDERATELY
Figure out which way the wind is blowing and position yourself downwind from your neighbors. Puff away, and deposit your butt in the nearest trash receptacle.

### ENGAGE IN RESPECTABLE HORSEPLAY
Keep the splashing around to a minimum, and limited to your party. Dunking of heads is best kept quick and painless; no more than three seconds or panic will ensue.

### PEE IN A POOL WITHOUT GETTING CAUGHT
Don't, for starters, unless a legitimate bathroom isn't an option. Then, and only then, should you find the filter along the edge of the pool and make your way toward it. Do your business.

## THE *Beach Bag*

- **The bag:** A tote that provides easy access to whatever you need.
- **The towel:** Terry cloth or plush cotton. Bold stripes or pattern. Any color.
- **The shades:** Dark, polarized lenses to protect your eyes from harmful rays.
- **The sunscreen:** The kind with UVA *and* UVB protection. Make sure to apply to face to avoid sunglass lines.
- **The MP3 player:** Or iWhatever. You need music, man.
- **The footwear:** Flip-flops.
- **Etc.:** Bottle of water, reading material, waterproof wallet, bocce balls.

*Bag by Jack Spade. Towel by J. Crew. Flip-flops by Coach. Sunglasses by Paul Smith. Sunscreen by Dermalogica.*

> "Get a sun lamp to keep you looking as if you have just come back from somewhere expensive."
> —*Aristotle Onassis*

# A (Healthier) Day at the Beach

*What were once relaxing activities can now become parts of a rigorous full-body workout.*

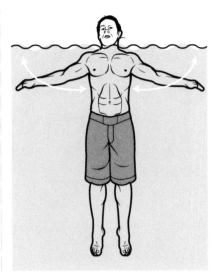

**1. WHEN YOU TOSS** a football, do it in shallow water. The resistance works your legs harder.

**2. PLAY SPORTS LIKE** Kadima or volleyball on the dry sand for a better calf-and-foot workout. Use your nondominant hand. This will challenge your brain (and your ability to throw like a man).

**3. GO OUT IN** the water where you can't touch. Tread water using only your arms.

# How to Take a Picture in the Sun

• Shoot in the late afternoon, when the light is softer and you get more pleasing, sculpting shadows.
• Stand between the sun and what you're shooting. Ideally, the sun should be at your back, about 30 degrees off to one side.
• If you're on the beach and you have a dark blanket, lay it in front of your subject (out of the shot) to cut down on reflected light.
• For a moodier look, close your aperture one to two stops, making the background more of a blur.
• Make sure your subject's hands are doing something. Even something simple like swinging, brushing hair, or holding a beer.

*With thanks to Michael Dweck, photographer, whose work includes the books* Habana Libre *and* The End: Montauk, N.Y. *and the photo above.*

# HOW TO WEAR SHORTS

*The basic rules of showing leg*

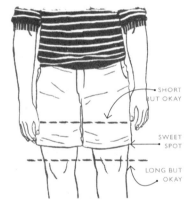

SHORT BUT OKAY

SWEET SPOT

LONG BUT OKAY

→ There is no single prescribed length for shorts, but there is a clear sweet spot: an inch above your kneecap. Consider it a starting point, and add or subtract from there based on your comfort level with your body.

If you are of thick leg or small stature, shorts that hit higher on the thigh will stretch you out a bit. (In order to avoid confusing bulges, the shorter your shorts, the fewer things you'll want to carry in your pockets.) If you are tall or have thin legs, the opposite is true—your shorts should fall closer to your knee. The longer they are, the more fitted they should be. You should also consider a cuff, which will give the illusion of heft. And unless you're actively harvesting clams, it's never okay to go past the knee.

## THE PERFECT BEACH DRINK

### THE CALIMOCHO

Coke and red wine make a perfectly delightful combination when mixed about 50-50 and well iced. The wine cuts the sweetness of the Coke, and the Coke adds zing to the wine. And it travels. Easily. —DAVID WONDRICH

TO PREPARE:
Take a 1.5-liter bottle of Coke and pour out half. Pour in one 750-milliliter bottle of dry (and cheap) red wine. Seal the bottle. Dispense into red Solo cups full of ice. Repeat.

## THE IDEAL BEACH SETUP
*Because a six-pack and a blanket just don't cut it anymore*

**1.**
An 8-by-8 sun shelter provides more shade than an umbrella. And unlike a tent, it won't get blown over in the wind.

**2.**
Lugging your gear to the beach should take no more than one trip from the car. **Rio's Hi-Tech Textilene Backpack Cooler chair** can be carried on your back, freeing up your hands for more important, drinkable things.

**3.**
**Dunhill's solar charger** packs 30 hours of charge time, but costs almost as much as the gadgets you'll charge with it. Keep an eye on it.

**4.**
The beanbag toss of beach games, **ladder golf** is kind of like lawn darts, if lawn darts were played with Eskimo yo-yos.

**5.**
You'll need a book— something light and entertaining that you can easily pick up at any time, like **Vengeance**, a collection of short stories about vigilante justice from Dennis Lehane, Karin Slaughter, and others.

**6.**
The **Coleman 50-quart wheeled Xtreme 6 cooler** purports to stay cool for six days, even in 90-degree heat.

---

## JUST SAY **NO**
*Where you'll find the harshest drug laws, from extensive jail time to death sentences*

| | | | |
|---|---|---|---|
| China | ☠ | Philippines | ⚷ |
| Indonesia | ☠ | Singapore | ☠ |
| United Arab Emirates | ☠ | Saudi Arabia | ☠ |
| Iran | ☠ | Sri Lanka | ☠ |
| Laos | ☠ | Thailand | ☠ |
| Malaysia | ⚷ | Tunisia | ⚷ |
| Morocco | ⚷ | Vietnam | ☠ |
| Oman | ☠ | | |

☠ = *DEATH PENALTY*    ⚷ = *JAIL TIME*

### (OTHER) *Local Delicacies*
*Where to enjoy narcotics in peace*

**Mexico:** As of 2009, no jail time or fines for small amounts of major narcotics.

**Portugal:** Since 2001, drugs have been decriminalized for personal use, possession, or acquisition. You are allowed to have up to a ten-day supply.

**Holland:** Marijuana is technically illegal, but those laws are famously not enforced in designated cafés, and police make no arrests for small amounts in possession. The country is moving forward with banning tourists from the cafés, however, so do some research before you go. Since 2007, there has been a ban on hallucinogenic mushrooms.

**Czech Republic:** Drug use legal since 1990; possession is still technically illegal, but law mostly not enforced.

---

HOW TO BE
# OUTSIDE
Solutions to outdoor situations
a man may face this summer

**THE SUN IS OUT:**
Unless you had horrible parents, we're not the first to tell you: Put on sunscreen. You want one that protects you from UVA rays, which age your skin, and UVB, which cook it. The American Academy of Dermatology recommends an SPF of at least 30, applied 15 minutes before going outside and every two hours after that. And don't forget your scalp. A few hair products even have SPF built in.

**THE SUN IS NOT OUT:**
Clouds block as little as 20 percent of UV rays. See above.

**A MAN HAS ASKED YOU TO "GET HIS BACK":**
If the man is a stranger, it's best to move on. If not—and if there's no one around with whom he might have a closer relationship—oblige him. You may need the favor repaid at some point.

**YOUR DEODORANT DOESN'T SEEM TO BE WORKING:**
As discreetly as you can, dry your armpits with something you won't need again: a paper towel or someone else's T-shirt. Removing the sweat reduces smelly bacteria.

**YOU HAVE A HAIRY BACK:**
If it's a special occasion (honeymoon, work picnic, reality-TV audition), four weeks before any expected disrobing, visit a spa for a wax. A few days after, scrub your back with a washcloth to limit clogged pores and breakouts, which look a lot worse than a backful of hair.

**YOU PLAN ON GOING BAREFOOT:** You need only two things—a pumice stone and some moisturizer—and two minutes of effort. Use the pumice stone to rub the dead skin from your heels, then apply moisturizer. And trim your nails. If you see any signs of fungus, do the right thing: Wear shoes.

**SOMEONE MENTIONS YOUR CALF IMPLANTS:**
Soak up the attention.

# Don't Forget to Try *The Crack Seed*

### ADVENTURES IN EATING LIKE A LOCAL

| HONOLULU, HAWAII | ST.-RÉMY, FRANCE | MARRAKECH, MOROCCO | BUENOS AIRES, ARGENTINA |
|---|---|---|---|
| ***Street food:*** Taro chunks and salmon belly wrapped in a leaf. | ***Street food:*** Grab a pissaladière, a pizzalike treat usually topped with caramelized onions, olives, and anchovies. | ***Street food:*** One can find babouche, or boiled snails, at street vendors across the city. | ***Street food:*** Head to a parilla for a hot-off-the-grill choripan (sausage sandwich) with chimichurri sauce. |
| ***Beer:*** Kona Brewing Company has been Hawaii's go-to microbrewery since 1996. Try the Longboard Lager. | ***Beer:*** Red wine. Local. | ***Beer:*** Flag Spéciale. | ***Beer:*** Antares Porter, a dark and delicious local brew. |
| ***Dessert:*** Malasadas, a Portuguese-inspired deep-fried beignet. | ***Dessert:*** Calisson, a frosting-topped marzipan wafer that supposedly helped stave off plague in the 17th century. | ***Dessert:*** Mouhalabieh, a traditional orange-flavored cream. | ***Dessert:*** It's hard to find a menu without dulce de leche and flan. Go for it. |
| ***And don't forget to try:*** Crack seed; it's dehydrated and preserved fruit, and the locals love it. | ***And don't forget to try:*** Brandade, a paste made of salted cod and olive oil. Some people like it; most of them are French. | ***And don't forget to try:*** Pastilla, a doughy delicacy filled with shredded pigeon (sometimes chicken), egg, and almonds and topped with sugary icing. The only pigeon-based dessert you'll ever eat. | ***And don't forget to try:*** All that amazing local wine. |

## THE ENDORSEMENT
### *Luggage Tags*

A luggage tag may seem unimportant—a small square of leather that you most likely won't check the next time you grab your bag from the carousel. It might even seem unnecessary, since every airline gives out paper tags at the counter. But nothing cheapens a beautiful bag faster than adding that ratty cardstock rectangle, notched and fading and clinging meekly to your suitcase by an elastic band the width of a thread. Respect your bag—and yourself. Buy something nice. Something worthy of the both of you.

# Planes, Trains, and Automobiles

### STYLING SUGGESTIONS FOR A MAN ON THE MOVE

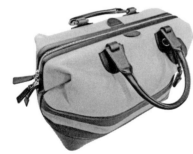

### Plane

***What you're wearing:*** Loafers, the better to slip on and off at security; a fitted but unstructured jacket to stow all the essentials, and keep the rest of your clothes loose—a polo or T-shirt, sweater, and khakis.

***Luggage restrictions:*** Just a few. Check with the airline for potential charges and restrictions, and never underestimate the good horse sense of FedExing your bags to your destination before you leave.

***Suggested piece of luggage:*** Something that will fit in an overhead bin.

*Polycarbonate trunk by Rimowa.*

### Train

***What you're wearing:*** Whatever you please, though it's the least climate controlled of all these options. Make allowances for changes in outside temperature, or just keep your bag within reaching distance.

***Luggage restrictions:*** They vary among carriers, but with Amtrak, two carry-on bags and three checked bags is the limit. No restrictions on toiletries, though, which is nice.

***Suggested piece of luggage:*** Something tough and light that won't ding or dent but can still stand up to some tight squeezes.

*Nylon duffel by Tumi.*

### Automobile

***What you're wearing:*** Sunglasses, obviously, and if you're in for a long drive, dispense with the belt and remove billfolds and keys from your trouser pockets to stay comfortable. You can also get in the spirit with a leather jacket and rubber-soled driving loafers.

***Luggage restrictions:*** Only what fits in the trunk of your car.

***Suggested piece of luggage:*** That luxury hold-all you're too nervous to hand over to baggage handlers.

*Cotton-and-leather duffel by Gucci.*

# CHAPTER THREE

# Women

PRACTICALLY EVERYTHING WE DO IS IN PURSUIT OF ATTAINING—AND KEEPING—A COMPANION.

YOU WILL MESS UP ALONG THE WAY. THAT IS A FACT. BUT MEETING AND WOOING A WOMAN

NEEDN'T BE CAR MAINTENANCE. THOUGHT, CONSIDERATION, AND EFFORT

GO FURTHER THAN ANY PICKUP LINE.

# Kissing Women

### The Air-Kiss
**REMEMBER:** *No lips to skin, and no cheek to cheek, either.*
**GOOD FOR:** *Casual acquaintance.*

### The Quick Peck
**REMEMBER:** *Go for her right cheek.*
**GOOD FOR:** *Your mom.*

### The European Kiss
**REMEMBER:** *Let her initiate the second peck.*
**GOOD FOR:** *Your wife's Italian cousin.*

### On the Mouth
**REMEMBER:** *No tongue in public.*
**GOOD FOR:** *Your wife or significant other. Or both.*

### On the Hand
**REMEMBER:** *Mouth lightly touches hand. And certainly never lick between fingers.*
**GOOD FOR:** *The pope's ring.*

---

## HOW TO APOLOGIZE. IN WORDS.
*Follow this script, adjust as needed, and sound like you mean it*

I want to apologize to you for (*description of your transgression*). I know what I did was (*percentage exceeding 100*) wrong, and if there's anything I can do to make it better, I will. I'm sorry that I have (*hurt/embarrassed/offended*) you and your (*friend/mother/rabbi*). I'm hoping you will forgive me and stop (*description of her punishment*). I promise it will never happen again. Probably.

---

> If women didn't exist, all the money in the world would have no meaning.
> —*Aristotle Onassis*

---

## NOTES ON WORRY-FREE OGLING
*No sunglasses? Here's how to appreciate a beautiful woman and get away with it.*

**HOW TO AVOID GETTING CAUGHT:**
Position yourself so that the person you wish to ogle is between you and something you're actually allowed to look at (e.g., the ocean at the beach, or the television at a bar).
Do it alone. By yourself, it's a discreet act of appreciation, like watching a sunset. When done with a couple other guys, however, you draw attention to yourselves, and what was harmless can seem predatory and disrespectful.

**YOU'VE BEEN CAUGHT: WHAT NOW?**
Shift your attention immediately to the object in the background and hope she understands that you weren't actually looking at her. Or . . .
. . . If she doesn't buy that, approach her and say, "Excuse me, but is your name [insert name here] and did you go to [insert name of your alma mater here]?" When she says no, apologize and say she reminded you of an old friend from college. Walk away and don't so much as breathe in her direction again. Or . . .
. . . Be bold. Maintain eye contact and smile, because if you act like what you did was wrong, then she's more inclined to think it was wrong. If you had any interest beyond ogling, go say hello. And, if applicable, remove wedding band. —*Ben Cake*

*Photo: Sean Combs, er, appreciating Jessica Biel at the 2007 Golden Globe Awards.*

---

## YOU LOOK
*[adjective]:*
**A few alternatives to "nice"**

**Acceptable:**
*Beautiful.*
*Gorgeous.*
*Amazing.*
*Fantastic.*
*Great.*

**Risky:**
*Lovely.*
*Stunning.*
*Spectacular.*
*Cute.*
*Fine*
*(pronounced fy-neh).*

**Unacceptable:**
*Adorable.*
*Delectable.*
*Divine.*
*Ravishing.*

# LEGENDARY SWORDSMEN
## THE INTERNATIONAL PLAYBOY'S GUIDE TO WOOING WOMEN

### Aristotle Onassis
*(Born Turkey, 1906)*

**Day job:**
*Shipping magnate*

**Famous conquests:**
*Jackie Kennedy, Maria Callas*

**Secret to his success:** *"I approach every woman as a potential mistress."*

**Philosophy:** *"Beautiful women cannot bear moderation; they need an inexhaustible supply of excess."*

**Downfall:** *Too many women.*

### Hugh Hefner
*(Born United States, 1926)*

**Day job:**
*Publisher*

**Famous conquests:**
*Playmates of the Year 1982, 1989; Barbi Benton*

**Secret to his success:** *"Every man should have a Hitachi Wand. It's a very good vibrator."*

**Philosophy:** *"I have slept with thousands of women, and they all still like me."*

**Downfall:** *N/A*

### Errol Flynn
*(Born Australia, 1909)*

**Day job:**
*Swashbuckler*

**Famous conquests:**
*Ingenues*

**Secret to his success:**
*He was Errol Flynn.*

**Philosophy:** *"I like my whisky old and my women young."*

**Downfall:** *Statutory-rape laws.*

### Casanova
*(Born Venice, 1725)*

**Day job:**
*Philosopher*

**Famous conquests:**
*Half of Venice*

**Secret to his success:** *"I've never made love to a woman whose language I didn't speak, because I like to enjoy myself in all my senses at once."*

**Philosophy:** *Love "is three quarters curiosity."*

**Downfall:** *Syphilis.*

### Porfirio Rubirosa
*(Born Dominican Republic, 1909)*

**Day job:**
*Race-car driver*

**Famous conquests:**
*Zsa Zsa Gabor, Barbara Hutton, Doris Duke*

**Secret to his success:** *In his lifetime, large pepper grinders were referred to as "Rubirosas," in honor of his endowment.*

**Philosophy:** *"Women like to be gay.… They want to be happy. I try to make them happy."*

**Downfall:** *Divorce lawyers.*

## PRELUDE TO A KISS
### SAM RODDICK, PROPRIETRESS OF THE FAMED EROTIC-GOODS EMPIRE COCO DE MER, ON SETTING UP FOR THE BIG SCORE

—BEFORE THE DATE even begins, build the anticipation by sending her a note, text, or e-mail during the day, letting her know that you can't wait to see her that evening.

—AN UNTIDY APARTMENT may be forgiven if the bed is clean and made.

—DO NOT, under any circumstances, answer your cell phone while you're with her, and don't even try texting when you think she isn't looking. Your undivided attention is vital.

—WOMEN DO NOT FEEL at all confident or sexy under the glare of interrogation-style lighting. Bright lights must be banished, and if you have dimmer switches, use them.

—A MASSAGE is always a welcome treat. A whisper in the ear and the anticipation of a light touch up and down the thighs will send a shiver up and down her spine, especially when wearing a blindfold. You can also use a blindfold to bind wrists together, so you can tease and torment into the early hours.

*For more information, visit cocodemerusa.com.*

## THE MOST IMPORTANT WOMEN IN THE HISTORY OF BATHING SUITS

BERNARDINI, M.
**1946:** Models first-ever modern bikini.

ANDRESS, U.
**1962:** First Bond Girl to don a bikini.

WELCH, R.
**1966:** First big star in a fur bikini.

FAWCETT, F.
**1976:** Models a red bathing suit.

DEREK, B.
**1979:** Reinvents the one-piece.

CATES, P.
**1982:** Takes it off. And how.

ANDERSON, P.
**1989:** Reinvents the red bathing suit.

---

### How to Apply Sunscreen to a Woman's Back

**1.** Wait until you are asked. Don't stand around with sunscreen on your hand.

**2.** Do not apply the sunscreen directly to her back. Instead, put it on your hands and begin rubbing on her back, making sure not to miss any spots.

**3.** Keep talking while you do it. There's nothing creepier than someone silently rubbing your back. Ask if you missed anything.

**4.** Leave the front to her. Unless she asks.

*With thanks to Daniel Post Senning, moderator of etiquettedaily.com.*

> A bikini is like a barbed-wire fence. It protects the property without disturbing the view.
> —*Joey Adams*

---

**CAN IT BE SAVED?**

## A SPECIAL
# *You-Called-Her-by-the-Wrong-Name*
## *EDITION*

**The problem:** You can't remember her name, or you didn't catch it the first time around.

**Can it be saved?** Yes.

**The solution:** Apologize and blame the noise level of the room in which you met.

**The problem:** You mispronounce her name.

**Can it be saved?** Yes, provided it's a minute difference. For instance, if her name is Cara, it's okay to say *care-uh* instead of *car-uh*.

**The solution:** Admit that you had a friend in the past with a similarly spelled name.

**The problem:** You called her by your ex-girlfriend's name.

**Can it be saved?** Yes, provided you do it only once.

**The solution:** Do not call her by your ex-girlfriend's name.

---

### HOW TO GIVE
# A FOOT MASSAGE

**1.** Prepare the feet with massage oil by first applying it to your hands and then in broad strokes over the feet.

**2.** Then, with one hand on top of the foot and the other on the bottom of the foot rub in circles.

**3.** Next, place both thumbs on top of the foot, with fingers wrapped around and under the foot's bones. Apply pressure up and down the length of the top of the foot, from ankle to toes.

**4.** Use a similar technique for the bottom of the foot: Firmly push down the center line of the sole with both thumbs. Try applying pressure for ten seconds on five different points from the heel to the tip of the toes.

**5.** Ask how good it was. Collect your reward.

*With thanks to Robyn Rubenstein at manhattanmassage.net.*

## FOUR WAYS OF THE PANTY
### WHAT SHE'S TELLING YOU WITH HER UNDERWEAR

**Briefs:**
I've got a million things to do today, and I'm not in the mood.

**Boy shorts:**
I'm looking to have some fun.

**Thong:**
Don't get too excited. I'm only wearing this so I don't have a visible panty line, okay?

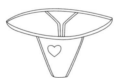

**G-String:**
My name is Fantasia. Need a date?

---

## HOW TO
# BUY LINGERIE

*Style expert Mary Alice Stephenson walks us through a place as menacing as it is rewarding: the lingerie store*

**1. Figure out her size.** Do this before you get to the store. Check her closet, or even the bra she left on the floor when she went in for a shower. And then be smart. For anything related to her breasts, err on the side of too big. For her ass, go small. Even if she has to return it, she'll be flattered. Keep in mind that higher-cut panties flatter shorter or thicker women by elongating legs. Boy shorts (see left) are hot on taller women or those who aren't so hippy. If you want to be extra safe, get something with a less specific size (small, medium, large), like a black lace robe or negligee.

**2. Figure out your store.** All women love La Perla, but that can be a little pricey, so try its Malizia line. It's just as nice, less expensive, and—most important—still says La Perla on the tag. Agent Provocateur is a good option if you want something more fantasy-related. And Victoria's Secret always works. It has a regular line, which is really affordable and well made, and also its Pink label, in case you want to see her in something more sweet and innocent.

**3. Pick a genre.** If kinky, try lace in black or red. For sweet, stick with cotton in pink, baby blue, or white. If you want something that'll make her hate you, try plaid or polka dot.

**4. Remember comfort.** Whereas most men want lingerie to come off as quickly as possible, women enjoy wearing it longer. They feel sexy in it, even if it's under their clothes.

**5. Ask questions.** Frank questions. Don't worry, the salespeople have heard worse. They're there to help.

**6. Pay.**

*—As told to Peter Martin*

---

## THE Visual Argument
### there is nothing new about cougars

Eleanor of Aquitaine

Queen Elizabeth I

Catherine the Great

Mae West

Mrs. Robinson

Susan Sarandon

Demi Moore

---

# *Arm Candy* THROUGH THE AGES

**Eleanor of Aquitaine**
*(1122 to 1204)*
**Assets:** Beauty, title to the better areas of modern-day France.
**But nobody's perfect:** Tried to overthrow her king, who was also her husband.

**Marie Antoinette**
*(1755 to 1793)*
**Assets:** Beauty, Austrian royal blood.
**But nobody's perfect:** Couldn't stick to a budget.

**Lauren Bacall**
*(b. 1929)*
**Assets:** Beauty; promising career; sensual voice.
**But nobody's perfect:** Yes. That's why we like her.

**Jacqueline Kennedy Onassis** *(1929 to 1994)*
**Assets:** Beauty, sophistication.
**But nobody's perfect:** Came off as frigid.

**Carla Bruni**
*(b. 1967)*
**Assets:** Beauty, decent singing voice.
**But nobody's perfect:** Dated Donald Trump.

## AND NOW A FEW WORDS ON SEX

Sex is interesting, but it's not totally important. I mean it's not even as important (physically) as excretion. A man can go 70 years without a piece of ass, but he can die in a week without a bowel movement.

—CHARLES BUKOWSKI

Sex at age 90 is like trying to shoot pool with a rope.

—GEORGE BURNS

That man that hath a tongue, I say, is no man, If with his tongue he cannot win a woman.

—SHAKESPEARE, *THE TWO GENTLEMEN OF VERONA*, ACT 3, SCENE I

# How to Read Her Face

### A VISUAL GUIDE

*Highly controlled anger*

*Disgust*

*A mix of anger and enjoyment*

*Polite smile*

*Concentration*

*Pleasure*

WITH THANKS TO PAUL EKMAN, CREATOR OF THE FACIAL ACTION CODING SYSTEM AND AUTHOR OF *EMOTIONS REVEALED*.

---

## HOW MUCH IS TOO MUCH?

THE SEXUAL SUGGESTIONS OF A BOLD MAN

PROSECCO

CHOCOLATE-DIPPED FRUIT

ROSE PETALS

SCENTED OILS

MENTHOLATED RUBS

SALVIA

(BOUNDARY OF GOOD TASTE)

CLOTHESPINS

BRADS

SPECULUM

SOFT SWINGING

LIGHT ASPHYXIA

CATTLE BELLS

CATTLE PRODS

CATTLE

---

Lady Nancy Astor: "Winston, if I were married to you, I'd put poison in your coffee."
Winston Churchill: "And if you were my wife, I'd drink it."

# Compliment a Woman

IT IS AS MUCH A SKILL AS IT IS A NECESSITY.
A FEW RULES AND EXAMPLES TO GUIDE YOUR WAY.
ADAPT. REPEAT.

You can say that her hair is an improvement, but not so much of an improvement as to imply that you didn't like it before.
TRY:
"I like what you're doing with your hair."

As basic as it sounds, women love to hear that a color looks great on them.
TRY:
"That color looks really nice on you."

When complimenting her chest or ass, try to avoid sounding lascivious.
TRY:
"That color looks really nice on you."

Never harp. It seems disingenuous.
TRY:
"Love your hair. When's dinner?"

Your niece looks cute or pretty. Your wife looks gorgeous, stunning, beautiful, or amazing.
TRY:
"You look [any of the words above]."

Nothing says sincerity more than the look on your face. Either that or a well-placed expletive.
TRY:
"You look fking amazing."

When in doubt, go simple.
TRY:
"Wow."

---

The Big Black Book

# RESPONSE GENERATOR

Situations that may arise with the woman in your life, and how to handle them

|  | NEW RELATIONSHIP | LONG-TERM RELATIONSHIP |
|---|---|---|
| SHE SNEEZES | "Bless you." | "Bless you." |
| SHE SAYS "I LOVE YOU" | "I really care about you." Anything but "Already?" | "Love you, too." Never: "Still?" |
| HER DOG DIES | Hugs Space Donation to the local shelter, or maybe just a stuffed animal | Hugs Space Flowers (gardenias are nice) Framed picture of the dog A new dog (when she's ready) |
| SHE BREAKS WIND AT A COCKTAIL PARTY | Pretend it didn't happen. Take her to get another drink. | Heroically take credit. |
| SHE WANTS TO HAVE BRUNCH | Pick a sweet place and take her to brunch. | Tell her to have a good time. |

*COOL*

---

A FEW WORDS ON WOMEN

*"The motto of chivalry is also the motto of wisdom; to serve all, but love only one."*
—HONORÉ DE BALZAC

## "WOMEN ARE MADE TO BE LOVED, NOT UNDERSTOOD."
—OSCAR WILDE

*"Never try to impress a woman, because if you do she'll expect you to keep up the standard for the rest of your life."*
—W. C. FIELDS

---

*HOW TO*
## Date at Work
(ABRIDGED)

The chances of it all working out are slim.

◆

That said, it happens.

◆

Your relationship will remain secret for no more than three weeks, no matter how hard you try— and you must try.

The good news: No one will really care. At least not after the first day or two. The only real problem is when one of you is the other's boss. You could maybe get fired.

◆

Don't bring your work home with you. Conversely, no canoodling, bickering, or lovemaking at the office.

◆

Exit strategies are limited to a job change and marriage.

# Female Troubleshooting

**PROBLEM:** She's giving you the silent treatment.

**SOLUTION:** Say "I love you" and smile innocently.

**PROBLEM:** Where's dinner?

**SOLUTION:** "You know what would be so great? That [fantastic dish here] that you made a couple of weeks ago."

**PROBLEM:** Her friend is extremely attractive.

**SOLUTION:** Avoid direct eye contact.

**PROBLEM:** Her chin is quivering.

**SOLUTION:** Immediate hug.

**PROBLEM:** She won't have sex with you.

**SOLUTION:** Give her a back rub; kiss her neck.

**PROBLEM:** She's running a temperature.

**SOLUTION:** Two Tylenol and fluids.

---

# AN IMPROMPTU TRIP

*Suede duffel by Ralph Lauren.*

**{ 1 }**
On Thursday afternoon, check the weather. If it's going to be a nice weekend in your vicinity, proceed.

**{ 2 }**
Pick a place somewhere between two and three hours away, so you can leave work early, pick her up, and be there by eight.

**{ 3 }**
Book a B&B. Of course you don't want to sit in a sunroom and have breakfast with some other couple who doesn't want to chat with you, either, but a surprise trip demands a B&B. She'll enjoy a B&B. And always call. Don't reserve online. The person you talk to on the phone is more than likely going to be there when you arrive. They want to please you as soon as possible.

**{ 4 }**
Call her up and say, "Let's get away. You deserve it." Establish that this trip is a gift. But a modest one.

**{ 5 }**
Lower expectations. On the way there, say things like "You know, it's not a fancy hotel or anything." Or "It's probably going to be dead in Mystic this time of year." The worse you set it up, the more magical the weekend.

---

## HOW TO
## Slow Dance

HAVE A DRINK OR TWO. Lead her to the floor by the hand.

**POSITION HER** so that the center of her sternum is lined up with just inside your right shoulder.

PLACE YOUR RIGHT HAND on the small of her back and hold your left out to the side, at chest level. Your hands should be interlocking C's, not intertwined.

SPACING IS KEY. Three to six inches. The goal is an intimacy that still allows her to move freely.

MOVE CLOCKWISE. Your right foot is the anchor. Shift all your weight to one foot, then every time you hit the one of the four-beat count, shift your weight to the other. And so on.

SLOW DOWN.

NO DIPPING.

AN ADMITTEDLY SIMPLISTIC GUIDE TO

# WOMEN AROUND THE WORLD

### TOKYO
*Wow, she looks like:*
Mia Hama from *You Only Live Twice*
*What she's drinking:*
Umeshu
*How to say "beautiful":*
Utsukushii (you-tsu-ku-shi)
*How to say "sorry":*
sumimasen (su-mi-ma-sen)
*Word to the wise:*
Blowing your nose in front of her is the equivalent of asking her to watch you use the toilet.

### STOCKHOLM
*Wow, she looks like:*
Elin Nordegren
*What she's drinking:*
A shot of aquavit
*How to say "beautiful":*
Vacker (va-ker)
*How to say "sorry":*
Förlåt (furr-lawt')
*Word to the wise:*
Swedes are funny about personal space. Make sure you stay at least three inches away from her. At first, anyway.

### ST. PETERSBURG
*Wow, she looks like:*
Natalia Vodianova
*What she's drinking:*
A shot of chilled vodka
*How to say "beautiful":*
Krasivaya (krah-see'-vah-ya)
*How to say "sorry":*
Izvinite (eez-vee-neet'-yeh)
*Word to the wise:*
Never sip vodka. You must down it in one gulp, lest she think less of you.

### RIO DE JANEIRO
*Wow, she looks like:*
Gisele Bündchen
*What she's drinking:*
A caipirinha
*How to say "beautiful":*
Linda (leen'-dah)
*How to say "sorry":*
Desculpe (dish-kool'-peh)
*Word to the wise:*
Making the OK symbol with your fingers means anus—or, quite literally, asshole—and is therefore not okay.

### PARIS
*Wow, she looks like:*
Brigitte Bardot
*What she's drinking:*
Pastis
*How to say "beautiful":*
Belle (behl)
*How to say "sorry":*
Je suis désolé (juh swee de'-zo-lay)
*Word to the wise:*
It's considered rude to place your hands below the table during dinner. Always keep them where she can see them.

## HOW TO HANDLE A **HOT WOMAN**

*Solutions for a woman who is not enjoying the heat*

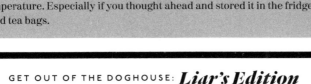

**SPICY FOOD:** Is she hungry? Are you near your kitchen or that of a person who charges to cook things in his? Counterintuitive as it may seem, spicy food causes you to sweat without raising body temperature. That sweat will evaporate and cool her skin.

**TEA:** Put a couple of used tea bags in an airtight container in the fridge to cool. Take them out and place them near the pulse points on her inner wrists. They'll help her feel cooler, and, if you had the foresight to pick peppermint tea, will have the refreshing sensation of menthol.

**ALOE VERA:** Lotion with aloe vera (or a stalk from the plant) instantly lowers her skin temperature. Especially if you thought ahead and stored it in the fridge. You know, next to your used tea bags.

GET OUT OF THE DOGHOUSE: *Liar's Edition*

*Occasionally, you have to lie to your wife. For her sake. (At least that's what you can tell yourself.) But when you get caught, sometimes a simple apology isn't enough.*

YOU LIED ABOUT LIKING...

$

**...*her dress.***
L'EAU DU TRENTE-QUATRE FRAGRANCE
by Diptyque.

**...*her new haircut.***
HAND-ENGRAVED CUSTOM STATIONERY
by Crane & Co.

**...*that woman who walked by.***
PATENT-LEATHER HEELS
by Nicholas Kirkwood.

**...*her friends.***
LEATHER BAG
by Alexander Wang.

**...*her mother.***
SOLID-GOLD AVIATORS
by Lindberg.

**...*your middle child.***
DIAMOND WATCH
by Harry Winston.

$$$

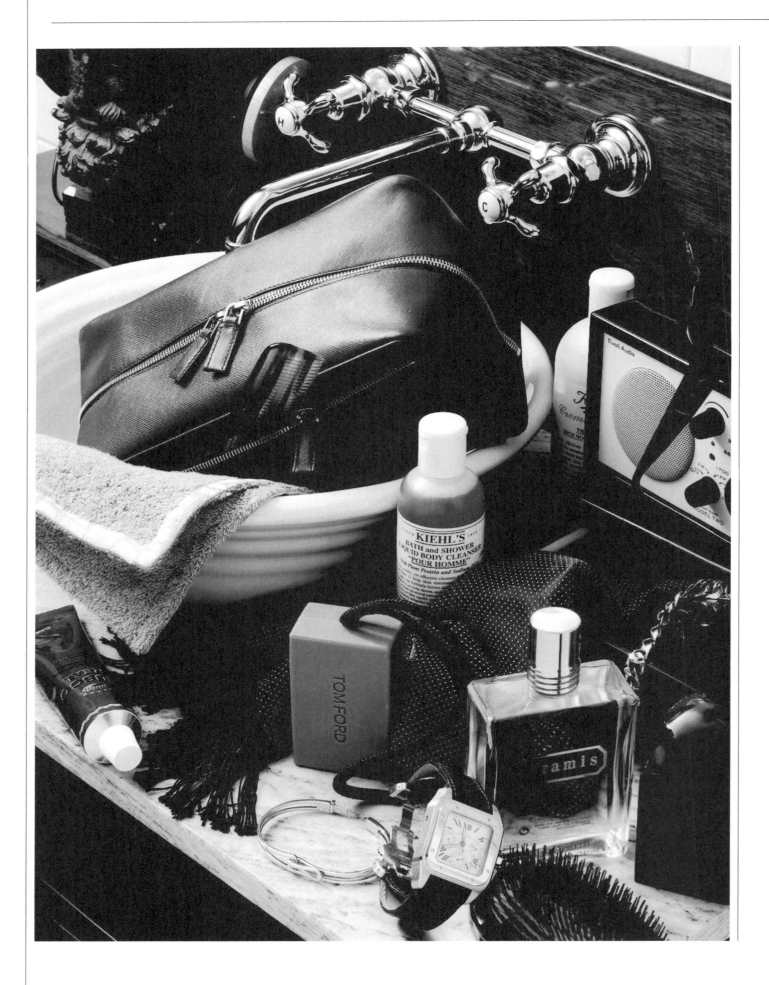

# CHAPTER FOUR

# Fitness & Grooming

THE CARE AND KEEPING OF YOU—BE IT TAMING YOUR BUSHY EYEBROWS OR TACKLING

THAT EXTRA FEW POUNDS YOU'RE CARRYING—IS MORE ABOUT TIME THAN ANYTHING.

TIME SPENT SHAVING. TIME SPENT EXERCISING. TIME SPENT AT THE BARBER.

HERE ARE THE BEST WAYS NOT TO WASTE IT.

# FIVE TERMS
## *To Use With Your Barber*

YOU KNOW HOW YOU WANT YOUR HAIR TO LOOK, BUT YOU DON'T KNOW HOW TO EXPLAIN IT. HERE ARE FIVE TERMS YOUR BARBER WILL UNDERSTAND.

| THINNED OUT | LAYERED | CHOPPY | RAZORED | TEXTURIZED |
|---|---|---|---|---|
|  |  |  |  |  |

**THINNED OUT:** When the barber breaks out thinning shears (which look like regular scissors but have matching sets of "teeth" with gaps between them), which allow some of the hairs to be cut short and others to remain at their full length. Good for thick, unmanageable hair.

**LAYERED:** When longer hair rests on top of shorter hair, and your hair appears to have some movement and depth. Good for thin hair.

**CHOPPY:** When hairs are all different lengths, which gives hair a thicker appearance. It's good for fine or thinning hair.

**RAZORED:** When a barber uses a razor (instead of scissors) to trim the ends of your hair. Your hairs will have a tapered edge (rather than a blunt, straight-cut edge), which will give them more texture and volume.

**TEXTURIZED:** Like choppy, only shorter.

### *Words a Man Should NEVER USE with His Barber*
"Sexy" • "Hip" • "Like Bon Jovi" • "I don't care" • "Who's your pick for *American Idol*?"

---

A SIMPLE GUIDE TO
# BODY-HAIR REMOVAL

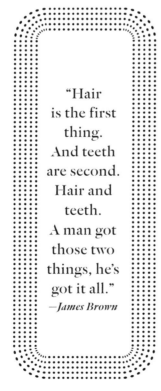

"Hair is the first thing. And teeth are second. Hair and teeth. A man got those two things, he's got it all."
—*James Brown*

| BODY PART | NECESSARY? | TOOL | HAZARDS | HOW OFTEN? |
|---|---|---|---|---|
| Nose | Yes | Small scissors; electric nose-hair trimmer. | With scissors, you could pierce your septum. Otherwise, none. | Check for errant hairs once a week and act accordingly. |
| Ear | Yes | Shaving razor for lobe; small scissors. | Inserting anything into your ear canal could lead to damage. Don't. | As needed. |
| Back | Only if your back hair makes you uncomfortable. If not, leave it. | Wax (administered by professional). | Bursts of pain followed by horrendous acne breakouts. | Once a year, six weeks before you'll take your shirt off in public. |
| Chest | Only if the hair becomes obtrusive. | Small scissors or electric hair clipper. | Cutting yourself; overtrimming your way back to early puberty. | As soon as the hair becomes visible through a thin polo shirt. |
| Nether regions | Only when mandated by a physician or significant other. | Small scissors. | Too many to count, too horrible to name. | As rarely as possible. |

# 3 TOOLS EVERY MAN SHOULD OWN

**NAIL FILE.** Most emery boards will work, but according to the guys at Truman's Gentlemen's Groomers, a New York City spa for men that gives manicures but refuses to call them that, you should get one that's low grit (it's measured in coarseness, like grits of sandpaper, and will be clearly marked on the packaging), like this durable stainless-steel model. Start with the rougher side and then smooth your nail tips with the other. Even if you don't appreciate it, your girlfriend will. *The Art of Shaving nail file.*

▼

**NAIL CLIPPERS.** When a German knife company starts producing grooming implements, you can be sure of three things: They'll be expertly crafted, they'll be sharp, and they probably won't have a sense of humor. That they look this masculine is just a bonus. These Ultra-slims fold completely flat, and if you're ever dissatisfied, you can return them. *Zwilling J.A. Henckels pour Homme ultra-slim nail clippers.*

▼

**HAND MOISTURIZER.** No one's going to notice your nails if your hands look like a topographic map of Death Valley. A daily moisturizer is the first step toward keeping this from happening. No longer pouring battery acid on your hands is the second. *Anthony Logistics glycerin hand and body lotion.*

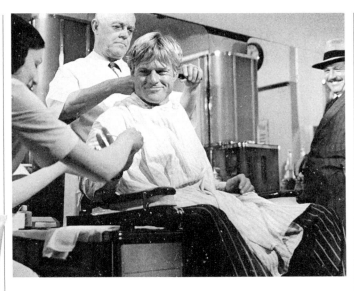

## THE MAN'S GUIDE TO
# HAND CARE

*John Allan owns four spas for men in New York City and has a line of hair-care, skin-care, and shaving products and accessories. He has seen jagged edges, chewed-up hands, and bloody hangnails. Here's his advice for how to avoid them.*

**{ 1 }**
First, stop using your teeth.
Don't bite, chew, or gnaw on nails, hangnails, or cuticles.
This is what separates you from the animals.

**{ 2 }**
If you're cutting your own nails, use a nail clipper
to trim them just to your fingertip, but no shorter.
You should be able to pick up a penny off a table,
though we'd counsel against doing this in public.

**{ 3 }**
During or after your shower, gently push your cuticles back
with your fingertip. (That's the thin layer of skin
that covers the base of the nail.) This will give your nails
a cleaner, healthier look.

**{ 4 }**
Follow up with a hand moisturizer to keep
your hands and cuticles from drying out.

**{ 5 }**
If you've got a hangnail, cut it away
with a pair of sharp scissors. Don't bite.

> "Bathe twice a day to be really clean, once a day to be passably clean, once a week to avoid being a public menace." —*Anthony Burgess*

BEFORE

## THE BASICS OF
# Eyebrow Maintenance

**{ STEP ONE }**
Buy a good pair of tweezers from a brand like Mehaz ($33; mehaz.com) or Tweezerman ($20; tweezerman.com). Be sure to get slanted tips; pointed tweezers are more likely to pinch your skin.

**{ STEP TWO }**
Take a shower. The hairs are easier to pull out after a warm shower.

**{ STEP THREE }**
Put the pad of your thumb between your brows; whatever hair it covers needs to be gone.

**{ STEP FOUR }**
Grab the individual hair and yank it out in one swift pull. If you can't get a hair by the third try, leave it alone. It's not ready to come out.

**{ STEP FIVE }**
Using your fingers, brush your brows up and trim the hairs that stray over your brow line with a pair of scissors. Don't mess with your lower brow line.

*(With thanks to John Allan of John Allan's salons in New York City.)*

AFTER

# THE PERFECT DOPP KIT . . .

**THIS IS THE PERFECT DOPP KIT.** To the untrained eye, it may look like other, non-perfect Dopp kits, but here's why it's perfect. It's made of nylon, so it's washable and suited to the messy rough-and-tumble of travel. For another, it's a shallow rectangle that you can stack in your bag. Finally, it's roomy enough to hold all of this, which is more or less what every man should carry. *Prada Dopp kit.*

## . . . AND WHAT TO PUT INSIDE IT

Molton Brown Recharge Black Pepper body wash

Tom's of Maine deodorant

Kiehl's lip balm

Fusion Chrome razor by Gillette and the Art of Shaving

Kiehl's shaving cream

Bumble and Bumble shampoo

toothbrush and toothpaste

Peter Thomas Roth moisturizer-sunscreen combo

Zwilling J. A. Henckels nail clippers

lint roller

extra pair of contact lenses

Band-Aids

Airborne

earplugs

floss

condoms

ibuprofen

**RULE NO. 294:**

Always keep a dopp kit in your office. In addition to normal hygiene products, include collar stays, static guard, a nip bottle of scotch, and a clean pair of socks.

## The History of the Dopp Kit

**IT SEEMS A SIMPLE ENOUGH IDEA:** make a small bag that holds your toothbrush, your shaving cream, and any other stuff you need while you're on the road. But it took a German leather-goods maker living in Chicago, Charles Doppelt, to come up with what became known as a Dopp kit in the early 20th century. Doppelt's business was limited until the U.S. Army issued them to millions of GIs in the Second World War. Demand soared when the boys came home, and the name and the bags have been around ever since.

A GUIDE TO

# *THE THINKING MAN'S HAIRCUT*

*They're mainly famous for what went on inside their heads, but that's nothing compared with what went on outside. A groundbreaking study of hair and thought.*

ARISTOTLE 384–322 B.C.
*Shtick:* metaphysics, wavy caesar.

DESCARTES, R. 1596–1650
*Shtick:* rationalism, radical mullet.

LEIBNIZ, G. 1646–1716
*Shtick:* optimism, heavy-metal hair.

# ⚠ *The Problem Areas*

### *How long should my sideburns be?*

Keep everything in proportion: If you have a longer face, go a little longer with your sideburns; if it's shorter or rounder, go for shorter. Whatever you do, you want to keep the length to the base of the ear or above—the closer you get to the base, the less conservative you'll look. This *[Fig. 1]* is a good, not too stuffy length. To make sure your sideburns are the same length, find a part of the ear, perhaps at a particular ridge, and cut to that point; then find the same spot on the other ear and repeat. If one ear is higher than the other, clip one side, then use a comb to create a straight line across your face and clip the other.

[Fig. 1]

### *Should you shave your neck when you have a beard?*

For a cleaner, more upscale look, shave the neck clean where the jaw meets the neck *[Fig. 2]*. Another option is to use a selectable trimmer to keep the neck hair shorter than the facial hair *[Fig. 3]*, which is a great option for those with strong stubble. In any case, shaving a clean line on the low side, say around or below the Adam's apple, just tends to look a bit odd.

[Fig. 2]

### *Should my barber finish the back of my head with a square or rounded cut?*

If you've got wavier, slightly longer hair, a rounded back looks more natural; if you've got straighter hair or a shorter cut, lean toward a clean-looking square cut.

[Fig. 3]

# *What Your Toothbrush* **Says About You**

Gingivitis is no laughing matter. *Oral-B.*

I also use Prada toothpaste. *Paul Smith.*

My arthritis is killin' me. *Radius.*

Zip-a-dee doo-dah. *Creations by Alan Stuart.*

I'm saving up for platinum. *Janeke for the Conran Shop.*

## How to Maintain **A MAGNIFICENT BEARD**

*If you're man enough to grow a beard, you sure as hell better be man enough to maintain it. And you can't whine about the work: Two wet shaves and a clipper trim each week are all it takes to keep things from going the way of Grizzly Adams.*

**1. Twice a week:** Hop into the shower to soften up the scruff. Then apply shaving cream to your cheekbones just over the sides of your beard, along your neck from the collarbone up to below the jaw, and in the space between your nose and the top of your 'stache. Wet-shaving these areas will define the lines of your beard.

**2. Once a week:** Following a wet shave, rinse and dry your face, and pull out your clippers. Be sure to get a set that's adjustable and has guards so that you have flexibility in terms of beard length. Because you've already cleaned the lines of your beard, you're just making sure your beard is consistent in length and thickness.

**3. After wet shave or clipper trim:** Thoroughly rinse your beard and work with your fingertips to get cleansers and moisturizers into the skin beneath it. Be lazy about it and a world of skin problems await come spring when you opt for a clean shave.

VOLTAIRE 1694–1778
*Shtick:* enlightened wit, jheri curls.

THOREAU, H. D. 1817–1862
*Shtick:* transcendentalism, neck beard.

NIETZSCHE, F. 1844–1900
*Shtick:* nihilism, proto-quiff.

SARTRE, J. P. 1905–1980
*Shtick:* existentialism, movie-star slick.

DERRIDA, J. 1930–2004
*Shtick:* deconstruction, bedhead.

SIMPSON, H. 1989–
*Shtick:* thoughtlessness, comb-over.

# A BRIEF HISTORY OF
# Q-TIPS

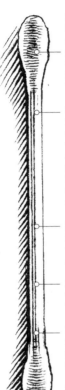

**1923:** Upon observing his wife applying wads of cotton to toothpicks, inventor Leo Gerstenzang has an idea and starts making "Baby Gays."

**1926:** Realizing this name might cause confusion, he switches to Q-tips Baby Gays. Q stands for "quality," tips for the tip; he eventually loses the whole Gay thing altogether.

**1960s:** Painter Ed Ruscha pioneers the use of Q-tips in drawing.

**1970:** The rapper Q-Tip is born in New York.

**1976:** Mickey Goldmill swabs Rocky Balboa's face with a Q-tip.

**1998:** Q-tips antimicrobial cotton swabs debut. A nation celebrates.

---

THE BEGINNER'S GUIDE TO
# NOSE MAINTENANCE

**To remove excess nose hair:** Take a warm shower to moisten up the hairs, and then position yourself in front of a well-lit mirror. Holding a small pair of eyelash scissors at a 45 degree angle to your septum and with your head tilted slightly back, begin snipping away at only those hairs you can see in the mirror. Don't insert the scissors into your nose any more than absolutely necessary and don't turn up your nose to get hard-to-reach hairs. If you can't see it poking out of your nose, leave it be. Or invest in an electronic trimmer (Panasonic makes a good one) and save yourself the anxiety.

**To clear up large pores and blackheads:** Open up your pores by applying a warm towel to your nose for about ten minutes. Then apply an exfoliant with buffing grains and massage gently for two minutes before washing clean. Moisturize.

*With thanks to stylist and makeup artist Michele Shakeshaft.*

---

# *Three Ways* To Go Bald

HOW TO MAINTAIN YOUR STYLE WHEN YOU'RE LOSING YOUR HAIR

### The Short Crop
•

Best for a moderately receding hairline. Ask your barber to make the top and sides the same short length—it'll make your hair appear thicker. Similar to the butch, the crew cut, and the ass slapper.*

*There is no such name.

### The Shaved Top
•

Best for a severely receding hairline and/or a thinning crown. Tell your barber to take off the top and keep the sides short. No comb-overs, not ever. Approach any compensatory facial hair with extreme caution.

### The Full Shave
•

The nuclear option for those with receding hairlines and thinning crowns. Use a manual razor every other day, or even every day if you want that nice, intimidating shine. Make sure to apply sunscreen.

---

# *CAN IT BE SAVED?*

YOUR BODY EDITION

 **YOUR HAIRLINE**
*Before there's a problem:* Baldness is a genetic time bomb, but you can do a few things to lengthen the fuse. Use lightweight grooming products without harsh straightening properties and natural-bristle brushes that are more gentle on follicles.
*And after:* Thickening shampoos can help once you start to lose locks, and of course there are heavy-duty products like Rogaine and Propecia.

**YOUR HAIR COLOR**
*Before there's a problem:* Some scientists claim that UV rays cause pigment cells in your scalp to go dormant. Use products with UV protection to slow that process.
*And after:* Color-boosting shampoos help retain shine and partially cover grays, or you can do the allover dye (but for the love of all that is good, maintain your roots). Or just embrace your gray. She might like it.

**YOUR FACE**
*Before there's a problem:* Wear sunscreen (or moisturizer with SPF) to help prevent wrinkles, and drink plenty of concord-grape juice. The antioxidant polyphenols preserve the skin's elasticity.
*And after:* Facial creams containing alpha hydroxy acids (AHAs) help iron out wrinkles. But they also make you more sensitive to sun damage, so be sure to pair with SPF 15 or higher.

**YOUR TEETH**
*Before there's a problem:* Brushing, flossing, and regular dentist visits.
*And after:* Over-the-counter whiteners have improved in recent years. Apply twice a day for 30 minutes, using a toothpick to be sure the strips fill the gaps between your teeth.

 **YOUR EYES**
*Before there's a problem:* UV filters on eyeglasses and sunglasses help prevent conditions like cataracts.
*And after:* Don't delay in getting reading glasses. They alleviate headaches and eye strain and won't accelerate macular degeneration. Be sure glasses have antireflective coatings, and use drops to keep the eyes lubricated.

## *The Before and After of*
# GOOD POSTURE

**BEFORE:**
Slouching squeezes the spinal disks and increases core muscle tension, both of which lead to muscle fatigue. It also makes you look meek.

**AFTER:**
Lift the sternum, let the shoulders slide back slightly, keep chin level. Maintain and run for president someday.

### THE GOOD-POSTURE WALL EXERCISE

**1)** Stand with your head, shoulders, and back against a wall.

**2)** Position your feet about six inches away from the wall.

**3)** Flatten your back against the wall while maintaining the fixed position of your feet. Ignore stares of passersby.

**4)** Push away from the wall by arching your lower back while keeping your shoulders and head against the wall.

**5)** Repeat movement 10 to 15 times twice a day.

*With thanks to Dr. Daniel Mazanec, associate director of the Cleveland Clinic Center for Spine Health (my.clevelandclinic.org/spine).*

---

### THE OVERWORKED MAN'S
# GUIDE TO EYE CARE
### How not to look strung out and tired when you're strung out and tired

#### Bags under your eyes:
**short-term solution:** Apply cool tea bags over the area for 15 minutes. The caffeine helps temporarily improve skin tone in the area. Also: hemorrhoid cream, applied sparingly and discreetly to the puffy skin.
**long-term solution:** Prescription products containing Vitamin A, or over-the-counter products containing Retinol (such as RoC Retinol Correxion eye cream) can potentially reverse signs of aging and sun damage with long-term use.

#### Bloodshot eyes:
**short-term solution:** Over-the-counter artificial tears; get the nonpreserved ones for sensitive eyes.
**long-term solution:** Anti-inflammatory drops (prescription required).

#### Red-rimmed eyes:
**short-term solution:** Try cleaning your irritated eyelids with lid scrubs, which, aptly enough, are little pads that get rid of the flakes and debris. A good brand is Ocusoft (prescription required).
**long-term solution:** Eat more Omega-3 fatty acids. It'll take three to six months before you see any signs of a cure, but it's the best way to tune up your lubrication.

---

## THE
# LIFE-CHANGING HAIRCUT
### We help three men make a somewhat late transition from boy to man

*Rogen, S.*

**Before:**
It's pretty much one length all around, which rounds out his face and makes him look young. But not in a good way. Like in a kindergarten way.

**After:**
Your barber should make sure the sides are shorter than the top and that the hair is "texturized," or debulked. Finish the sides with a matte (or dry) paste.

*Blagojevich, R.*

**Before:**
The bangs fall too close to the eyebrows, making his already too-close-together eyes look even more too close together. Plus, bushy hair that isn't tamed makes an already round face look even rounder.

**After:**
Ask your barber to cut the sides close to emphasize the angles of your face. And for up top, ask for a shorter, "chopped into" fringe that removes some of the volume. Finish it off with a soft side part.

*Bon Jovi, J.*

**Before:**
This is no kind of do for a grown-up. Too long and too wild—plus, the widely flicked-out sides narrow the face. Who does he think he is—Pat Benatar?

**After:**
Your barber should shorten the sides, back, and top, all of which will bring out the strength of the jawline; finish with a matte paste or cream. It'll keep Benatar comparisons at bay.

*With thanks to Hillel Ulysses, hairdresser at Serenity Salon in New York City.*

# AN "EAU" GLOSSARY

**EAU DE COLOGNE:** A solution consisting of 3 percent perfume in a water-and-alcohol base. Can be splashed on generously. Best worn when expecting close encounters.

**EAU DE TOILETTE:** A solution containing 3 to 8 percent perfume oil in alcohol. A good daily scent that's not overpowering.

**EAU DE PARFUM:** A solution containing 10 to 15 percent perfume oil in alcohol. A strong, long-lasting scent; use when you want to make a statement.

**EAU-DE-VIE:** Strong, coarse, and colorless brandy distilled from fermented fruit juice. Wear only in the presence of old, forgiving friends.

### OTHER COMMONLY USED TERMS

**ABSOLUTES:** Pure, natural, nonsynthetic extracts from flowers and other materials.

**ACCORD:** The mixture of various aromas to produce a harmonious effect.

**BASIC NOTE:** The third olfactory note sensed by the nose, after the top and middle notes.

**BODY:** A fragrance's main theme, or middle note. Considered the heart of a scent.

**COLOGNE:** A city in Germany where the precursor of modern perfumes was first produced.

**ENFLEURAGE:** The classic method of extracting fragrant absolutes, whereby flowers and other materials are combined with fat and then pressed to produce a pomade filled with the material's essence.

**FATIGUE:** When prolonged exposure to one fragrance causes the nose to become desensitized to said aroma.

**MIDDLE NOTE:** The heart of a scent and the main blend that classifies it in the wider taxonomy of fragrance. Also called the *body*.

**SYNTHETICS:** Artificial scents that mimic materials that occur naturally.

**TOP NOTE:** The first olfactory impression one notices when smelling a fragrance. Typically a light scent.

---

## Great Men *and* Their Colognes
### (which are all still available)

**George III**
Creed Royal English Leather

**George Washington**
Caswell-Massey Number Six

**Napoleon Bonaparte**
Jean Marie Farina Eau de Cologne by Roger & Gallet
*(new name, same formula)*

**Winston Churchill**
Creed Tabarome

**James Bond**
Floris No. 89
*According to Ian Fleming's books, it's the only fragrance he wears.*

**Cary Grant**
Creed Green Irish Tweed, *made exclusively for Grant*

---

## *The Four Scent Groups:* An Olfactory Guide

*Top notes, base notes, fougère, chypre... The nomenclature of the fragrance counter can be downright mystifying. Luckily, the majority of scents fall into a handful of categories. Here are the big four:*

| AROMATIC | CITRUS | ORIENTAL | WOODY |
|---|---|---|---|
| Armani *Acqua di Gio*, Davidoff *Cool Water* | Dior *Eau Sauvage*, Calvin Klein *CK One* | Cartier *Must pour Homme*, *Helmut Lang* | Tommy Hilfiger *Tommy*, Burberry *Touch for Men*, Ralph Lauren *Polo* |
| These traditional, herb-based scents, which sometimes incorporate citrus or spice, are naturally masculine and crisp. Approximately 70 percent of colognes belong to this group. | Lemon, orange, and more-exotic fruit scents get beefed up by aromatics (botanical oils, animal musk) or spices for a fresh and energizing scent. | Exotic and spicy, these fragrances feature heady ingredients like amber, resin, and wood oils, made sweeter with a dash of vanilla or mossier with synthetic tobacco. | Ingredients such as cedar, sandalwood, and patchouli become less treelike with the addition of aromatic citrus notes. |

---

## THE RULES OF *SHOWING CHEST HAIR*

No jewelry. The hair is decoration enough.

No more than three buttons undone at any given time.

If you take off your shirt, it wouldn't kill you to trim...

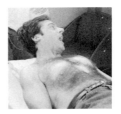

And trust us: Trimming is always better than waxing.

---

## AN INTRODUCTION TO ELECTRIC SHAVING

▸ THE FIRST ELECTRIC SHAVER was patented by an American inventor (and World War I veteran) named Jacob Schick in 1928. Schick's prototype featured a heavy motor tethered by a metal cable to a razor-equipped shaving head, but a later, more commercially successful model combined the motor and the head in one unit.

▸ THERE ARE TWO TYPES of electric shavers: foil and rotary. Foil razor heads have a single perforated metal strip. Rotary shaver heads usually have three individual discs that can pivot around the contours of your face.

▸ FOIL SHAVERS are usually thought better at providing close shaves. Rotary shavers are usually thought to be easier to maneuver around tricky areas like the chin and neck.

▸ THINGS WORTH CONSIDERING before purchasing any new razor: Is it waterproof? How long does it take to recharge to full capacity? How often do you need to clean it?

▸ JACOB SCHICK BELIEVED that regular shaving could extend a man's life to 120. He died at age 59, though his death had nothing to do with shaving.

---

## ALL ABOUT

**How to avoid it:** Before you shave, soak your face with a warm washcloth to saturate the skin and prevent irritation. Use a shaving cream with aloe—it will help soothe the skin. And here's the important part: Always shave in the same direction as the grain. Sure, it's not as close a shave, but it's a hell of a lot less irritating.

**How to deal with it:** Use an over-the-counter hydrocortisone cream on the affected area, and hold off on shaving for a few days if at all possible. If you can't make it to the pharmacy for the hydrocortisone, create an at-home compress by soaking a towel in a solution of a teaspoon of salt and a pint of warm water. Lay the towel on the affected area for 10 to 15 minutes before and after work. The salt will calm the inflammation and soothe the skin.

*With thanks to Dr. Bruce Katz and the JUVA Skin and Laser Center.*

# Get Fit Like a Canadian

OR A ROMAN OR A SUMO. THREE CLASSIC WORKOUTS THAT DON'T REQUIRE A GYM

## 5BX

Developed by the Royal Canadian Air Force in 1959. Rumored to be practiced by Prince William and other members of the British royal family.

**Exercise 1 *(30 reps)*** With feet shoulder width apart and arms above your head, bend down and touch the floor. Stand back up and do a backbend to complete one rep.

**Exercise 2 *(23 reps)*** Lie on your back. Sit up into a vertical position.

**Exercise 3 *(33 reps)*** Lie on your chest with your palms under your thighs. Raise your head, chest, and legs for one rep.

**Exercise 4 *(20 reps)*** Push-ups.

**Exercise 5 *(500 reps)*** Run in place. Each step with the left foot counts as a rep. Every 75 steps, do ten jumping jacks.

*Complete in 11 minutes or less. Repeat daily. (A copy of the complete workout can be found online. We recommend Googling "5bx PDF.")*

## The Legionnaire

FLIP-FLOPS

Based on a regimen used by Roman legionnaires, as described in Flavius Vegetius Renatus's *On Roman Military Matters*. Adapted into a slightly more contemporary version by Mark Merchant, co-owner of Alta Health and Fitness Center and As One in New York.

**1. (a) Frog jumps:** Squat like a frog, with your fingertips touching the ground in front of you. Jump as high as you can, then return to a squat. **(b) Clap push-ups. (c) Sit-ups,** holding some sort of weight, e.g., a rock, your copy of the *OED*, the nearest baby. *Do each exercise ten times, then repeat. But* *this time do only nine reps, then eight, etc., all the way down to one.*

**2. (a) Put on a backpack** containing two 30-pound bags of sand, a ten-pound sledgehammer, and two buckets. Hike four miles. **(b) Use the sledgehammer** to hit a downed log—15 times with a right-handed grip and 15 times with a left-handed grip. **(c) Put a sandbag** in each bucket. Carry up a small hill and return. Repeat sledgehammer-strike/bucket-walk cycle for 30 minutes. **(d) Pack up and hike** the four miles back.

*The entire circuit should take you three hours. Complete once or twice a week.*

## The Sumo Wrestler

JEANS

Practiced by the Japanese for centuries, the art of sumo is about more than morbid obesity. These guys are strong, too.

**1. Shiko** Stand with your feet wide and knees bent 90 degrees. As you raise your right leg as high as you can, straighten out both legs. Stomp your right back down to the ground and squat as deep as you can. Fifty reps per leg.

**2. Matawari** Sit on the ground with your legs spread in front of you. Lean forward until your head and chest touch the ground. If you can't touch, have someone push on your back. Hold one minute.

**3. Teppo** Find a tree. A big, smooth one. Stand three feet from it. Bring your right arm back, then step forward with your right leg and smack the tree with your right hand. Repeat 24 times. Switch hands.

*With thanks to Dan Kalbfleisch, six-time U.S. sumo champion.*

## Exercise Anywhere

Easy workouts for anywhere you might find yourself

*With thanks to Washington, D.C., trainer Stu Carragher.*

**IN A HOTEL** Do three sets of ten for each of the following: **air squats, jumping lunges, clap push-ups, chair dips, planks** (like holding a push-up, but resting on your forearms—3 reps of 60 seconds), **side plank** (only one forearm and your feet should touch the ground—3 reps of 45 seconds per side).

**IN A MEETING Leg extensions** (briefcase against your shins for resistance), **calf raises** (briefcase across your lap), **oblique dips** (briefcase in your hand, lowered slowly to the floor by bending sideways), **core flexes** (flex and hold your abs—3 reps of 30 seconds), **glute flexes.**

**ON A PLANE** Hold each of the following stretches for 30 seconds: **glute stretch** (with one foot on your opposite knee, lean forward; switch legs and repeat), **hamstring stretch** (try to touch your toes without bending your knees), **neck stretch** (look down as far as possible, look up as far as possible), **rotator-cuff stretch** (with your elbow bent 90 degrees and pinned to your side as a pivot, make a fist and move it from in front of your stomach to just outside your shoulder; switch arms and repeat ten times per side), **calf stretch** (resting your toes against something, push your heels forward).

# YOU GONNA EAT THAT?

↓

→ Whether you're trying to put on muscle or just live to see your 60s, one of the most important things you can do for yourself is eat right. (And change the batteries in your smoke detector, but now we're just nagging.) Here, a brief guide to acceptable foods.

## THINGS YOU SHOULD EAT[1]
Fish, eggs (with the yolk), vegetables, milk-based proteins, oatmeal, brown rice, sweet potatoes.

## THINGS YOU CAN EAT[2]
Beef, chicken, pork, fruits (they're high in sugar and carbs), breads (whole wheat), cereals, white rice, potatoes.

## THINGS YOU SHOULDN'T EAT[3]
Bagels, doughnuts, beer, liquor, and everything else that tastes good.

1. You can never go wrong with plants. Or (lean) protein.
2. Even natural sugars and whole-wheat carbs present some dangers. Enjoy in moderation.
3. The fewer ingredients you recognize in something, the less likely you should eat it.

# T Minus Three Months

*Spring is here and, with it, plans of summer. And with those plans, the awareness that you'll be taking your shirt off in public at some point in the near future. Here's a three-month workout plan that will get you ready for that moment. \**

## WEEKS 1 TO 6
Choose a weight that allows you to perform three sets of 10 to 12 reps per exercise.

### DAY 1
- Barbell squats
- Dumbbell lunges
- Barbell step-ups
- Kettlebell swings
- Shoulder press
- Standing lat raises

### DAY 2
- Bench press
- Dumbbell decline press
- Incline barbell press
- Stability-ball cable flies
- Standing barbell curls
- Preacher curls
- Reverse-grip cable curls

### DAY 3
- Dead lifts
- Wide-grip pull-ups
- Lat pull-downs
- Seated rows
- Close-grip upright rows
- Back extensions
- Skull crushers
- Bench dips
- Rope triceps extensions

### DAY 4
- 30 min running, biking, or elliptical
- 10 min on the rowing machine
- Plank (1 min, 3 times)

- Stability-ball crunches (3 sets of 15)
- Leg raises (3 sets of 15)

### DAY 5
- 30 min running, biking, or elliptical
- 10 min on the rowing machine

- Cable wood chop (3 sets of 15)
- Oblique dips (3 sets of 15)
- Medicine-ball rotations (3 sets of 15)

### DAYS 6 TO 7
- Rest

## WEEKS 7 TO 12
Choose a weight that allows you to perform 4 sets of each exercise. For the first set, 12 reps, then 10, then 10, then 8.

### DAY 1
- Front squats (do air squats between sets)
- Walking lunges
- Box jumps
- Bulgarian split squats
- Kettlebell high rows
- Stability-ball seated

barbell press
- Cable lat raises

### DAY 2
- Reverse-grip bench press (superset with decline push-ups)
- Stability-ball dumbbell press

- TRX chest press
- Decline barbell press
- Barbell three-grip curls (close grip, wide grip, and shoulder-width grip; 1 set of 8 reps each)
- Dumbbell-curls drop set (start with 12 reps, then grab the next-lowest weight and immediately do 10 reps, grab the next-lowest weight and do 8 reps, then grab the next-lowest weight and do 8 reps)
- Barbell preacher curls

### DAY 3
- Dead lifts
- Wide-grip pull-ups (superset with close-grip pull-ups)
- Bent-over rows
- Dumbbell rows
- Wide-grip pull-downs

(superset with close-grip pull-downs)
- Dips
- Single-arm overhead triceps extension
- Triceps kick-backs

### DAY 4
- Cable-rope crunches
- Bench leg extensions
- Stability-ball weighted crunches
- Cable rotations
- Medicine-ball slams

- GHD sit-ups
- Treadmill sprints: Run hard for 2 min, jog for 1; repeat to 25 min total
- Bike sprints: 1 min hard, 2 min light; 20 min total

### DAY 5 (as a circuit, repeated 8 times):
- Jumping squats, 30 sec
- Box push-ups, 30 sec
- Burpees, 30 sec
- TRX rows, 30 sec
- Plank, 30 sec

### DAY 6
- Do the circuit below.

### DAY 7
- Rest

*IF YOU'RE NOT YET FAMILIAR WITH BULGARIAN SPLIT SQUATS (SEE WEEK 7), OR ANY OTHER MOVE MENTIONED HERE, GO TO VIDEOS.BODYBUILDING.COM.*

## IF YOU CAN SPARE ONLY 20 MINUTES A DAY...

→ Do the following circuit 3 times, resting 1 min between rounds, and watch the pounds come off.

- Air squats, 1 min
- Push-ups, 1 min
- Bent-over dumbbell rows, 1 min
- Burpees, 1 min
- Dumbbell shoulder press, 1 min

*With thanks to Washington, D.C., trainer Stu Carragher.*

"I work out for two hours every morning, seven days a week. I hate it. But I love the result! That's the key, baby." —*Jack LaLanne*

# THE VAGUELY INTERESTED MAN'S
# GUIDE TO THE GYM

**1.**
Check in. Be sure to grab a towel. Smile!

**2.**
Start with at least five minutes of cardio to warm up.

**3.**
A treadmill at incline 12.0 and speed 3.5 burns as many calories as running.

**4.**
Weight machines operate on fixed planes, so they're less likely to cause an injury. If you don't really know what you're doing, start here.

**5.**
Never block a weight rack or a person's view of the mirror (often used to monitor form). It's just rude.

**6.**
It's perfectly acceptable to ask the nearest person for a spot.

**7.**
It should be common sense, but still: If you're filling a water bottle, let the guy behind you grab a drink first.

**8.**
Stationary bikes can be great for cardio, but only if you really push yourself. Which is to say, you shouldn't be able to read a magazine.

**9.**
In the locker room: Keep eye contact, banter, and requests for mole checks to a minimum. And don't forget flip-flops.

## Do You Need a Trainer?

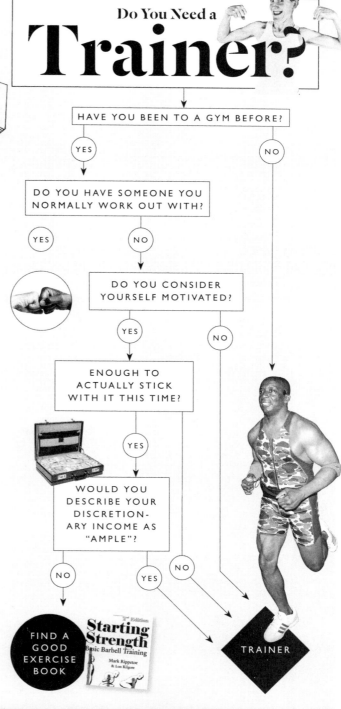

HAVE YOU BEEN TO A GYM BEFORE?

— YES
— NO

DO YOU HAVE SOMEONE YOU NORMALLY WORK OUT WITH?

— YES
— NO

DO YOU CONSIDER YOURSELF MOTIVATED?

— YES
— NO

ENOUGH TO ACTUALLY STICK WITH IT THIS TIME?

— YES

WOULD YOU DESCRIBE YOUR DISCRETIONARY INCOME AS "AMPLE"?

— NO
— YES
— NO

FIND A GOOD EXERCISE BOOK

**Starting Strength**
2nd Edition
Basic Barbell Training
Mark Rippetoe & Lon Kilgore

TRAINER

---

## A Brief Tour of Name-Brand Diets

**Atkins:** The idea behind it is that limiting carbohydrate consumption in order to moderate glucose and insulin levels will cause the body to burn fat. *Good for:* People who love bacon.

**Raw Food:** Adherents believe cooking food destroys nutrients and may cause numerous other ills. *Good for:* Fans of Dr. Bronner's soaps.

**Mediterranean:** Emphasizes healthy staples like olive oil (over butter), fish, cheeses (for dairy), and high consumption of fruits and vegetables. Maybe even a little wine. You know, for the antioxidants.
*Good for:* Fans of Greek food.

**South Beach:** Advocates consumption of nutrient-dense foods with lots of fiber, like fish, nuts, lean protein, and legumes, thus regulating blood sugar and food cravings and achieving gradual weight loss. *Good for:* Those with patience.

**The Zone:** A balanced intake of carbs (40 percent), fats (30 percent), and protein (30 percent) purported to prevent physical and mental illness. The most important factor is balance, not foods consumed. *Good for:* Christian Scientists.

# THE CREATIVE TRASH-TALKER

Your game is weaker than my neighbor's wireless signal.

You've missed more shots than a homeless guy with smallpox.

That shot was luckier than seeing a nip slip on the Food Network.

You're going down faster than a nativity scene in a city that doesn't also prominently feature a menorah.

You've thrown away more balls than the janitor at a sex-change clinic.

If your forehead were a Facebook page, I'd have just posted a picture of my balls on it. And two people have already liked it.

You play so bad that if Isiah Thomas still ran the Knicks, he'd trade a first-round draft pick for you.

You've been blocked more than a guy searching for porn at work.

You move slower than the last season of *Lost*.

*By Ferdinando DiFino*

---

## THE VISUAL ARGUMENT

NO ONE EVER NEEDS DIRECTIONS TO THE GUN SHOW.

Schwarzenegger, A.

LaLanne, J.

Hulk, T.I.

Hercules

Bluto/Brutus

---

## YOU
### AND THE
## GYM

Don't leave your towel on one machine if you're using another.

Don't leave your dirty clothes on the bench in the locker room. Use a locker.

Don't flex in the mirror unless someone asks you to.

Scratch that:
Don't flex in the mirror, especially if someone asks you to.

Wipe down the machine.

Use a towel.

If you grunt under weight or pressure, learn to do it quietly.

Know where and how much you sweat. Dress accordingly.

Don't spit in the drinking fountain.

Don't impatiently ask someone how many more sets he has. And don't hover and glare. Go to another machine and wait your turn.

---

## How to Win the Game
### *Without Coming Off Like an Asshole*

▶ A little light gambling is devoutly to be desired. Gets everyone focused.

▶ Early in the round, give your opponents a few three-footers. Makes you seem like a nice guy but doesn't let them get comfortable with the short putts. The four-footer on 17 with $50 on the line will look a whole lot longer.

▶ Praise but don't go overboard. "Golf shot" is plenty.

▶ Every time your opponent tees off on a par-3, shout, "I've never seen one! Oh, my God, I've never seen one!" It's either really funny, or it will drive him to distraction.

▶ During the round, there's never a bad time to buy everyone a drink. If there's money on the line, you don't have to actually, you know, drink.

▶ Act like you don't want their money when they're settling up.

▶ Enjoy your drink. Talk about how well everyone played. Commiserate over that putt on 17.

▶ Two cans of balls. Don't be the dick who shows up empty-handed.

▶ Ignore your friend's foot-faulting. Ninety-four percent of recreational players foot-fault. It's just part of the game.

▶ Line calls you make: If it's close, it's in.

▶ Line calls he makes: Third bad call, walk halfway to the net, peer toward the spot the ball landed, then walk back to the baseline and resume play.

▶ A little light cursing is fine, shows you care, suggests that you are trying. Unless there are children on the next court.

▶ No throwing the racket. If you must, a racket dropped with just the right measure of disgust is every bit as effective.

▶ As Red Auerbach once said to Charlie Pierce, "If you're keeping score, win."

▶ And then buy the beer.

*—David Granger*

---

## THE
## VISUAL
### TIMELINE

100 YEARS OF ATHLETIC STYLE

**1900s**

**'10s**

**'20s**

**'30s**

**'40s**

THE INJURY-PRONE MAN'S GUIDE TO

# PAIN

### Knee

**CAUSES:** Any activities involving repetitive and varied knee stress.

**PREVENTION:** Shoes that fit, proper stretching.

**IF YOU DO GET HURT:** Ice for 48 hours. A heated sleeve can also provide relief.

**IF IT BECOMES CHRONIC:** Time for a brace. Just try not to rely on it too much, as that can weaken the surrounding muscles and lead to repeat injuries.

### Back

**CAUSES:** Lifting heavy objects, bad posture.

**PREVENTION:** Strengthen your core.

**IF YOU DO GET HURT:** Minimize movement. Ice eight times a day. After 48 hours, try light stretching, but don't hold the positions more than a few seconds, as this will make your muscles even tighter than before.

**IF IT BECOMES CHRONIC:** Stretch first. Even if you're only picking up a baby.

### Tennis Elbow

**CAUSES:** Tennis, for one. Pull-ups, chin-ups, grocery bags—anything that stresses the tendons on the outside of your upper arm.

**PREVENTION:** Take more time to recover.

**IF YOU DO GET HURT:** Rest. Massage. Ice. Flex your wrist up and down to keep the tendons stretched.

**IF IT BECOMES CHRONIC:** Focus on wrist flexion and extension exercises. Strengthening shoulders could help.

### Ankle Sprains

**CAUSES:** Any activity with jumping and sudden lateral movement.

**PREVENTION:** Wear shoes that fit correctly.

**IF YOU DO GET HURT:** Ice, compression, and elevation. To help retain your range of motion during recuperation, try to write the alphabet with your big toe while lying down.

**IF IT BECOMES CHRONIC:** Brace or tape your ankle before activity.

### Rotator Cuff

**CAUSES:** Unexpected jerks, especially when your arms are raised.

**PREVENTION:** Take a break. Also, fix your posture.

**IF YOU DO GET HURT:** Keep the joint moving. Massage.

**IF IT BECOMES CHRONIC:** Lie stomach-down on a bench, arms dangling, holding light weights. With thumbs up, raise your arms parallel to floor; pause, shift 30 degrees toward shoulders. Three sets of ten.

## AURAL INSPIRATION: THE PERFECT PLAYLISTS

### *Weight lifting*

THE ROOTS (FEATURING GREG PORN), "Stomp"

COMMON, "Ghetto Dreams"

30 SECONDS TO MARS, "Vox Populi"

CHEVELLE, "Face to the Floor"

RENE AMESZ & BAGGI BEGOVIC, "Smells Like Teen Spirit"

WOLFGANG GARTNER, "Wolfgang's Fifth Symphony"

AIRBOURNE, "Steel Town"

METALLICA, "Hate Train"

ANTHONY HAMILTON, "Back to Love"

### *Cardio*

MIGUEL, "Sure Thing"

SAM SPARRO, "Black & Gold"

PAROV STELAR, "Booty Swing"

DUCK SAUCE, "Barbra Streisand"

LUPE FIASCO, "The Show Goes On"

LMFAO, "Sexy and I Know It"

PITBULL (FEATURING CHRIS BROWN), "International Love"

THE BLACK KEYS, "Lonely Boy"

GARY CLARK JR., "Don't Owe You a Thang"

KILL THE ALARM, "Fire Away"

VIZA, "Trans-Siberian Standoff"

**'50s**
**'60s**

**'70s**
**'80s**
**'90s**

**2000s**

# SCIENCE in the SEAMS

CAN MEN OF SPORT ALSO BE MEN OF STYLE? BY MARTIN MARKS

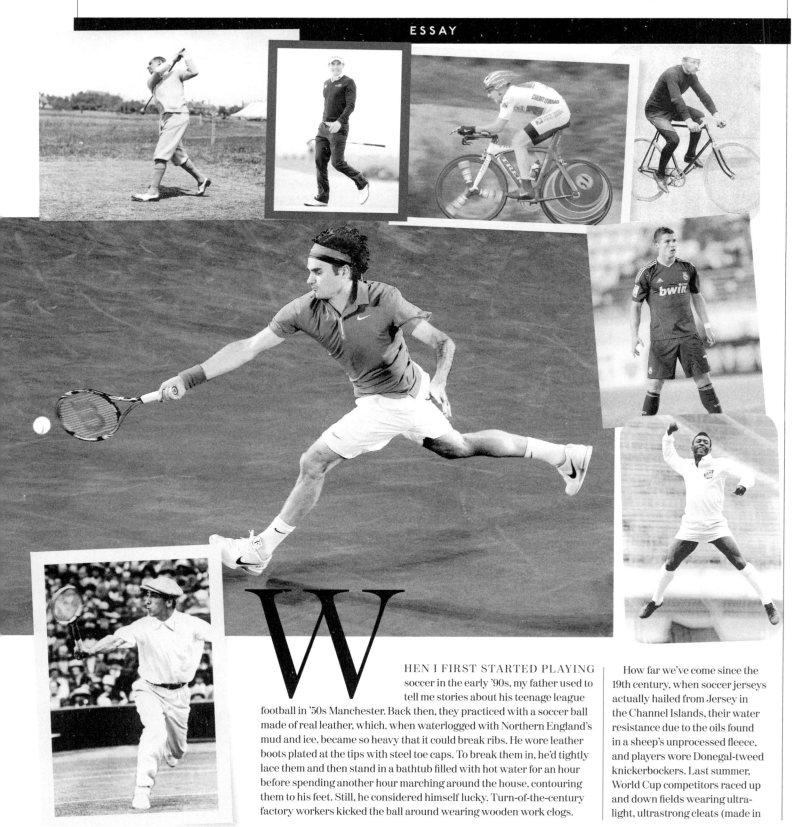

**W**HEN I FIRST STARTED PLAYING soccer in the early '90s, my father used to tell me stories about his teenage league football in '50s Manchester. Back then, they practiced with a soccer ball made of real leather, which, when waterlogged with Northern England's mud and ice, became so heavy that it could break ribs. He wore leather boots plated at the tips with steel toe caps. To break them in, he'd tightly lace them and then stand in a bathtub filled with hot water for an hour before spending another hour marching around the house, contouring them to his feet. Still, he considered himself lucky. Turn-of-the-century factory workers kicked the ball around wearing wooden work clogs.

How far we've come since the 19th century, when soccer jerseys actually hailed from Jersey in the Channel Islands, their water resistance due to the oils found in a sheep's unprocessed fleece, and players wore Donegal-tweed knickerbockers. Last summer, World Cup competitors raced up and down fields wearing ultra-light, ultrastrong cleats (made in part from carbon fiber) and high-tech polyester jerseys equipped with features like ClimaCool and Dri-FIT. Tennis players, meanwhile, have traded in the white cotton shirts of René Lacoste for the mesh-and-Velcro extravaganzas of Rafael Nadal and Roger Federer. Professional golfers, once under the cool, patrician influence of Walter Hagen, seem hell-bent on dressing more and more like extras from *Star Trek*. Today every sport worth playing requires cutting-edge clothes that would look and feel utterly alien to our grandfathers, and from courses and courts to playing fields around the world, men of sport have somehow ceased to be known as men of style.

You can thank, or blame, DuPont and its ilk for the technical revolutions of the past 60 years. Until the 1950s, the materials that went into sports gear were largely elemental—cotton, wool, leather, metal. But as the shorts grew shorter and the hair grew shaggier, scientists started to make molecular-level advances in fabric technology, producing an alchemical blend of performance textiles to keep athletes ahead of the game. Neoprene, acrylic, and polyester wound their way into the looms—reinforcing traditional materials like wool and cotton—and onto the bodies of running, jumping, swimming, climbing enthusiasts the world over. To complicate matters further, technical sportswear started expanding beyond the playing fields en masse in the late 1970s, and by the time Reagan took office, one couldn't walk down the street without seeing someone in a polyester (or, woefully, velour) tracksuit and shapeless windbreaker, the college letters of yore replaced by the logos of Sergio Tacchini, Nike, or Adidas.

The importance of function, or the appearance of function, completely subsumed the imperatives of form, and too many of us got it in our heads that it didn't matter what you looked like so long as you were playing (or pretending to play) the game.

But a man who cares about his style as much as he cares about his score has options. Over the past decade, athletic companies such as Adidas and Puma have attracted new legions of followers thanks to collaborations with cutting-edge designers. (See: Messrs. Yohji Yamamoto and the late, great Alexander McQueen, respectively.) Giorgio Armani and Miuccia Prada are among the mainstream designers who frequently incorporate synthetic materials into their sportswear. Dolce & Gabbana outfits entire soccer teams in its native Italy, and also England's Chelsea Football Club. One unexpected source of pitch-perfect athletic wear is Ralph Dunning, a former Ironman turned clothing designer who started Dunning Sportswear at a time when uncomfortable fits and slapdash construction were the norm. His clothes, often made by combining traditional materials such as merino wool and cotton with polyester, spandex, and Coolmax, are both wearable and functional, and by avoiding the garish fluorescent colors and uncomfortably cloying fits of most athletic wear, he makes clothes that you won't be embarrassed to wear on the court (or course) or off.

That's all it takes, really: an awareness of how you look and a commitment to looking, if not your very best, then at least good enough. Pay attention to the fit. Make sure you can move. And remember that cotton and wool, while seemingly old-fashioned today, were good enough for some of the greatest athletes of the 20th century. They might—might—just be good enough for you.

*Martin Marks is a writer in New York City. He no longer plays soccer.*

# The New Breed

## 21ST-CENTURY SPORTSWEAR

**The Evolution of Polo Shirts**
From left: Cotton polo shirt by Lacoste. Polyester polo shirt by Dunning.

**The Quick-Drying Swim Trunks**
Near right and center: Polyamide swim trunks by Orlebar Brown. Far right: Nylon swim trunks by Victorinox Swiss Army.

**The Technical Jackets**
From left: Recycled-polyester Ecotene jacket by Zegna Sport. Polyester sailing jacket by Brooks Brothers. Polyester fleece by Nautica.

# CHAPTER FIVE

# Home

FROM BED TO BATH AND BEYOND.

THE TIME YOU SPEND HERE IS YOUR PERSONAL TERRITORY. MAKE YOUR MARK WITH THESE TIPS.

# BATH TAKING

### When is it okay to take a bath?
- Any era prior to the 1930s.
- When entering into any sort of contract with Russian businessmen.
- Whenever you are concerned your sperm count is too high.
- When your muscles ache. (Hot water increases circulation, similar to massage.)
- When you are invited to by someone you care about.
- Whenever you feel like it.

### What accessories do I need?
- Soap and shampoo, if actually bathing.
- Bath salts, if dealing with soreness (legal variety only).
- Long-handled brush, if arthritic.
- Bubbles, if accompanied.

### What bath accessories do I never need?
Rubber ducky, action figures, battleship, bathing suit, candles, toaster.

### Should I feel environmentally friendly?
Not really. The average bath uses anywhere from 30 to 50 gallons of water. With a 1.5-gallon-per-minute showerhead, that's the equivalent of a 20-to-30-minute shower, which even you don't need.

### How long should my bath last?
If you're in there to soothe sore muscles, ten minutes should be enough to allow the hot water to help flush out any lactic acid. Otherwise, take as long as you want. We're not here to judge.

---

**BATHROOM TIP! No. 1**

Before you begin trimming your beard with an electric razor, make sure that you have a full charge. Unless you don't care for symmetry.

---

## The *Well-Dried* Man

▶ Towels made of cotton or bamboo are more absorbent than synthetics, so that's a good place to start. For best results, look for 100 percent Egyptian, Turkish, or pima cotton towels, which have long-staple fibers that are more durable and thus will stay soft and fluffy. You can tell by feeling the towel. Good options will be soft, of course, but they will also have a bit of weight and fibers that stand up rather than lay flat.

▶ In terms of color, there's really only one rule to follow: Pick something you like. Okay, there is a second rule: Nobody likes neon. Whatever you choose, be sure to buy at least one matching hand towel. Guests should never be forced to consider drying their hands with your bath towel.

▶ Always wash your new towels before you use them. You never know where they've been. And if you ever notice a musty, mildewy smell, add a cup of white vinegar to the next wash cycle.

*With thanks to Annie Graham at John Matouk & Co. Inc.*

---

## And a Few Tips **For the Shower**

Shower behavior explained. Or at least categorized.

### ENCOURAGED
General cleansing. ● Shaving. (The steam softens follicles and opens pores.) ● Oral irrigation for healthy gums. (Get an irrigator that hooks to your showerhead. You'll save yourself a lot of hassle—and all that drooling over the sink.)

### DISCOURAGED
Urinating. (Yes, we've also heard that urine is sterile. No, we don't care.) ● The "farmer's blow." (Wait for a tissue.) ● Consumption of any foodstuff. (You don't need us for this one.)

### PERSONAL CHOICE
Tooth brushing. (Convenient, only moderately repulsive to those who share your shower.) ● Singing. (The acoustics make your voice sound better. Scientific fact.) ● Beer drinking. (In the case of an extreme hangover only.)

---

**12 MINUTES IN THE BATHROOM**

The bathroom is a sanctuary any time but in the morning. We walk in a mess. So what do we do? We insult our bodies. We blast ourselves with hot water. We scrape our faces with a blade. And we start to feel fantastic. We have been renewed, redeemed. All in about 12 minutes. Here, a guide to making your morning ritual count, the best way we know how:

**THE CLEANING OF THE SKIN AND HAIR**
If you have dry skin, look for a soap-free cleanser. Oily skin? Something with glycolic or salicylic acid. As for hair, wash it only every other day. Otherwise you can strip it of its natural oils. Conditioner will then reseal the hair and keep dirt from getting back in.

## A BRIEF HISTORY OF **THE TOILET**

### *(With a few appearances by a toilet's best friend, the bidet!)*

**3000** *B.C.*
People in what is now Scotland build their huts with special drains, thereby establishing some of the first known primitive toilets.

**1596**
John Harington, the godson of Queen Elizabeth I, writes a political screed that includes a design for the first flush toilet, which is built and installed in the queen's palace.

**MID 18TH CENTURY**
The bidet is popularized in France. Its name comes from the French word for pony, because both are straddled in a similar fashion. Early models use hand pumps to shoot water.

**1857**
The first packaged toilet paper, marketed as "medicated paper," is introduced.

**1880s**
Thomas Crapper, a plumber and inventor, installs several lavatories in British royal palaces. Crapper receives no patents for his toilets, but does receive one for the floating ball cock.

**1880s, TWO DAYS LATER**
The first floating-ball-cock joke is made.

**EARLY 20TH CENTURY**
Advances in plumbing technology result in the bidet's long overdue move from the bedroom to the bathroom.

**1940s**
The first port-o-pot is installed in Long Beach, California.

**1980**
Australian engineers invent the dual-flush toilet. Although making it nearly impossible to distinguish between the two buttons is not an intended part of their design, it will somehow be replicated by all manufacturers to come.

**1980s**
Bidet-loving Japanese companies bring to the masses models with automatic controls and built-in dryers.

**1986**
Crocodile Dundee is the first person bold enough to admit that he's not sure how to use a bidet. And to wonder why it's still included in nice hotels.

**1992**
The U.S. Congress passes legislation requiring toilets' water usage to be cut by more than half, to 1.6 gallons per flush. (Older toilets used up to 7 gallons per flush, which probably made for a rewarding *whoosh*, but wasn't that environmentally responsible.)

**2000s**
Toto and other Japanese toilet makers announce plans for new toilets, including portable and Internet-connected models that can monitor users' health.

**2005**
Only 60 years after the port-o-pot's introduction, some method of cleaning your hands is added to each structure. If you're lucky.

**2007**
The iPhone is introduced, forever changing where most of the e-mails you receive are written. (And, admit it: where you write most of your e-mails.)

**2015**
That guy from marketing still refuses to flush the urinal at work.

## THE VAGUELY INTERESTED MAN'S GUIDE TO SHOWER-HEADS

### BASIC
Usually uses 2.5 gallons of water per minute (GPM). You'll have little to no control over stream type or intensity, but it's cheap, and the result is not entirely unpleasant. While it could be worse, it could also be much, much better.

### LOW-FLOW
A low-flow showerhead can emit no more than 2.0 GPM. A few will aerate the water, making droplets feel larger and less disappointing. The only real side effect is extra noise.

### MULTIFUNCTION
Most mid- to high-end showerheads let you customize the width and style of your stream. In general, options that require rotating the bezel offer less variety and distinct settings than those that require rotating the entire showerhead, but they look a lot nicer. Your call.

### RAIN
If you want a rain shower, either hire a contractor or change your mind. This showerhead needs to be mounted from the ceiling; otherwise, the gentle flow has no pressure. Adapters for standard pipes do exist, but they look terrible—more at home in a science lab than a bathroom.

### HANDHELD
Incredibly ugly. Favored by Europeans.

*With thanks to Travis Rotelli at Kohler.*

### THE CLEANING OF THE FACE
*Use a washcloth for a better scrub. Focus on the center of your forehead and your nose, where oil glands are concentrated. Once a week, use an exfoliating scrub to even your complexion and allow moisturizer to penetrate deeper. And be sure that moisturizer has an SPF.*

### THE SHAVING OF THE WHISKERS
*If you shave in the shower (or after), the heat will open your pores and soften your beard, giving you a closer shave. Pre-shave oil protects your skin, and a brush raises your whiskers a bit, helping you get closer to the root. It also makes you feel fancy.*

# THE TOOTHBRUSH MATRIX

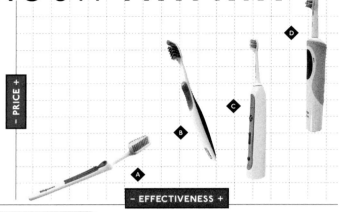

### A. MANUAL BRUSH
Used properly, a manual brush can be as effective as an electric. Less expensive options are fine, as long as they have the ADA-approved label, which means they use round-edged synthetic bristles that won't irritate your teeth and gums. *By Walgreens.*

### B. MANUAL BRUSH YOU SPENT TWO MORE DOLLARS ON
Brushes with extra-long bristles at the end of the head can help reach areas in the mouth that regular brushes can't. *By Oral-B.*

### C. INEXPENSIVE ELECTRIC
You're not going to get much in the way of actual power, but the extra agitation from the brush's automatic movement doesn't hurt. *By Oral-B.*

### D. EXPENSIVE ELECTRIC
There's little evidence to suggest that electric toothbrushes work any better than correctly used manual brushes. But there's plenty of evidence that most of us don't use our manual brushes correctly. Hence the need for electric toothbrushes. *By Philips Sonicare.*

*With thanks to Dr. Richard Price of the American Dental Association.*

**− PRICE +**

**− EFFECTIVENESS +**

---

**BATHROOM TIP!**
*No. 2*

Although in-office procedures get the best results, at-home tooth-whitening kits are no longer the joke or effort they have been in the past. Especially if you ignore the directions to space out application over days or weeks and use the product back-to-back-to-back, with 15-minute intervals. All the whitening, nowhere near the commitment.

---

# THE WELL STOCKED MEDICINE CABINET

**Toothbrush**
**Toothpaste**
**Dental floss**
Unless you have large gaps between your teeth, stick to a flat floss rather than thick dental tape.
**Eye cream**
The skin around your eyes is among your body's thinnest and thus the most prone to damage. Especially after you hit 30. Look for anti-aging ingredients like coenzyme Q10, polyphenols, vitamin A, and alpha-hydroxy acids.
**Deodorant**
Although Dr. Mehmet Oz says you shouldn't wear anything, as it blocks your body's pheromones.
**Razor**
**Shaving cream**
Pre-shave oil isn't necessary but does add an extra bit of lubrication, in case you have sensitive skin.

**Moisturizer**
As with eye cream, the best incorporate anti-aging elements. Choose one with built-in SPF, too.
**Comb**
**Hair product**
Higher-end options have better silicones and conditioning agents, keeping your hair healthier—which is to say not brittle and flaky. (See opposite page to pick what works best for you.)

**Nail clippers**
**Tweezers**
Good for splinters. And errant ear hair.
**Cologne**
In general, the more expensive the cologne, the more natural ingredients contained within. And really, would you rather smell like actual citrus or a scientist's approximation?
**OTC painkiller**
For rough mornings.

---

## LET THERE BE (FLATTERING) LIGHT

Move over incandescents. Halogens, too. Now that LED bulbs are common (and have lost that strange, greenish tint), prepare yourself for a better bathroom experience—in terms of lighting, at least.

Yes, LEDs are more expensive than traditional bulbs. But they can last for decades. Plus, they emit far less heat than other types of bulbs and can fit in less obtrusive fixtures. Most important of all, they actually produce something that looks like natural light. Every morning, for better or worse, you get to see yourself the way the rest of the world does.

Not just any bulb will do. Choose something with a warm color temperature (the level of color on a scale from healthy orange to cadaver blue), around 2,700 Kelvin. And look for a Color Rendering Index (CRI, a way of measuring color accuracy) of 82 to 92. Mount the lights on the sides of the mirror to light your head and face without casting shadows on your neck. It's better for shaving—and it may finally force you to come to terms with that double chin.

We kid. You really do look great.

*With thanks to Xavier Yager, certified lighting consultant, Chicago.*

---

*12 MINUTES* IN THE BATHROOM (CONT'D)

### THE MANAGEMENT OF THE HAIR
*Style your hair first, then add product. If you put product only where you need it, you'll be less likely to look greasy or shellacked. Whatever amount you currently use, you really could get away with half.*

### THE BRUSHING OF THE TEETH
*Soft bristles. Always. Medium or hard can wear away enamel. Use a back-and-forth stroke on biting surfaces and a gentle, circular motion everywhere else. For chronic bad breath, try brushing your tongue. And please floss. The ones you want to keep, at least.*

*BATHROOM ACTIVITIES*

# She Does Not Want You to See

- The use of Q-tips.
- The use of dental floss.
- The use of tweezers.
- The use of nail clippers.

- The use of nose-hair trimmers.
- The use of ear-hair trimmers.
- The use of the toilet.
- The close inspection

- of any sort of blemish, peeling skin, or newfound hair.
- Intimate grooming of any variety.
- Discreet sobbing.

## THE ENDORSEMENT:
### *THREE-STEP FACE CARE*

You use a moisturizer. Good for you. Moisturizers smooth your skin, mask imperfections, and generally help you avoid conditions that might be referred to as beardruff. So what more could you need? Two things, actually. With a three-step system from a company like Murad, you can do more than just protect your skin. You can repair it. After washing your face, the first step is toner, applied as a mist. It feels silly, but toner prepares the skin for serum, allowing it to penetrate deeper than moisturizer. Serum gets down to where the cells are grown and bolsters new production. After that, it's the tried-and-true moisturizer, which packs on a protective outer layer. Does the system work? Yes. Will other people notice? Probably not right away. But will you feel like you're doing everything you can to prolong the youthful appeal of that face of yours? Absolutely. One more minute in the morning gets you the satisfaction of knowing that your face is aging at the slowest rate possible. And that, to us, is a worthy trade.

HOW TO HAVE A
# STEAM-FREE MIRROR

**If you think ahead:**
Take a dollop of regular shaving cream, something like Barbasol, and polish it into the mirror with a paper towel. No condensation. Reapply when necessary.

**If you just got out of the shower:**
Run cool water over a towel, wring it out, and use that to wipe down the mirror. The lower temperature of the water can prevent steam from reappearing.

---

**BATHROOM TIP! No. 3**

Cleaning your mouth is about disturbing plaque. You'll never get rid of all of it—not even a dentist can—but if you stir up bacteria every so often, you're helping to prevent it from banding together with friends and causing real damage. Which is to say that while you should floss every night, if you get to it only every two or three days, you'll still be in pretty good shape.

---

# *The Rules of* Overnight Guests

## *YOU'RE THE HOST*

Fresh sheets. Clean towels on the edge of the bed.

Unless they were involved in your birth or that of your wife, let them find their own way from the airport.

Stock the fridge. Beer, milk, eggs, maybe a few cheeses. Humboldt Fog and aged Gouda are nice.

You're not a tour guide, but you do know the lay of the land. Share it. But only if they ask.

Have a spare set of keys handy. It'll help your guests feel less like they're inconveniencing you.

Always be the first one up.

No sex.

## *YOU'RE THE GUEST*

Arrive on time. If you'll be more than 15 minutes late, call to let them know.

Don't show up empty-handed. Try Sequoia Grove Napa Valley cabernet sauvignon (safe) or Vieux Pontarlier absinthe (adventurous).

Unless you are out with your hosts, you should be home by 11. Not everyone's on vacation.

Things you should always offer to do: wash the dishes, strip the sheets.

If you wanted to sleep late, you should've splurged on a hotel. Get up when you hear others are awake.

Send a thank-you note.

No sex.

# A CHAIR OF ONE'S OWN

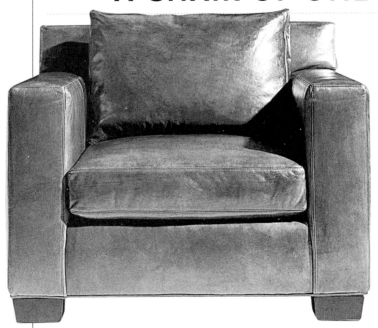

**THE ARMCHAIR** doesn't get enough respect. For decades it was a man's throne, a plush, inviting four square feet of private reprieve from the Sturm und Drang of daily life. More important, it was his chair and his alone.

Most of us now sit on couches, sofas, or, worse, love seats. Four square feet of retreat has turned into an overstuffed sectional of stress, and the stolen moments we once enjoyed in the armchair— reading the paper, catching up on a book, thinking—have been replaced with arguing with our kids about American Idol.

Our suggestion? Buy a chair of your own. A leather one with beefy arms and some give in the seat. Something like this.

*Armchair by Ralph Lauren Home.*

## THE MOST IMPORTANT MEAL OF THE DAY

*Breakfast, according to these champions*

•

**JAMES BOND:**
Scrambled eggs with chopped chives, served on hot buttered toast with pink champagne.

**ABRAHAM LINCOLN:**
An egg, a cup of coffee.

**WINSTON CHURCHILL:**
Poached egg, toast, jam, butter, coffee and milk, a jug of cold milk, cold chicken (or meat), a grapefruit (with a sugar bowl), a glass of orange squash (with ice), whiskey (with soda), cigar.

**PEE-WEE HERMAN:**
Eggs and bacon arranged in a happy-face shape atop a pancake. Topped with cereal.

## FOOD THAT BELONGS IN BED...

STRAWBERRIES

CAVIAR

CHOCOLATE TRUFFLES

ICE CREAM

HONEY AND TOAST

CROISSANT

CLUB SANDWICH

BACON SANDWICH

## THE BEST-MADE BED

*NOTE: Use only crisp, flat sheets processed with light starch and softener for the proper emotional experience. No fitted sheets.*

**1.** With your first sheet, cover the top of the mattress from left to right and top to bottom. Tuck the edges of the sheet underneath the bed while creating boxed corners (i.e., tight tucks). This is the only sheet you will tuck.

**2.** Cover the first sheet with a second sheet, and then fold the top half of the second sheet over the bottom half so that the foot of the bed is the only part covered with the second sheet. This is called a foot fold, and it is good.

**3.** Place a feathered duvet on top of the first and second sheets. This will serve as simply a coverlet.

**4.** Take your top sheet and lay it over the comforter and the other two sheets; fold both the comforter and the top sheet from the top down a foot away from the headboard.

**5.** Adorn the top of the bed with feather pillows. Stare in amazement.

**6.** Find a woman who can help you mess it up. She'll do.

*With thanks to Margie Garay, director of housekeeping at the Four Seasons Hotel, New York City (not pictured).*

## FOOD THAT DOES NOT BELONG IN BED...

MEATBALLS

CHICKEN AND/OR RIBS

SUSHI

CURRY

BANANAS

HOT DOGS

BURGERS

PASTA

BEEF STROGANOFF

**Velvet**
Constructed with slight heel,
monogram, or bullion-
embroidered coat of arms.
Sense of humor essential.
*Slippers and pajamas by Tom Ford.*

**Slides**
Quick and convenient
with a soft suede exterior.
*Suede calfskin slippers by Hermès.*
*Pajamas by Ascot Chang.*

**Moccasins**
Shearling slippers without a
sole. Good for slipping out to the
mailbox or garage on dry days.
*Suede slippers by Bottega Veneta.*
*Pajamas by L.L. Bean.*

**Quilted**
Superwarm and luxurious.
Ideal for cold stone floors.
*Cashmere slippers by Loro Piana.*
*Pajamas by L.L. Bean.*

**Purloined**
Must be from a reputable
establishment. Unique is better.
*Slippers courtesy of the*
*St. Regis Hotel, New York City.*
*Pajamas by Tom Ford.*

LEAST HOITY

THE ENDORSEMENT:
# PAJAMAS

**NOT PJS. NOT JAMMIES.** Not the silky lounge acts favored by over-the-hill playboys. Classic cotton pajamas—long pants and a matching shirt, liberally cut and dignified. You remember dignity, don't you? That feeling you had when you could wake up and walk around the house without exposing yourself to innocent bystanders? It's been a while, we know, and though there's something convenient about sleeping in your underwear and something appealing about sleeping in the buff, there ain't nothin' dignified to it. For that you'll need to wear pajamas, and if the matching pants and shirt are too Father Knows Best for you, stick with the pants and offer your wife the top half to sleep in. Now you're in business.

## 5
(Really Good)
# BOOKS
To Put You to Sleep

*Swann's Way,*
by Marcel Proust
*Moby-Dick,*
by Herman Melville
*The Metaphysical Club,*
by Louis Menand
*Infinite Jest,*
by David Foster Wallace
*Gravity's Rainbow,*
by Thomas Pynchon

## 5
(Gently Rousing)
# ALBUMS
To Wake You Up

*The Earth Is Not a Cold Dead Place*
by Explosions in the Sky
*Takk...,*
by Sigur Rós
*Ambient 1: Music for Airports,*
by Brian Eno
*December,*
by George Winston
*Reiki the Healing Bird Song,*
by David Sun Productions

# SO. MANY. PILLOWS.
AND WHAT TO DO WITH THEM
WHEN YOU'RE MAKING THE BED

*The base layer should be the pillows you sleep on. Lay them at a slight angle against the headboard, then work your way out from largest to smallest, keeping every row centered relative to the headboard. Eventually, you want to form a rough triangle. The cute little bear always goes last.*

# A User's Guide to SLEEPWEAR

## PAJAMAS

**BENEFITS:** Warm; projects dignity and modesty; color-coordinated; in a pinch, can be worn to answer the door.
**DRAWBACKS:** Constricting; could mark one as uptight and/or aged.
Cotton pajamas by Derek Rose.

## LONG JOHNS

**BENEFITS:** Very warm; folksy.
**DRAWBACKS:** A little silly looking outside arctic climates; extremely silly looking outside your bedroom.
Long-sleeved wool crewneck and wool long johns by Icebreaker

## BOXERS AND A T-SHIRT

**BENEFITS:** Convenient; comfortable; moderately attractive.
**DRAWBACKS:** Drafty; inappropriate in mixed company; the possibility of jailbreaks (you know, when your business slips out).
Sea Island cotton T-shirt and boxer shorts by Sunspel.

## NOTHING AT ALL

**BENEFITS:** Convenient; lightweight; cost-effective; nothing to launder...
**DRAWBACKS:** ...Except, maybe, your sheets.
Eye mask part of travel set by Frette.

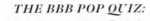

---

### THE BBB POP QUIZ:
# SHOULD YOU DON A ROBE?

Only if you answer *yes* to one or more of the following questions:

**Were you born before the Great War?**
☐ Yes ☐ No

**Do you own a smoking jacket?**
☐ Yes ☐ No

**Are you the founder of a famed international pornography empire?**
☐ Yes ☐ No

**Is it chilly in here?**
☐ Yes ☐ No

**Are you in a luxury hotel?**
☐ Yes ☐ No

**Are you about to get a massage?**
☐ Yes ☐ No

**Do you consider yourself a man of elegance and high style?**
☐ Yes ☐ No

**Even when no one is looking?**
☐ Yes ☐ No

**Do you live on a secluded street and just need to get the newspaper?**
☐ Yes ☐ No

**Are you naked and for whatever reason feel the need to answer the door?**
☐ Yes ☐ No

**Is that a pipe you're smoking?**
☐ Yes ☐ No

**Are you about to enter the Octagon?**
☐ Yes ☐ No

# A LITTLE HELP | TIME-HONORED TRICKS FOR GETTING SOME REST

| | | WHAT IT IS | PROS | CONS |
|---|---|---|---|---|
| | WHITE-NOISE MACHINE (OR PHONE APP) | A combination of all frequencies of sound that absorbs other noises. | Eliminates almost any type of noise. | 10% to 20% of people will be bothered by even this sound. Also, possibly addicting. |
| | EYE MASK | A mask that goes on your eyes. | Blocks out all light. | Looks ridiculous. |
| | EARPLUGS | Plugs for your ears. | Block out all noise. | Hearing your own breathing can be surprisingly disturbing. |
| | BENADRYL | Over-the-counter antihistamine that works for mild, short-term sleeplessness. | Works fast. As a bonus, it also alleviates allergy symptoms. | Potential next-day confusion. Less effective if used regularly. |
| | AMBIEN, LUNESTA, ETC. | Prescription drugs that enhance the effect of GABA amino acid, easing the brain into sleep. | Minimal grogginess the next day. Resultant hallucinations can be entertaining. | Grogginess not always minimal. Can be habit-forming. |
| | MAGNESIUM | Over-the-counter mineral supplement. | Can induce sleep and relieve restless-legs syndrome and muscle cramps. | Evidence mostly anecdotal. Can cause diarrhea. |
| | VALERIAN ROOT | Herbal remedy that can improve the overall quality of your sleep. | Doesn't cause wooziness if you wake up in the middle of the night. | May take a few weeks to kick in. Smells (and tastes) like sweaty socks. |
| | WARM MILK | Drinkable by-product of cows. | Cheap. Natural. | Will make you want a cookie. |

## SCIENCE: GOING TO SLEEP

If you get less than six hours of sleep a night, you're in trouble. You need sleep more than you need food. When you're always tired, you actually age faster than you should. Here is your new nightly routine:

1. Dim the lights an hour before bedtime. This mimics sunset. In response, your pineal gland releases melatonin, the hormone that readies the mind and body for sleep.

2. If certain things weigh on you—tomorrow's meetings, errands—write them down before bed to sweep them out of your mind.

3. If you're still awake after 15 minutes, get up and do something quiet, like reading a book. No Internet, no TV, no exercise. You have to let your body and mind slow down.

4. Sex. It releases endorphins and relaxes you.

## SCIENCE: WAKING UP

1. You should be waking up at the same time every day, give or take an hour on the weekends. Otherwise, you're basically creating jet lag. And don't let yourself hit the snooze button. Your body has started revving up for the day. Hitting the snooze button interrupts that process and makes it even harder to wake up later.

2. Ideally, you want to be woken up gradually—not by a sudden burst of beeps or the newsy drawl of Steve Inskeep. Look for an alarm that starts softly, using either beeps or music, and slowly increases in volume. Or find one that doesn't use sound at all. Lighted alarms will brighten your room like a sunrise does, signaling your internal clock that it's time to get up.

3. And when you do wake up, don't lie in bed. Getting up and walking around, even if just to the kitchen for coffee, helps jolt your body out of its sleep state.

Adapted from an April 2008 *Esquire* article by Dr. Mehmet Oz, a heart surgeon and the coauthor of *You: Staying Young*.

*"'Tis the current coin that purchases all the pleasures of the world cheap; and the balance that sets the king and the shepherd, the fool and the wise man, even."* —Cervantes, *Don Quixote*, on sleep

## Everything You Need to
# SLEEP

**Mattress:** Memory foam provides the most support, but some people find it uncomfortably hot. Plus, if you're a restless sleeper, the foam has to readjust every time you change position, which can be unpleasant. The most common option is innerspring, which has a little less support but is slightly less expensive. You can ask about spring gauge and coil density, but the most important thing is how the mattress actually feels. Lie on it for a while at the store—longer than you're comfortable, like ten minutes—in the position you normally sleep. The more you weigh, the firmer the bed should be. Pillow tops can be nice, but they tend to flatten out relatively quickly. Maybe try a replaceable insert instead. And if you still use satin sheets and consider yourself a man of leisure, head straight to the water-bed section.

**Sheets:** Don't be suckered by thread count. Some companies weave threads together (the tag will say multi-ply instead of single ply), which increases thread count but does little for softness, and actually reduces strength. Look for all-cotton or a cotton-silk blend. Unless it is a very special occasion (say, the '70s), silk will always be kind of creepy. And then there's pattern. Don't be fixated on matching. Choose an assortment of designs and shades. You could always buy multiple sets of complementary sheets and mix them together. And don't even try to fold a fitted sheet neatly. It's just not possible.

**Pillows:** Many people prefer down for its softness. Spend more for full feathers. Cheaper options are made with bits and pieces that don't retain the same level of fullness—and have a better chance of jabbing you in the cheek at night. If you're allergic, quality synthetics offer similar traits, but you'll want to find something a little thicker than true down, since synthetics condense much faster. Aside from the heat issues mentioned above, memory-foam pillows mold perfectly to the contours of your neck, shoulders, and head—excellent for support, terrible for feeling like a pillow. And then there's the catchall: polyester. It's as common as it is mediocre. You'll save money, but at the expense of support. No matter what variety of pillow you go with, know that within a year a large portion of a pillow's weight will be mold, fungus, dust-mite feces, and dead skin. So you might consider replacing your pillows. Frequently.

**Flair:** Your sheets and duvet can have patterns and color, but they should all be subtle. If you want character—and you probably do, just a little—get a couple masculine throw pillows or a bold patterned blanket like the ones at left.

*From top: Cashmere blanket by Brunello Cucinelli. Wool blanket by Faribault. Wool-and-cashmere blanket by Hermès.*

With thanks to Dan Schecter at SleepBetter.org.

**PLATFORM:** You have modern decor and don't mind sleeping close to the floor.

**SLEIGH:** You prefer something a little more ornate and substantive for a versatile, vintage feel.

**FOUR-POSTER:** You embrace the traditional look and find comfort sleeping in an enclosed space.

**FUTON:** You are in college. Possibly a halfway house.

**RACE CAR:** You are nine years old.

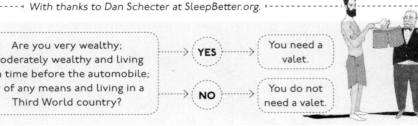

**DO I NEED A VALET?**

A VERY BRIEF FLOWCHART

Are you very wealthy; moderately wealthy and living in a time before the automobile; or of any means and living in a Third World country?

YES → You need a valet.

NO → You do not need a valet.

## The Visual Argument: Slippers are a way to express yourself

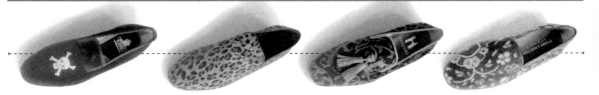

*"It's called swagger."* By Crockett & Jones.

*"I can be an animal."* By Jimmy Choo.

*"Still formal!"* By Hadleigh's.

*"Yeah, what of it?"* By Stubbs & Wootton.

# THE ANNOTATED **NIGHTSTAND**

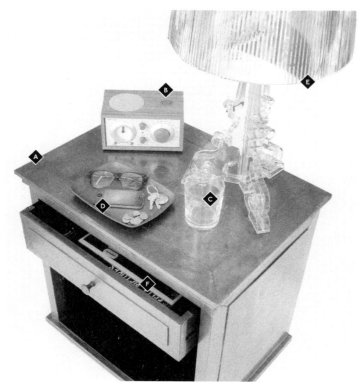

**[A] NIGHTSTAND**
Pick your bed first, then find a nightstand (Restoration Hardware) that complements the bed's style and that is the height of your mattress or a little lower for easy access. One drawer.

**[B] ALARM CLOCK**
You can use your phone as an alarm, but a good clock radio does more for the room. Find one that has a classic look that belies the innovation inside.

**[C] DRINKING GLASS**
Sometimes people get thirsty, and a drinking glass (Ralph Lauren) can be as decorative as it is functional. Unless your nightstand is metal, like this one, don't forget the coaster—and to wash the glass once in a while.

**[D] CATCHALL**
Solve clutter by giving it a home. With a small leather tray you can dump the contents of your pockets in a way that actually looks kind of nice. Glasses by DKNY. Key chain by Paul Smith.

**[E] LAMP**
Your lamp, like this Bourgie, should be a statement piece. Stick to bulbs under 60 watts: Stark lighting will never be confused with mood lighting.

**[F] READING MATERIAL**
Books may make you look smart, but you really shouldn't be reading in bed. According to Dr. Mehmet Oz, your bed should be reserved for sleeping and recreation.

At some point before, after, or midsleep, she will want some water. It's science.

☾

No matter the temperature, keep an extra blanket at the foot of the bed for her.

☾

If you wake up first, no more than one snooze.

☾

Bodily noises emitted involuntarily during the night are off-limits for discussion the next morning.

☾

If you can't afford a Kindle Paperwhite, a book light will run you maybe six dollars. Invest in one. Show you care.

☾

You are entitled to two coughing fits before you should hit the couch.

☾

The last person to get under the covers has to turn out the lights. Unless it's not you.

## On My Nightstand
World travelers (and world-class fashion designers) tell us the one thing they need near them while sleeping

**STEVEN ALAN**
"Our Good Candle in cedar scent reminds me of being in the country—a trip to Taos, where everything smelled like piñon."

**ANDY SPADE, OF PARTNERS AND SPADE**
"I never like to be without a pad of paper and a pencil to write down ideas."

**NEIL BLUMENTHAL, OF WARBY PARKER**
"A half-eaten bag of trail mix that I bought in the airport and unfortunately served as my dinner."

**GEORGE ESQUIVEL**
"A soft vachetta-leather valet tray that holds my watch and my phone, which I use to snap inspirational images and as my alarm."

**TODD SNYDER**
"The L'Occitane Lavender Pillow Mist. With it, I fall asleep in about five seconds. Without it, I stare at the ceiling for hours."

# PRATESI SHEETS:
## *AN ACTUAL LOVE STORY*

Remigio Pratesi's wife saw his bedsheets long before she ever saw his bed. According to company lore, he was smitten after seeing her doing embroidery. Asking her out was frowned upon in early-20th-century Italy, so instead he bought a set of linens and asked her to embroider them. Love blossomed—and then a new linens business. Over the ensuing decades, Pratesi would become the favored brand of European royals and American celebrities. (According to the company, although Jennifer Aniston got rid of things she'd shared with Brad Pitt after their divorce, she liked the sheets so much she bought replacements.) The company's linens are still made in a factory in Tuscany from ultra-high-end Egyptian cotton, and its embroiderers train for up to three years before they're qualified to make the hand-rendered designs.

# CHAPTER SIX

# Food & Drink

THE BEST HOST, LIKE THE BEST GUEST, IS A GRACIOUS ONE.

WHETHER YOU ARE OUT TO DINNER, AT THE BAR, OR IN YOUR BACKYARD,

HERE ARE A FEW RULES TO ENSURE EVERYONE HAS A GOOD TIME.

# *The Well-Stocked* Wet Bar

YOU'RE NOT A BARTENDER, AND YOU DON'T LIVE IN A BAR. BUT YOU DO, ON OCCASION, LIKE TO ENTERTAIN,
AND YOU WANT TO KNOW THE ESSENTIAL INGREDIENTS AND TOOLS REQUIRED
TO MAKE MOST OF THE COCKTAILS YOU'D EVER WANT TO MAKE.
YOU, SIR, ARE IN LUCK.

*By David Wondrich*

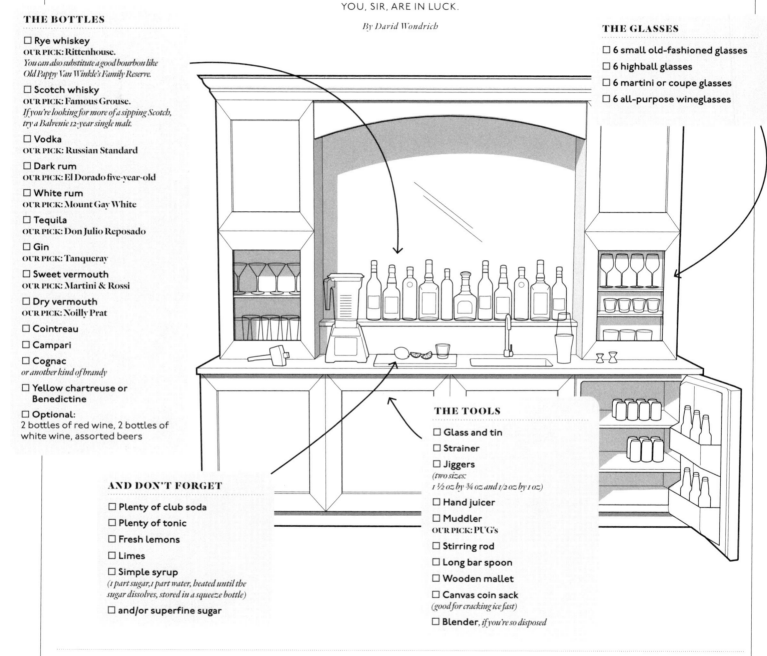

## THE BOTTLES

☐ **Rye whiskey**
OUR PICK: Rittenhouse.
*You can also substitute a good bourbon like Old Pappy Van Winkle's Family Reserve.*

☐ **Scotch whisky**
OUR PICK: Famous Grouse.
*If you're looking for more of a sipping Scotch, try a Balvenie 12-year single malt.*

☐ **Vodka**
OUR PICK: Russian Standard

☐ **Dark rum**
OUR PICK: El Dorado five-year-old

☐ **White rum**
OUR PICK: Mount Gay White

☐ **Tequila**
OUR PICK: Don Julio Reposado

☐ **Gin**
OUR PICK: Tanqueray

☐ **Sweet vermouth**
OUR PICK: Martini & Rossi

☐ **Dry vermouth**
OUR PICK: Noilly Prat

☐ **Cointreau**

☐ **Campari**

☐ **Cognac**
*or another kind of brandy*

☐ **Yellow chartreuse or Benedictine**

☐ **Optional:**
2 bottles of red wine, 2 bottles of white wine, assorted beers

## THE GLASSES

☐ 6 small old-fashioned glasses
☐ 6 highball glasses
☐ 6 martini or coupe glasses
☐ 6 all-purpose wineglasses

## AND DON'T FORGET

☐ **Plenty of club soda**
☐ **Plenty of tonic**
☐ **Fresh lemons**
☐ **Limes**
☐ **Simple syrup**
*(1 part sugar, 1 part water, heated until the sugar dissolves, stored in a squeeze bottle)*
☐ **and/or superfine sugar**

## THE TOOLS

☐ **Glass and tin**
☐ **Strainer**
☐ **Jiggers**
*(two sizes: 1 ½ oz by ¾ oz and 1/2 oz by 1 oz)*
☐ **Hand juicer**
☐ **Muddler**
OUR PICK: PUG's
☐ **Stirring rod**
☐ **Long bar spoon**
☐ **Wooden mallet**
☐ **Canvas coin sack**
*(good for cracking ice fast)*
☐ **Blender**, *if you're so disposed*

# Great Men *and* Their Tipples

F. Scott Fitzgerald
GIN RICKEY

William Faulkner
MINT JULEP

Raymond Chandler
GIMLET

Ben Franklin
MADEIRA WINE

Franklin D. Roosevelt
GIN MARTINI

Homer Simpson
DUFF BEER

# The Hierarchy of
# CORKSCREWS

### The Double Lever:
The best thing to happen to winos
since the '86 Montrachet.

### The Double Wing:
Keep one handy for when your Double Lever
breaks. Which it probably will.

### The Waiter's Friend:
What they give away at liquor stores
when they run out of Miller T-shirts.

---

THE MASTER LIST OF
# HANGOVER REMEDIES

| THE POISON | THE SYMPTOMS | THE REMEDY |
| --- | --- | --- |
| **Beer** | The grains and yeast contained in beer lead to bloating and diarrhea. | Alka-Seltzer Plus. The carbonation soothes your nausea, while the aspirin takes care of the headache. |
| **Red wine** | The tannins lead to sharp, migraine-esque headaches. | Gatorade and aspirin. The aspirin eases headaches while the Gatorade helps replace the fluids you've lost around the brain. |
| **White wine** | The sugar content in some white wines can trigger dehydration and headaches. | Rehydrating with some water over the course of the day and an ibuprofen for the headache. |
| **Dark liquors** | These contain congeners, substances that when metabolized can lead to intense nausea. | A whiskey and lemonade (preferably with home-made lemonade). Lemon stimulates digestion while whiskey decreases withdrawal symptoms. Or: See red wine. |
| **Carbonated mixed drinks** | The carbonation causes you to absorb the alcohol faster and increases the likelihood of dehydration. | See red wine. |

*With thanks to Frankie Thabeld, mixologist, and Mitch Earleywine, associate professor of psychology at the University at Albany.*

---

### RULE NO. 1401

## A little fresh grated nutmeg
## will enhance the flavor of any rum.

---

**Wait to order near
the taps. It's where
the bartender will
most often be.**

Brief eye
contact only. He'll
get to you.

Overtip on the
first round.
Your bartender
will remember
you when you
come back.

No matter your
hunger level, never
eat garnishes out
of the fruit tray.

If this is 1964 and
you're celebrating
O'Malley's
retirement from
the force, then,
and only then,
should you yell for
the "barkeep."

Know where you
are. Which is to
say, don't order an
old-fashioned at a
sports bar, a beer
at a cocktail bar, or
a Long Island iced
tea at a beer bar.

In fact, never
order a Long
Island iced tea.

---

*Snap Judgments:* # WHAT TO MAKE OF YOUR BARMEN

**The Easy
Listener**

YOU'LL KNOW HIM BY HIS:
Plaid shirt and baggy jeans.
HABITAT: Sports bars
DISPOSITION: Friendly.
May call you "Buddy."
Unlikely to interrupt your
conversation but contributes
happily when invited.

**The
Mixologist**

YOU'LL KNOW HIM BY HIS:
Facial hair and/or ironic
eyewear.
HABITAT: Cocktail bars
DISPOSITION: Considers
his work a craft. Looks
down on you for ordering
a gin and tonic.

**The
Drink
Butler**

YOU'LL KNOW HIM BY HIS:
Tuxedo.
HABITAT: Hotel bars, high-
end restaurant bars
DISPOSITION: Personable
but removed. Committed to
good service. Knows how
to pronounce Auchentoshan.

**The
Old Man**

YOU'LL KNOW HIM BY HIS:
Lightly stained apron.
HABITAT: Dives
DISPOSITION: Initially
prickly, thanks to years spent
serving cheap tippers. Good
with advice, but not until
you're on your second drink.

# *The 6 Drinks* Every Man Should Master

HOSPITALITY DEMANDS MORE THAN A VODKA TONIC. START WITH FOUR KINDS OF GLASSES, STOCK UP FOR THESE RECIPES, AND YOU'LL HAVE ALL THE DRINK YOU'LL NEED.

*By David Wondrich*

### Paloma

Squeeze 1/2 a lime into a tall glass full of ice and drop in the rind. Add 2 oz 100 percent agave reposado tequila. (Cuervo Tradicional is a great, economical choice.) Add a pinch of kosher salt and top off with 3 to 4 oz grapefruit-flavored soda. (If you can't find such a thing, use Fresca or Squirt with a splash of grapefruit.) Stick a straw in and serve.

### Dry Martini

Stir well with lots of ice 2 oz Tanqueray or Beefeater gin and 1 oz Noilly Prat dry vermouth. Strain into a chilled glass and twist a thin-cut swatch of lemon peel over the top. Note: You can also substitute Russian vodka—Stoli, Imperia, Russian Standard—for the gin, though martini purists chafe at the notion.

### Hemingway's Daiquiri

Shake well with cracked ice 2 oz white rum, such as Flor de Caña or 10 Cane, the juice of 1/2 a lime, 1 tsp Luxardo maraschino liqueur, and 1 tsp fresh-squeezed yellow grapefruit juice. Strain into a chilled martini glass and float a thin wheel of lime on top.

### Hot Whisky Toddy

Rinse a mug with boiling water. Then add 1 teaspoon raw sugar, 1 oz boiling water, and a longish swatch of thin-cut lemon peel, and stir briefly. Add 2 oz single-malt Scotch (Glenlivet or Glenrothes if you like it smooth; Laphroaig, Bowmore, or Ardbeg if you like it smoky) and another 1 oz boiling water. Drink up.

### Old-Fashioned

Put a sugar cube into a small tumbler, then add 3 dashes Angostura bitters and 1 tsp water. Crush the sugar and stir until it's dissolved. Add 2 oz good, strong bourbon, such as Wild Turkey, and stir. Add 3 or 4 ice cubes, stir again, and twist a sliver of orange peel over the top. Let sit for a couple of minutes. Serve with a stir stick or short straw.

### Caipirinha

Cut the ends off a lime, slice it into 4 rings, and cut each ring into quarters. Put the cut-up lime and 2 tsp of sugar in a smallish, heavy-bottomed tumbler and mash everything together with a wooden muddler. (Press just enough to extract all the lime juice, not so much as to make a paste.) Add 2 oz cachaça—Beleza Pura or Água Luca are good brands. Add cracked ice and stir.

---

**FINAL LIST OF INGREDIENTS**

**One (1) bottle each:**
Tanqueray *gin*
Stolichnaya *vodka*
Wild Turkey *bourbon*
Glenlivet *single-malt Scotch*

Flor de Caña *white rum*
Cuervo Tradicional *agave reposado tequila*
Noilly Prat dry *vermouth*
Beleza Pura *cachaça*
Luxardo *maraschino liqueur*

Angostura bitters
Assortment of lemons, limes, oranges, grapefruits
Sugar cubes

---

# FIVE WAYS TO OPEN A CHAMPAGNE BOTTLE

Tilt bottle, pop cork with thumbs. **Good for:** New job.

Hold cork, twist bottle slowly. **Good for:** New baby.

Knock off top with spoon. **Good for:** New house.

Knock off top with sword. **Good for:** New marriage.

Break bottle over bow of a ship. **Good for:** New ship.

## THE ART OF
# Small Talk

**❝ Arrive early.** When you show up late, groups have already formed, and it's much harder to break into a group of people who have been talking for a while than to find individuals also looking for someone to talk to."
—Bernardo J. Carducci, author of *The Pocket Guide to Making Successful Small Talk*

**❝ For smooth,** economical conversation, I recommend having a team of producers. If you don't have that, talk about kids, neighbors, pets—anything to help you make every conversation the most interesting conversation ever."
—Jimmy Kimmel, host of *Jimmy Kimmel Live!*

**❝ Ask open questions.** Anything that begins with who, what, where, why, when, or how will get people talking."
—Nicholas Boothman, author of *How to Connect in Business in 90 Seconds or Less*

**❝ Ask what they do** for a living and how they got into this field. You can also ask about the best way to break into their field, making them the expert."
—Bill Broydrick, founder of lobbying firm Broydrick & Associates

**❝ Read the newspaper,** paying attention to the first paragraph or two in every section. Then think of three to five items you can bring up if there's a lull in conversation."
—Susan RoAne, author of *How to Work a Room*

**❝ Never ask** 'Are you married?' or 'Do you have any kids?' If the answer to either of these is no, you've hit a dead end."
—Debra Fine, author of *The Fine Art of Small Talk*

**❝ Don't memorize** a generic script for conversation. People respect honesty and sincerity."
—Richard S. Schneider, DDS

# "WHAT MORE CAN I SAY?"
### A PRIMER FOR THE NONCOMMITTAL COMPLIMENT

"It was so interesting!"

"I've never seen/ tasted anything like this before."

"What can I say? It's really, really something."

"You must've been practicing forever. How did you find the time?"

"Wow. Where did you get your formal training?"

"You've done it again!"

"I'm blown away, really."

"Congratulations! You must be so proud."

## THE
# BEST HOST GIFTS
*You've been invited to stay over. Don't show up empty-handed.*

• Bottle of host's favorite spirit or champagne. *(When in doubt: a good single-malt Scotch. Will last forever.)*

• Box of milk-chocolate truffles. *Vosges.*

• A package of good steaks. *Lobel's, the "Weekender" collection of filet mignons, porterhouses, and strip steaks.*

• Block of Parmigiano Reggiano cheese.

• Handmade ice cream in one of 22 flavors. *Graeter's Ice Cream.*

• Good bottles of olive oil. *Yellingbo Gold Extra Virgin Olive Oil.*

## HOW TO GET INVITED FOR A *Weekend Away*

The only way you can get invited without actually inviting yourself is through subtle tactics.

**Lay the foundation:** Make it known once and only once that you'd love to see his place—anything more seems desperate.

**Then build from there:** Drop hints whenever possible that you have no plans for the weekend, and hope your friend picks up your cues.

### THE SOCIAL DILEMMA:
# YOUR PARTY GUESTS WON'T LEAVE

**(1)**
Subtly taper off the entertainment. Gather glasses and bottles and put away any remaining food.

**(2)**
Start loading the dishwasher. Yawn and say, "Honey, we should really go to sleep. These people want to get going."

**(3)**
Openly use cleaning products. Ask them to help by taking out the trash. Or going out and getting in their car.

# Dinner
## for Ten

HOW TO THROW
A MEDIUM-SIZED
DINNER PARTY
WITHOUT A HITCH

> They've arrived! Now get a drink in your guests' hands quickly. Could be champagne, could be a cold beer, could be a martini—something. There is no shame in offering a selection of, say, three drinks, and that's it, and you should make sure to have something for nondrinkers other than water and Diet Coke. (Seltzer with fruit garnishes is good.) Also, there's a reason it's called a cocktail hour—people drink too much and get too hungry if it lasts much longer.

> Don't overstuff people with too many apps or munchies upon arrival—one or two options (including a well-stocked antipasti plate they can graze on) should be plenty.

> When inviting your guests, ask if they have any dietary restrictions and plan your meal accordingly. And never, ever try to pull off a dish you've never made before. Keep it simple and remember that just because you're into, say, Mongolian-Brazilian fusion right now doesn't mean your guests will agree.

> If you're entertaining a senator, that's one thing. But for normal humans, cook stuff people like to eat. Follow the well-worn path set by restaurants: a light salad, a bread basket, the main course (a protein, a starch, and a vegetable), and a dessert with coffee.

> Keep the place setting simple. If people want baby forks and eight different wineglasses, they can go to a restaurant. For home, it's two forks (salad and dinner), two plates (dinner and bread), two glasses (water and wine), a knife, a spoon, and a napkin.

> Be aware of how much alcohol you drink. Getting too drunk at your own party has consequences, not the least of which is that you'll overcook the food.

> Buy at least one bottle of wine per person, and when in doubt, buy more red than white.

(White-wine drinkers generally don't mind switching to red; red drinkers generally do mind switching to white.)

> Opt for low light, but not so low that things devolve into an orgy—unless that's what you're going for—and if you go with candles (always a good move), make sure they are low enough that they're not in anyone's field of vision.

> Pick a mellow and interesting but unobtrusive playlist—try mixing contemporary, low-key rock (i.e., the XX, Grizzly Bear) with your standard-issue Bowies and Lou Reeds.

> Keep a bottle of red open at either end of the table at all times so people can help themselves; keep a bottle of white chilled by your end of the table and refill people's glasses as needed.

> Boy-girl-boy-girl is still the best option for arranged seating, and when in doubt, put couples next to each other. (That way, if a man is next to an annoying stranger, he has his wife to talk to; if, however, he's next to a fascinating, beautiful stranger, his wife can fend for herself.)

---

THE WORST-CASE-SCENARIO
# GUIDE TO ENTERTAINING

**The foul:** You've burned dinner.
**The fix:** If you've burned soup, stew, or sauce, they're lost causes; if you've burned chicken or steak, simply cut away the offending burned skin or gently scrape off the charred crust using the back of a knife, then serve; if you've burned rice or pasta dishes, remove the burned layer(s) and serve the rest.

**The foul:** A guest has spilled wine on your carpet.
**The fix:** Blot up as much as you can, and then, using a clean white cloth, apply a solution of one tablespoon dish soap, one tablespoon white vinegar, and two cups warm water. Blot with a dry cloth until the stain disappears, and then sponge with cold water and blot dry.

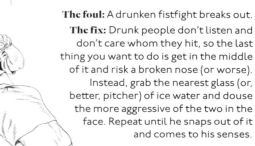

**The foul:** Someone starts choking.
**The fix:** Stay calm! Wrap your arms around the choker's waist, make a fist, and place the thumb side of your fist against her upper abdomen below the rib cage around the navel. Grasp your fist with your other hand and thrust into the upper abdomen until she is able to breathe. Allow her to thank you for saving her life.

**The foul:** A drunken fistfight breaks out.
**The fix:** Drunk people don't listen and don't care whom they hit, so the last thing you want to do is get in the middle of it and risk a broken nose (or worse). Instead, grab the nearest glass (or, better, pitcher) of ice water and douse the more aggressive of the two in the face. Repeat until he snaps out of it and comes to his senses.

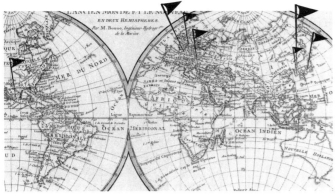

**Order the best thing on the menu:** Trust your appetite: If something jumps out, put the menu down and look no further. And be wary of specials: they're often just experiments auditioning for a regular spot, so skip them unless they include a super-seasonal ingredient.

**How to return a dish:** Keep the exchange businesslike. Say, "I don't like this dish as much as I thought I would," and then let the waitstaff know whether you'd like a different dish, the same dish recooked, or to move on to the next course.

**Tip when you've had bad service:** Servers make most of their income from tips, and service issues can often be out of their hands. However, there's no excuse for bad behavior. In that case, reduce or eliminate your tip and have a word with the manager. And never be afraid to seek assistance from a host or manager midmeal if things are going poorly. They can often turn the meal around or invite you back as a guest under better circumstances.

### THE INTERNATIONAL FOODIE'S

# GUIDE TO DINING OUT

### FRENCH
**When in doubt, order:** Boeuf bourguignon.
**When in doubt, avoid:** Aspic. (Beef should never be gelatinous.)
**You should know:** The salad and cheese often come after the entrée and before the dessert.
**How to say "cheers":** À votre santé (ah voh-tra sahn-tay).
**Best brew:** Kronenbourg 1664.
**Order her the:** Kir royale (champagne + Cassis, black currant liqueur).

### MEXICAN
**When in doubt, order:** Carnitas tacos.
**When in doubt, avoid:** Any dish with lengua. (That's tongue, and when it's bad, it's very bad.)
**You should know:** Good tequila should be sipped, not shot.
**How to say "cheers":** Salud (sah-lood).
**Best brew:** Negra Modelo.
**Order her the:** michelada (beer + lime + salt + hot sauce).

### CHINESE
**When in doubt, order:** Mu shu pork.
**When in doubt, avoid:** Stinky tofu. (Nothing is lost in translation.)
**You should know:** Set your chopsticks parallel on top of your plate when you're finished.
**How to say "cheers":** Gan bei (gahn bay).
**Best brew:** Tsingtao.
**Order her the:** Shao Hsing rice wine.

### KOREAN
**When in doubt, order:** Bibimbop (a mixed rice dish commonly topped with sautéed vegetables and meats).
**When in doubt, avoid:** Jeotgal (seafood fermented in salt).
**You should know:** Refill your dining companions' glasses when empty, but never your own.
**How to say "cheers":** Kumbae (kum-bay).
**Best brew:** Hite.
**Order her the:** Soju.

### GERMAN
**When in doubt, order:** Spätzle.
**When in doubt, avoid:** Milbenkäse (cheese ripened by mites).
**You should know:** Never cut boiled potatoes with a knife; always break them with a fork.
**How to say "cheers":** Prost (prost).
**Best brew:** Paulaner doppelbock.
**Order her the:** Riesling.

### JAPANESE
**When in doubt, order:** The tuna roll (or, for the fish averse, yaki udon, plump noodles with beef and veggies).
**When in doubt, avoid:** Futomaki. (These supersized rolls are nearly impossible to eat without showering yourself in fish parts.)
**You should know:** Use the pointed ends of the chopsticks for eating and the blunt ends for serving others.
**How to say "cheers":** Kanpai (cahn-pie).
**Best brew:** Asahi.
**Order her the:** Sake.

### GREEK
**When in doubt, order:** Moussaka. Or Greek salad.
**When in doubt, avoid:** Taramosalata. (Fish roe + olive oil + citrus = not for everybody.)
**You should know:** The coffee is never served with milk and generally has grounds at the bottom, so skip that last sip.
**How to say "cheers":** Stin iyia mas (steen ee-yah mas).
**Best brew:** Mythos.
**Order her the:** Ouzo if she's game; muscat if she's not.

# The Zoology of Waiters

### THE COLLEGE KID
**How you can tell:** Reads the specials off a piece of paper.
**Beware:** His recommendations. He's repeating what the manager told him to push.

### THE STARVING ARTIST
**How you can tell:** Those tattoos he's attempting to cover up.
**Beware:** Ordering anything too complicated. He hasn't slept in three days.

### THE EMPLOYEE OF THE MONTH
**How you can tell:** Sings "Happy Birthday" at the drop of a hat.
**Beware:** Speaking ill of him. He is always lurking, ready to serve.

### THE LIFER
**How you can tell:** Doesn't need to write anything down.
**Beware:** Talking down to him. The man's got a killer memory and he knows best.

### THE COCKTAIL WAITRESS
**How you can tell:** She asks what you're drinking.
**Beware:** Falling too hard for her. She's been flirting with you for one reason: tips.

## How to Negotiate a Party

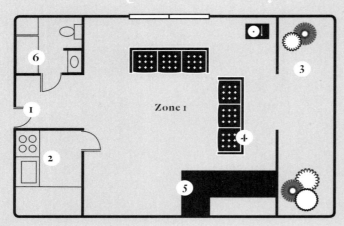

**Zone 1**

{1} DOOR: Let people know you have arrived by moving smoothly into Zone 1. Greet your host as soon as possible.

{2} KITCHEN: If hors d'oeuvres are being served, loiter on the fringes of Zone 1 to get the main traffic from the kitchen.

{3} OUTSIDE: It's for smokers, so leave complaints inside.

{4} SOFA: If you're invited to sit, choose the middle of the sofa— you'll look more social.

{5} BAR: Conversation is fine in the line for the bar, but leave the line once you have drinks.

{6} BATHROOM: As a courtesy, ensure that any bathroom visit does not involve sitting down.

---

## How to Give Yourself AN ADVANTAGE

Say your first and last name when trying to get a dinner reservation. People will think they're supposed to know who you are.

Pretipping an attendant at the parking garage will ensure quick exits.

Overtip a baggage handler at the airport and he may stick first-class tags on your checked bags.

Ask for something politely and honestly. Someone might just give it to you.

Send the concierge a generous tip before you check in to the hotel.

Apologize and take responsibility for what you've done. Someone will be more likely to forgive you.

---

### *The Complaint:* Bibs

**There comes a point** in every man's life when he must take responsibility for his actions. If he wants to drool, drop, and spill his way through dinner, he shouldn't try to hide behind some tucked-in napkin or some plastic bib with a lobster on it. He is a slob, and he should have the spotted shirt and tie to prove it.

---

## HOW TO BE A GOOD GUEST

**If you break something**, be a man and tell the host right away. Offer to pay for the damages.

**Say** thank you.

**If they ask you** to RSVP, do it. They need to know.

**Never bring** a guest unless you're explicitly invited to do so. If you're unsure, ask the host.

**If you're not** feeling well, stay in. Nobody invited you to their party so you could sit in the corner and bring everyone down.

**If it's a seated dinner**, always ask the host where you should sit. Engage with people on both sides of you, not just the cute one on your left.

**Never** be the first or the last to leave a party, don't leave under a cloud, and don't leave with a bang. If possible, thank the host discreetly.

**Write a note** of thanks by hand. Don't gush, but point out what you particularly enjoyed—the naked water polo, the sauna, the secret stash of Châteauneuf-du-Pape.

---

## Proper Attire Requested

How informal can you go at summer parties? It all depends . . .

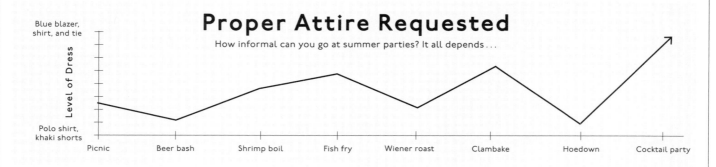

*Level of Dress* (vertical axis, from "Polo shirt, khaki shorts" at bottom to "Blue blazer, shirt, and tie" at top)

Horizontal axis: Picnic · Beer bash · Shrimp boil · Fish fry · Wiener roast · Clambake · Hoedown · Cocktail party

---

### THE CARDINAL RULES OF THE MEN'S ROOM

☞ **Flush.** It sounds basic, but you'd be surprised.

☞ **If you don't break wind** in front of colleagues outside the bathroom, don't do it at the urinal, either.

☞ **Even a G8 summit** held in the handicapped stall would not make bathroom handshaking okay.

☞ **A man should abide** by the same rules at the urinal that he would at a cathedral: No talking. No cell phones. No photos. Quiet reverence only, please.

☞ **A wordless look of disdain** is still the best reprobation for those who don't wash their hands.

## LESSONS FROM HISTORY'S GREATEST HOSTS

**Caligula:**
Have a good mix of men and women.

**Louis XIV:**
The more, the merrier.

**Truman Capote:**
People love a good theme party.

**Steve Rubell, Studio 54:**
Make sure things don't get out of hand.

**John Belushi, aka Bluto:**
Be the life of the party.

**Dennis Kozlowski, Tyco:**
Don't spend too much money.

## THE
# BEST BARBECUE
### *for Your Guests*

Grill master Steven Raichlen on everything you need when hosting a backyard burner

### THE MEAL:

A Texas-sized version of the most iconic dish in barbecue: spice-rubbed beef long ribs. SERVES EIGHT.

### THE INGREDIENTS:

- Four racks of beef long ribs, each about three pounds.
- Coarse salt, freshly ground black pepper, sweet paprika, chili powder, and mustard powder. Mix equal amounts of each to make a rub for the ribs.
- One bottle of your favorite barbecue sauce.

### PUTTING IT ALL TOGETHER:

Smoke-roast the spice-rubbed ribs, using the indirect-grilling method. (This means cooking the ribs next to, not directly over, fire; in a charcoal grill, which is best for smoke-roasting, rake the coals into two mounds at opposite sides of the grill. Then place an aluminum-foil pan between them in the center, place the ribs on the grate over the drip pan, and cover the grill.) Cook for 1½ hours at 350 degrees and brush on sauce during the last five minutes of cooking.

*Steven Raichlen is the author of* The Barbecue! Bible *and* How to Grill *(Workman Publishing) and host of* Primal Grill *on PBS. Visit his Web site at barbecue-bible.com.*

## THE
# Great Grill Debate
### A decision every host has to make

| | GAS GRILL | CHARCOAL GRILL |
|---|---|---|
| **Price:** | A good one often sets you back four figures and requires semifrequent maintenance. | Generally less expensive than gas grills, and, barring undue abuse and with semifrequent cleaning, a decent charcoal grill will last forever. |
| **Prep routine:** | Turn on the gas, press the igniter, and adjust the knobs to desired heat level; close grill. That's it. | Dump in natural lump charcoal or charcoal briquettes, ignite, and put on lid. Purists avoid lighter fluid because it could leave a taste on the food, but if you're in a hurry, it'll do. |
| **Prep time:** | Ready to cook in ten minutes. | Needs 20 minutes or more to heat up. If the briquettes are on fire, they're not hot enough to cook over. Look for a coating of white ash with a red glow coming through. |
| **Cooking:** | Most gas grills max out at around 500 degrees, so food can take longer to cook. Adjustable knobs allow for easy temperature control. | Depending on size of grill and intensity of fire, it can easily go above 500 degrees. Your food must be watched closely, and the temperature can be difficult to adjust. |
| **Flavor:** | Without a special smoke box, it's not so different from what you'd cook on an indoor griddle. | Smoky, charred, earthy: what barbecue is supposed to taste like. |
| **Cleaning:** | The grills are usually easy to clean and maintain. | Between the ashes and the grill, can be a bitch to clean. |
| **Biggest advantage:** | Convenience. | Authenticity. |

# *How to Throw a* **Summer Jammer**

GOOD FOOD, GOOD DRINK, GOOD MUSIC: ALL THE INGREDIENTS FOR A GOOD PARTY

## Cinco de Mayo

***Specialty drink:*** **Good margaritas.**
In a punch bowl, stir together with ice: 7 cups good tequila, 3 cups Cointreau, 2¼ cups fresh-squeezed lime juice, and ¾ cup simple syrup (mix superfine sugar and water in equal quantities). Strain into margarita glasses. Makes 24 drinks.

***Food:*** Steak tacos with guacamole, salsa, and lime crema (recipe available at esquire.com).

***Playlist:*** José Alfredo Jiménez, "El Rey"; Maná, "Oye Mi Amor"; Los Tigres del Norte, "Contrabando y Traición"; Alejandro Fernández, "Te Quiero"; Los Socios del Ritmo, "La Carreta"; El Chicano, "Viva Tirado"; Flaco Jimenez, "Marina"; Molotov, "Puto"; Sir Douglas Quintet, "Nuevo Laredo"; Son de Madera, "La Guanabana"; Plastilina Mosh, "Peligroso Pop"; War, "Cinco de Mayo."

## Kentucky Derby

***Specialty drink:*** **Mint juleps.**
In a mixing bowl, stir together 3 large bunches fresh mint, 4 oz water, 4 oz bourbon or dark rum, and ½ cup superfine sugar. Chop up the mint until fine and strain the resulting mint syrup into a punch bowl filled with ice. Pour in two 750-ml bottles bourbon and garnish with mint sprigs.

***Food:*** Easy Carolina pork-shoulder sandwich (recipe available at esquire.com).

***Playlist:*** Junior Kimbrough, "Stay All Night"; Dan Auerbach, "My Last Mistake"; Wendy Rene, "Bar-B-Q"; the Contours, "First I Look at the Purse"; Bill Black's Combo, "Smokie Part 2"; Furry Lewis, "I Will Turn Your Money Green"; Etta James, "Don't Lose Your Good Thing"; O.V. Wright, "A Nickel and a Nail."

## Memorial Day/Labor Day/ Fourth of July Pool Party

***Specialty drink:*** **Whiskey sours.**
In a punch bowl, stir together one 750-ml bottle whiskey, 6 oz fresh-squeezed, strained lemon juice, and 6 oz simple syrup. To serve, shake 3 oz per person with ice and strain into chilled cocktail glasses. Garnish with a cherry and an orange slice.

***Food:*** Coca-Cola-brined fried chicken (recipe available at esquire.com).

***Playlist:*** The Undertones, "Here Comes the Summer"; the Untamed Youth, "Pabst Blue Ribbon"; Casper & the Cookies, "My Heart Is in My Head"; DJ Quik, "Pitch In Ona Party"; Sea Ray, "Revelry"; the Dynamics, "Ice Cream Song"; Beulah, "Sunday Under Glass"; LCD Soundsystem, "Daft Punk Is Playing at My House"; Luna, "Ride into the Sun"; Deer Tick, "Dirty Dishes."

**And remember:** You can never have too much bug spray or too much ice. Have a backup plan in case of rain. And no roasting a pig on a spit.

# SUMMER ELIXIRS

THE BEST COLD ONES TO OFFER A FLUSHED FRIEND

### SOUTHSIDE

- Put 3 or 4 ice cubes into a tall glass.
- Pour 2 oz Bacardi Limón (instead of the traditional gin) 1½ oz simple syrup, 1 oz lime juice; add 3 or 4 fresh mint leaves.
- Shake well and strain over fresh ice in a pint glass.
- Top with club soda and garnish with fresh mint leaves.

### TOM COLLINS

- Fill a tall glass three quarters of the way with cracked ice.
- Pour in 2 oz London dry gin, 1 tsp superfine sugar, and ½ oz lemon juice.
- Stir and top with club soda or seltzer, garnish with lemon circle, and serve with stirring rod.

### GIN RICKEY

- Put 3 or 4 ice cubes into a tall glass.
- Squeeze in half a lime and drop in the rind.
- Add 1½ oz gin.
- Top off with chilled club soda or seltzer.

### RED WINE

- Stick a bottle of light, fruity red wine (Beaujolais and Barbera are reliable; Brouilly is unexpected) in the fridge for 45 minutes or an ice bucket for 15 minutes. (Take care not to chill it below 50 degrees.)
- Remove from fridge, uncork, and pour into glass.
- Inform your curious guest that some red wines are best enjoyed cold.

### ICE-COLD BEER

- Open, pour, repeat.

# THE STOCKED KITCHEN

### EIGHT THINGS EVERY MAN SHOULD HAVE ON HAND

**One block fresh Parmigiano-Reggiano**
*Good for:* Snacking, grating

**Tabasco sauce**
*Good for:* Adding kick

**One bar, dark chocolate**
*Good for:* Women

**Eggs**
*Good for:* Makin' eggs

**Olive oil**
*Good for:* Anything, everything

**Onions**
*Good for:* False tears

**Club soda**
*Good for:* Mixing drinks, removing stains

**Fresh herbs**
*Good for:* Enhancing flavors, smelling good

---

### THE BEST KINDS OF *ICE*

**Crushed:** Crushed ice cools the drink the fastest, but it also melts the fastest. Best for drinks that could use a little bit of watering down, like a mojito.

**Cracked:** Cracked ice will give you a middle-of-the-road balance of cooling and dilution. It works best with stirred or shaken drinks, like martinis that need rapid cooling with a little dilution.

**Cubed:** Cubed ice melts the slowest and causes the least dilution. It's best with liquor on the rocks, like a whiskey that you don't want watered down.

*With thanks to Charlie Hodge, bartender at the Amigo Room at Ace Hotel & Swim Club in Palm Springs.*

---

## HOW TO PACK A COOLER

**{1}**
First, chill everything overnight. Stuff that starts cold has a better chance of staying cold.

**{2}**
Cover the base with a layer of cans or bottles. Cans go on their sides. Bottles go straight up, side by side; fill the gaps with upside-down bottles. Check for malt liquor and discard.

**{3}**
Cover with ice. Repeat the layering until the cooler fills up. If there's room left over, throw in a Capri Sun for the driver.
*(With thanks to Pableaux Johnson, author of* Gameday Gourmet.*)*

---

# 5 WAYS TO COOL DOWN. QUICK.

**1)** Buy a can of cold soda or beer and press it against the back of your neck, one of the most exposed and easily over-heated areas of the skin. It should begin to cool your body within seconds.

**2)** Don't splash water on your face, unless you want to make a mess of yourself. Instead, run cold water on the insides of your wrists (i.e., the pulse points) or dip your elbow in cool water. This will help constrict the blood vessels that dilate when you overheat.

**3)** Head into a bathroom stall and remove your shoes and socks for a few minutes. Your body releases a lot of heat through your feet; by airing out your soles, you'll lower your body temperature.

**4)** Carry some cooling peppermint oil in your briefcase, and if you're feeling overheated, apply a few drops to your temples.

**5)** Ask for a glass of ice—hold the water. Then bring the cup up to your face and blow gently into it. The ice will cool down the air and it will blow back at you, forcing cold air onto your skin.

*With thanks to dermatologists Dr. Joel L. Cohen and Dr. Leslie Baumann.*

# Black Tie & Weddings

GETTING DRESSED UP IS FUN. SO IS GETTING MARRIED, OR AT LEAST GETTING DRESSED UP

AND GOING TO A WEDDING. HERE'S WHAT A MAN SHOULD THINK ABOUT WHEN HE THINKS ABOUT

FORMAL EVENTS AND WEDDINGS, WHETHER HIS OWN OR SOMEONE ELSE'S.

# THE BIG BLACK BOOK
# BOARD GAME

## How to navigate a formal event

Roll the die to make your way from front door to end-of-evening pleasantries

**START**

**CONGRATULATIONS!** You remembered to greet the host upon first entering the room. *Move forward 3 spaces.*

**ETIQUETTE BONUS:** You introduced your wife to the host, not the other way around. ("Mr. President, I'd like to introduce my wife.") *Move forward 2 spaces.*

**UH-OH.** You realize that your cummerbund has the vents pointed down. *Lose a turn while flipping it over in the bathroom.*

**TABLE ASSIGNMENTS!** You sat where you were told, recognizing the effort that went into those assignments. *Move forward 1 space.*

You tipped the **BARTENDER.** Right instinct, wrong event. *Go back 2 spaces.*

**GOOD JOB!** You left your napkin on the seat, not the table, so people don't have to see it. *Move forward 1 space.*

You forgot to **STAND UP** when your date returned to the table. It's antiquated, but still polite. *Go back 1 space.*

The **HORS D'OEUVRE** tray approaches, and you avoid anything that takes more than one bite or requires a toothpick. *Move forward 2 spaces.*

**CAUGHT CHECKING YOUR WATCH.** (As if you have somewhere better to be.) *Lose a turn.*

You tipped the **BATHROOM ATTENDANT.** Right instinct, right event. *Move forward 2 spaces.*

You performed a flawless **WALTZ**, the most common formal dance other than the box step. *Reward yourself by moving forward 3 spaces.*

Did you just say "CUM*BER*BUND"? *Start over.*

You smoothly exited a **BORING CONVERSATION.** (Maybe you simply said, "It's been a pleasure chatting with you.") *Move forward 2 spaces.*

**NICE JOB!** You made it through the whole night without removing your tuxedo jacket. *Move forward 1 space.*

**THANK THE HOST** on your way out. (You must land on this space before finishing the game.) *Them's the rules.*

**FINISH**

## *Famous Failures:* RED-CARPET EDITION

**Offender:**
NOLTE, N.
*Offense:*
Unless you're at an outdoor event or visually impaired, leave the sunglasses at home.

**Offender:**
WILLIAMS, P.
*Offense:*
Too much flash with the trim on the lapels and vest. Also: Giant bow tie, small man.

**Offender:**
BRAND, R.
*Offense:*
Midnight-blue tux is fine. Midnight-blue-plaid shirt is not.

**Offender:**
HOFFMAN, P. S.
*Offense:*
Black on black on black on black. Plus: hat.

**Offender:**
GORESKI, B.
*Offense:*
Inseam a bit too short.

### Things You Can Get Away With Saying Only While Wearing a Tux

*M'lady*

*Good day*

*Bravo*

*Simply riotous*

*What the devil?*

*Now that's a horse of a different color.*

*Give me your keys, and I'll park your car.*

---

# BLACK-TIE HAIR
### How to dress up a casual haircut
*By Rodney Cutler*

**YOUR USUAL LOOK:** Short, textured, and messy.
**YOUR BLACK-TIE LOOK:** Use a grooming cream like Kiehl's Creme with Silk Groom to bring your hair forward and push it to the side.

**YOUR USUAL LOOK:** Medium length, parted.
**YOUR BLACK-TIE LOOK:** Slick your hair down and add some shine with Murray's pomade. Move the part much lower on your head.

**YOUR USUAL LOOK:** Longish, but not longish enough for a ponytail.
**YOUR BLACK-TIE LOOK:** Use Paul Mitchell Mitch Steady Grip Gel to pull your hair straight back and off your face.

---

## BLACK-TIE RULE NO. 2

# SEEING IT AT THE OSCARS DOESN'T MAKE IT OKAY.

---

# A DANDY AND HIS WRIST
### The attributes of the ideal black-tie watch

Traditionally, watches weren't worn at formal events, as they suggested the wearer had better things to do. But if your watch is subtle, that rule is better when broken.

**THE SLIMMER THE WATCH,** the less noticeable it will be beneath your sleeve. When it was introduced, this Piaget Altiplano was, at 5.25mm, the thinnest automatic movement ever made.

**THE LACK OF** numbers reinforces the idea that a formal watch should not be a talking point.

**WHEN IN DOUBT:** Steel is timeless. Also, not flashy.

**OPPORTUNITIES** to use a chronograph are rare at a gala. The fewer dials the better.

*White-gold Altiplano watch by Piaget.*

---

## THE ENDORSEMENT:
# Proper Tuxedo Socks

Although few people will see them at a formal event, your ankles are not a place to be lazy. Or creative. Tuxedo socks should be black. Not heather or charcoal. Black. Look for fine-gauge silk, which is not only soft and comfortable but retains its color in the laundry better than cotton or wool. Socks should nearly reach your knee, virtually eliminating the possibility of your showing any flesh when you cross your legs. Which is good for everybody.

---

## HOW TO:
# STORE YOUR TUX

**1**
Take your tuxedo to the dry cleaner right after you've worn it, so when you go to wear it again, you won't have to scramble to get it cleaned.

**2**
Transfer your tux from the cleaner's wire hanger to a high-quality hanger with rounded edges to retain the shape of the jacket.

**3**
Place your tux in a garment bag and hang it in a dry place. If you are peculiar enough to have an airtight storage space, even better.

**4**
Just to be safe, open the bag back up and throw in a few mothballs.

**Bond, J.**
Shawl collar: always distinguished.

**Grant, C.**
Classic peak lapel: never out of place.

**Dujardin, J.**
Wing collar: if you know what you're doing.

**Warhol, A.**
Tuxedo jacket and jeans: if you are *reeeally* confident.

# THE *formalest* OF OUTERWEAR
### Black tie for the elements

There's no point in dressing well if you're just going to cover it with a bulky jacket. There's also no point in freezing on the way to your event. Cover up with something fitted, warm, and elegant. Like these things.

## ... THE HELL IS
# WHITE TIE?

Black tie, surprisingly enough, is considered semiformal. For the most formal of events, your host may indicate white tie, which requires you to wear a tailcoat, a white waistcoat, a wing-collar shirt, and, as you may have guessed, a white bow tie.

### A few rules:

→ Be sure it's requested. Wearing white tie to a black-tie event is almost as gauche as wearing a sweater to a wedding.

→ Tailcoats are made to fit the contours of your body without being buttoned. Never use the buttons.

→ There is no such thing as creative white tie. Show your personality in your conversation.

→ You are welcome to wear a top hat, assuming you are British or have invented a time machine.

*Wool evening suit, cotton marcella piqué waistcoat, and cotton piqué bow tie by Hackett. Cotton piqué formal shirt by Paul Stuart.*

## *How Not to Look Like* A Waiter

No notched lapels—peaked or shawl lapels only.
One-button jacket, not three-button.
Wear a proper evening shirt. • Wear a cummerbund.
Tie your own tie. • And stop filling other people's glasses.

## THE
# Well-Shod Man

You have three basic options. None is a wing tip.

### OPERA SLIPPERS
**What they are:** Low-cut slippers (officially called *pumps*) typically made of black calfskin or patent leather with a silk bow.
**When they're appropriate:** White-tie events.
**What they say about you:** You do not consider the word *dandy* to be pejorative.

### PATENT-LEATHER LACE-UPS
**What they are:** Oxfords or derbies with little to no ornamentation.
**When they're appropriate:** Any black-tie event.
**What they say about you:** You are a man of classic and suitable taste.

### VELVET SLIPPERS
**What they are:** Simple, informal slippers with a slim sole, typically made of black velvet with an embroidered crest or design.
**When they're appropriate:** Less-traditional events, evenings at the Playboy mansion.
**What they say about you:** You are stylish but not uptight. You most likely own a robe.

*With thanks to Steven Taffel at Leffot in New York City.*

BLACK-TIE RULE NO. 3

# THIS IS A BLACK TIE. IT IS NOT BLACK TIE.

# FABTQ

With thanks to Robert Gillotte at Turnbull & Asser, New York City.

( Frequently
Asked
Black-Tie
Questions )

**Q. How big should the tie be?**
As formal wear is by nature discreet, extreme proportions should be avoided. The tie should not be broader than the neck and/or extend beyond the collar, nor should it be excessively tiny.

**Q. What are acceptable materials for formal ties?**
While casual bow ties can come in a variety of adventurous materials and weaves, formal ties should be black silk, in either a satin, twill, or barathea weave.

**Q. Why those three?**
So that the texture of the tie corresponds to the facings on your tuxedo's lapels. Satin is for satin lapels. The other two weaves are paired with grosgrain.

**Q. Can I wear a clip-on? What about a pre-tied?**
If we are going to stickle, we would say stick to a tie you tie yourself. It's the proper way. That said, if that's a life skill too far, no one in this day and age will shoot you for wearing a pre-tied tie. In fact, for some of the sleeker, trimmer suits going the rounds at the moment, the narrower bow tie that goes with the look is almost impossible to tie yourself.

**Q. I've followed this advice. Is there still a chance I'll look like a waiter?**
See opposite page, "*How Not to Look Like a Waiter.*"

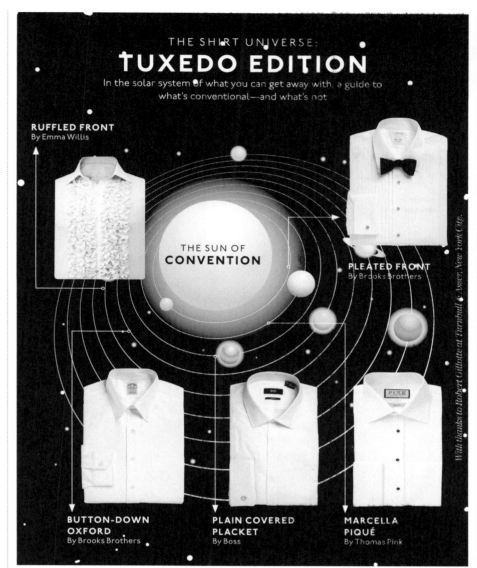

THE SHIRT UNIVERSE:
## TUXEDO EDITION
In the solar system of what you can get away with, a guide to what's conventional—and what's not

**RUFFLED FRONT**
By Emma Willis

**PLEATED FRONT**
By Brooks Brothers

THE SUN OF
**CONVENTION**

**BUTTON-DOWN OXFORD**
By Brooks Brothers

**PLAIN COVERED PLACKET**
By Boss

**MARCELLA PIQUÉ**
By Thomas Pink

THE ENDORSEMENT:
## *WING COLLARS*
**By Nick Sullivan**

**In the early '80s**, nostalgic movies and TV serials pitched youth headlong into a mania for 1920s and '30s garms in which black tie figured prominently. Clothes were more important than anything else (cf. Mr. Pacino in *Scarface*, 1983). Fast-forward three decades and a similar wave of nostalgia roars in on the dapper coattails of *Boardwalk Empire* and *The Artist*. After long years when the upturned, spread tips of the wing collar played second fiddle to the less showy turned-down collar, now is the time to experiment. Just bear in mind a few lessons: The points of the wing collar should sit behind the bow tie. The collar should have a stiffness to it and not buckle under the tie. Look for deeper collar bands and larger points. Embrace starch. Finally, a pretied bow tie, while barely passable with other collars, is nearly impossible to conceal on the naked flanks of a wing collar, so consider finally mastering the self tie. Then again, no one would have argued this point with the likes of Tony Montana.

THE
HIERARCHY
OF
**AFFECTA-TION**

**UNASSUMING**

POCKET SQUARE

BOUTONNIERE

GLOVES

CANE

SPATS

TOP HAT

CAPE

**BOLD**

# THE "IN-BETWEEN" SUIT

*Between the work suit and the tuxedo lies a specialized breed. It has a little more edge than the workday kind. It should have narrower-than-normal lapels for a subtly crisper silhouette (the outline of the suit), and the fabric should have a slight sheen to it.*

•

**The shirt should complement the suit—** and not just in terms of color. The narrow lapels of the jacket demand a narrow- collared shirt. Got wide lapels? Wear a bold spread collar that can stand up to them.

•

**The tie can make a statement,** including, "Work's over—I've taken mine off." If you do go without neckwear, though, don't skip the pocket square—one with a little color in it.

•

**The shoes should be something interesting.** Which is different from flamboyant. Classic brown wing tips don't beg for attention; they simply draw it to themselves.

## THE RULES

• Dress for the occasion. Don't complain about it. Be a man.

• If it's been a few months since you last wore the in-between suit (or a tux), make sure it still fits.

• It's always better to be slightly overdressed than slightly underdressed.

# The Annotated Tux

Men are returning to the notion of being properly attired for the event at hand— which means no more cutting corners on your evening wear. You don't need all the bells and whistles, but you do need a tux and a handful of the right accessories.

### The Tux

Peak lapels, single- or double-breasted. Notched lapels make you look like a waiter. Black wool barathea is classic, but a lighter plain weave is better for summer comfort. Grosgrain lapels last longer; satin has a habit of snagging and showing its age quicker. Midnight blue is very cool.

### The Pocket Square

In cotton or linen, not silk, which will slip.

### The Cummerbund

The cummerbund (from the Hindi for waistband), anachronistic or not, is still essential. Without it, you look as if you're not trying.

### The Shoes

You do not need patent-leather shoes, although they do look sharp. A good pair of well-polished cap-toe oxfords will suffice.

### The Shirt

White piqué cotton, bib-front or with vertical razor pleats, pressed until it's immaculate. French cuffs are essential. Try to find a fine, lightweight cotton for comfort. A turn-down collar is more comfortable; a wing collar is more dressy.

### The Bow Tie

Silk satin or silk grosgrain, black. Adjustable versions make tying easier. But you should tie it yourself (see opposite page).

### The Cuff Links

In gold or silver. Steel is also perfectly acceptable. Whatever you choose, the dominant hue should match your watch.

### The Watch

Leave the gas-station digital at home. If you've not saved up quite enough for a TAG, wear nothing.

*Wool tuxedo by Ermenegildo Zegna. Cotton shirt, cotton pocket square, silk bow tie, and silk cummerbund by Brooks Brothers. Leather shoes by John Lobb.*

## THE INVITATION TRANSLATOR

| What it says | What it implies | What it really means |
|---|---|---|
| Black tie | Tuxedo only | Tuxedo only, and not a black suit |
| Cocktail attire | A suit, shirt, and tie | Don't look as if you came straight from the office, even if you did (see above left) |
| Black-tie optional | You can choose between black tie and a suit | Black tie |
| Alternative black tie | Black tie, but with a twist | Black tie |
| Business casual | Polo shirt, chinos | A dress shirt that's not a polo shirt. No sneakers, no jeans. |
| Come as you are | Take a shower, at least | Dress any way you like |
| P.B.A.B. | Please bring a bottle of wine | Bring a bottle of good wine |

# *Great Moments in* **Tuxedos**

Allen, W., 1979

Martin, D., 1988

Astaire, F., 1930s

Bogart, H., 1942

Charles, R., 1967

Warhol, A., 1973

Corleone, V., 1972

# THE BOW TIE

## EVERY MAN SHOULD KNOW HOW TO DO THIS

**1.**
Make a simple knot with both ends, allowing slightly more length (one to two inches) on the end of **A**.

**2.**
Lift **A** out of the way, fold **B** into the normal bow shape, and position it on the first knot you made.

**3.**
Drop **A** vertically over folded end **B**.

**4.**
Then double **A** back on itself and position it over the knot so that the two folded ends make a cross.

**5.**
The hard part: Pass folded end **A** under and behind the left side (yours) of the knot, and through the loop behind folded end **B**.

**6.**
Tighten the knot you have now created, straightening any crumples and creases, particularly in the narrow part at the center.

## THE ESSENTIAL RULES OF
# *Black Tie*

Wearing a tuxedo can be a lot like speaking an unfamiliar language. The smallest mistake can ruin the whole effect. Here's how to get it right.

> You can add personal touches after you've nailed the standard. For your basic tux, stick with tradition. This dictates a one-button jacket with peaked lapels, a true pleat-front or marcella-front shirt (with French cuffs), black wool or silk socks, and black patent-leather lace-ups or polished oxfords. Bow tie only, in red or black (and tied yourself—it's the mark of a gentleman). And a cummerbund, of course.

> The pleats of the cummerbund should face upward.

> Your cuff links should match your watch: gold with gold, silver with steel, and so on.

> Leave your wallet at home and take a money clip instead. It's smaller, so it won't distort the lines of your tux.

# *Three Ways of* **the Wedding**

### HOW TO DRESS, DRINK, AND DANCE LIKE THE LIFE OF THE PARTY

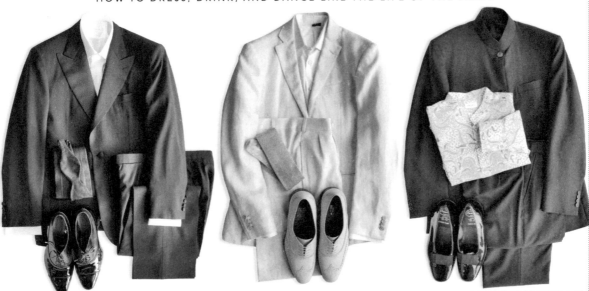

|  | BLACK TIE | BEACH | THEME |
|---|---|---|---|
|  | One-button wool tuxedo, cotton formal shirt, silk cummerbund, silk bow tie, and patent-leather shoes by Brioni. | Linen suit and cotton shirt by Ermenegildo Zegna. Silk tie by J. Press. Leather-and-canvas shoes by Salvatore Ferragamo. | Wool Nehru-collar suit and cotton Nehru-collar shirt by Ascot Chang. Patent-leather loafers by Church's. |
| **Attire** | Black tie means black tie—bow tie, cummerbund, the whole shebang. Oh, and "black tie optional"? They mean they would really prefer it but don't want to come off as stiff. | Unless the invite dictates otherwise, keep it simple with a linen suit or khakis and a blazer. Wear a tie, but if you're the only one wearing one, feel free to remove it and go open neck. | If the invitation specifies a certain kind of dress—like, say, Indian—go along with it or don't go at all. No one wants to be the guy in the boring blue suit while everyone else is decked out. |
| **Dancing** | One-on-one with your date. No grinding or feigned ass slapping—and do not, under any circumstances, throw your hands in the air like you just don't care. | Keep it light and PG-rated. If a clapping circle forms around a drunk and possibly break-dancing guest, make sure you are not that guest. | Follow the host's lead and be a good sport. Don't make a mad dash for the bar the minute they start in on the hora or square dancing. |
| **Drinking** | Cocktails to start, wine with dinner, and, if at all possible, pace yourself. | This is your one opportunity to partake in pink drinks or fruity mixers without judgment. | If there's a specialty drink, try it, and bring one over for the groom as well. Then it's back to your regularly scheduled drinking. |
| **And for what it's worth** | Women don't like being dipped nearly as much as you think they do. | Hold your date's shoes when walking in the sand. | No matter how crazy the ritual may seem, participate and look happy doing it. |

### WEDDING GIFTS NO MAN SHOULD GIVE

Unicycle  Lawn darts  Nunchucks  Kittens  Slim Jims  Doggie stairs  Puffy toilet-seat cover

*How to Buy*

# A FAKE DIAMOND
### (If You Must)

**Imitations have grades** the same way real diamonds do— cubic zirconia, for example, range from A (low quality) to AAAAA (high)—meaning some fakes will look better (and cost more) than others.

**Know your options.** CZ has better clarity, but moissanite is more brilliant because it is doubly refractive. If you want to opt for crystal, remember, what you're really doing is replacing a stone with glass.

**Always compare** your imitation side by side with the real thing before you buy it.

**Don't go too big.** For starters, unless you're a Saudi prince, people will know it's fake. Plus, CZ weighs about one and a half times more than diamond, so the bigger the rock, the more likely the recipient can feel the difference.

# SO YOU WANT TO BUY A DIAMOND

WHAT WE TALK ABOUT WHEN WE TALK ABOUT DIAMONDS

### COLOR

There are pink and yellow and even black diamonds, but she probably wants a white one. The whiter the stone, the higher the price, with the official grade range running from D (colorless) to Z (a light yellow). Anything higher than an I (i.e., D to H) will appear white enough for the most discerning eyes.

### CUT

You've got plenty of options, and keep in mind that the deeper the stone, the more light it will reflect and the more sparkle it will give off. Here are a few popular cuts:

| EMERALD | MARQUISE | OVAL | PEAR | PRINCESS | ROUND | ASCHER |

### CLARITY

Or: How jewelers describe the number and degree of the stone's flaws and/or "inclusions" (i.e., blemishes that interfere with light passing through the diamond). It's tough to find diamonds of the highest grade, Flawless (FL), so you should be okay with the next three levels down: Internally Flawless (IF); Very, Very Slightly Included (VVS1, VVS2); and Very Slightly Included (VS1, VS2).

### CARAT

You know the drill here, and here are some life-size examples of what we're talking about:

| 0.25 | 0.50 | 0.75 | 1.0 | 1.5 | 2.0 | 3.0 |

She will tell you that she doesn't care about size, and maybe she's telling the truth. Maybe.

### COST

There are a multitude of factors in determining the cost of a diamond, but generally speaking, you can get a pretty good one-carat diamond for $5,000 to $7,000. Budget accordingly.

## AND DON'T FORGET THE OTHER STONES

| **ruby** | **emerald** | **sapphire** | **garnet** |
|---|---|---|---|
| **Best color:** Pigeon blood | **Best color:** Deep green, no light green | **Best color:** Dark blue, but not a black blue | **Best color:** Mandarin |
| **Best cut:** Oval | **Best cut:** Rectangular | **Best cut:** Oval | **Best cut:** Round |
| **Best for:** Earrings. They retain sparkle even at night, good for being in view. | **Best for:** Necklace. Emeralds are fragile and not good for casual wear. | **Best for:** Bracelet or necklace | **Best for:** Big statement pieces |

*With thanks to Nicolas Luchsinger, New York store director and heritage curator for Van Cleef & Arpels.*

## THE REASONABLY ENTHUSIASTIC GROOM'S TO-DO LIST

Because she's not the only one with responsibilities

- ☐ PROPOSE.
- ☐ SUBMIT engagement announcement to the local paper, town gossip, or AOL Patch blogger.
- ☐ CHOOSE your best man (see page 94 for help) and groomsmen.
- ☐ DETERMINE budget. Add 20 percent.
- ☐ BUILD a guest list. (Matrimony tip: The more weddings you've had, the fewer people you invite.)
- ☐ BOOK venue, officiant, music, photographer, florist,

wedding planner, caterer, hotel block, invitation designer, rehearsal-dinner location, honeymoon, et cet.
- ☐ DON'T let her know you referred to anything as "et cet."
- ☐ OBTAIN marriage license.
- ☐ BUY rings.
- ☐ SELECT gifts for your groomsmen.
- ☐ ESTABLISH reception hashtag (for the Instagramming!).
- ☐ PANIC. Briefly.
- ☐ SHOW up.
- ☐ SMILE.
- ☐ EAT.
- ☐ DANCE a bit.
- ☐ SMILE.
- ☐ SLEEP.
- ☐ BRUNCH.
- ☐ HONEYMOON.

## Everything You Need to Know About a Wedding
# *You Can Learn from the Invitation*

### Yes, really.

The invitation reads:

> *Mr. and Mrs. Barack Obama*
>
> REQUEST THE HONOUR OF YOUR PRESENCE
>
> AT THE MARRIAGE OF THEIR DAUGHTER
>
> *Malia Ann*
>
> TO
>
> *Mr. Justin Drew Bieber*
>
> AT THE CHICAGO BOTANIC GARDEN
>
> SATURDAY, THE FIFTEENTH OF JUNE
>
> TWO O'CLOCK IN THE AFTERNOON
>
> TWO THOUSAND AND TWENTY-FOUR

**A Paper Stock:** Pick up the invitation and throw it. The farther it goes, the heavier the stock and the more expensive the invitation. If the invitation goes far, you can expect a top-shelf open bar and decent food; if it falls slowly to the ground, hit the ATM to pay for the cash bar and have a sandwich before you leave.

**B Font:** Calligraphy? The fancier the script, the more formal the wedding. Polish your shoes and get ready for a long night. Raised glossy type? A very big affair. Basic sans-serif type? Probably a little more casual and low-key. Wacky font? Consider staying home.

**C The Announcement:** First, are the parents a package deal, e.g., Mr. and Mrs. So-and-So? If so, they're still together; if not, they're probably divorced and there is bound to be some tension in the room. Second, is it just the bride's parents at the top, meaning they're your hosts, or is it the groom's too, meaning they're splitting the tab? Either way, it pays to know who your host is so you can thank people accordingly.

**D Spellings:** That extra u in honour? The time and year spelled out? These people take weddings very seriously. Long ceremony. Receiving lines. The works. Bring a flask.

**E Envelope:** The more envelopes and tissue paper in the whole package, the longer the cocktail hour will be.

---

### *Banned:* A FEW WEDDING RITUALS WE COULD DO WITHOUT

Hour-plus time gaps between the ceremony and the reception • Throwing rice
Corinthians 13:4 (Google it) • Guest books
Bride and groom throwing/smearing wedding cake on each other
Pachelbel's "Canon in D Major" (for ceremony time) • "At Last" by Etta James (for the wedding song)
"Brick House" by the Commodores (for getting-down time) • The Electric Slide • The conga line

---

## THE TROUBLESHOOTING GUIDE
### TO WEDDINGS

**How is it possible not to get absolutely hammered when dealing with an open bar?**

First, realize you are not, in fact, 17 years old and sneaking rum and Cokes at your cousin Larry's wedding. Second, you can get hammered, although you should do it gradually. Start with something strong and drink it slowly—this will be your base buzz—and stick with drinks on the rocks. (The ice will help dilute the booze.) Alternate one cocktail with one glass of water, and beware free-flowing wine at dinner.

**How can I applaud a toast if I'm holding a glass?**

Just tap your glass. It's not the sound that counts but the gesture.

**Shit. I have to give a toast.**

Stand up. Begin by telling everyone in the room your relationship to the bride and groom. Avoid inside jokes that only a few people will understand. Keep it PG. Don't mention past relationships. Anecdotes are good. Don't end on a joke. Keep it under five minutes.

**I've spilled red wine on the bride's dress.**

Don't laugh. This happens, people. The only thing you can do is grab some napkins and a glass of water and promptly hand them to the bride. (Do not, under any circumstances, try to blot out the wine yourself—she's someone's wife now.) She will be upset, or laughing, or both, and the best you can do is apologize, keep a low profile, and drink water.

---

# A Biased Zoology of Women at Weddings

**THE BRIDE**

It's her special day and she won't let anyone ruin it. Rearrange the seating cards at your own peril.

**THE MOTHER OF THE BRIDE**

Crying. Always with the crying. Tell her she looks lovely and ask her to dance.

**THE SLUTTY BRIDESMAID**

If you're single, be afraid. If you're married, be very afraid. She's serviced more wedding guests than a caterer.

**THE HOMELY DISTANT RELATION**

Make small talk and her day with one simple, harmless compliment, e.g., "I like your dress."

**THE SPINSTER OLDER SISTER**

Avoid at all costs. She's jealous, pissed off, and liable to take it out on you.

# The Well-Dressed Honeymooner

### Ideal clothes for any destination

**ON THE MOUNTAIN**
Your priority is warmth, so layer, preferably with items from a specialty brand like Patagonia, which really knows what it's doing. Plus, you'll look like you actually know a thing or two about hiking. Down jacket by Patagonia. Cotton sweatshirt by Burberry London. Cotton pants by Moncler Grenoble. Boots by Red Wing Heritage. Socks by REI.

**ON SAFARI**
It'll be hot, so focus on lightweight cotton. Bring at least one long-sleeved shirt to protect you when you're hiking through the bush, and a jacket, because it will get very cold at night. Jacket by L. L. Bean Signature. Vest by Ermenegildo Zegna. Henley by AG Adriano Goldschmied. Pants by Michael Bastian. Boots by John Varvatos.

**IN EUROPE**
You don't need a tie, but the jacket is key, ensuring that you will fit in whether you're at a museum, a restaurant, or just strolling the streets. Let the only thing that announces your nationality be your accent. Two-button wool-silk-and-linen jacket by Luigi Bianchi Mantova. Cotton shirt by Boglioli. Cotton chinos by MAC. Leather shoes by John Lobb.

**AT THE BEACH**
If you're headed to a nice resort, it might be time to invest in a new swimsuit. Pick a pattern, which will be more forgiving if you haven't yet picked up a tan. If you're exceedingly brave, a sarong can be a useful cover-up. T-shirt by Todd Snyder. Swim trunks by J. Crew. Wrap by Brioni. Flip-flops by Havaianas. Sunglasses by Oliver Peoples.

## HOW TO MAKE YOUR MARRIAGE LAST

Helpful tips for keeping your new covenant
BY STACEY GRENROCK WOODS

Marry someone who likes all the same things as you. This may not seem like much, but if your wife consistently prefers a movie like *Lincoln* to, say, *G.I. Joe: Retaliation*, you may both lose interest, and your disinterest will be compounded daily.

More important, you two should hate all the same things, too. The thrill she feels when you lambaste, let's say, Megan Fox will go a long way.

Install good-quality locks on all bathroom doors.

Keep your marriage free of stress by avoiding prolonged contact with relatives, coworkers, alternative pets, and children of all ages.

Keep financial woes at bay by earning, inheriting, stealing, or otherwise amassing great wealth. That way, you can spend more time pursuing arts and leisure activities. (If you're having trouble with this, consult Kickstarter.)

Fill your home with large flat-screen televisions, and make sure you have enough DVR space for the Food Network, the Cooking Channel, the Military Channel, and a little Logo.

Develop a wide range of outside interests and encourage each other to play Words with Friends with all kinds of different people.

Stay fit!

When you masturbate, fantasize about her at least every third time.

Clear history.

Clear recent searches.

# HOW TO CHOOSE YOUR BEST MAN

Your best friend is not always your best choice.
Hand out to all interested parties.

**1. Are you the brother of the groom?**
a) Yes (100)
b) No (0)

**2. Are you the father of the groom?**
a) Yes (–50)
b) No (5)
c) Yes, but this is the South and it's tradition. (100)

**3. Would friends characterize you as responsible?**
a) Yes (10)
b) No (0)

**4. Fun?**
a) Yes (10)
b) No (0)

**5. Selfish?**
a) Yes (–5)
b) No (0)

**6.** If, for whatever reason, the groom is unable to perform his duties through this marriage, are you willing to step up?
a) Of course. (–10)
b) That's not real. (5)

**7. Breath mint?**
a) Sure, thanks. (0)
b) Always carry them. Here you go. (5)

**8. Beer pong?**
a) Where!? (5)
b) I am an adult. (–10)

**9. True or false:** If no one is dancing, it is the best man's responsibility to get things started.
a) True (5)
b) False (0)
c) I assure you that there will never be a time when no one is dancing, drinking, hugging, or attempting all three simultaneously. (15)

**10. What is your ideal bachelor party?**
a) A weekend away with ten or so good friends. Some beers. Some grilling. (10)
b) A strip club or something. (0)
c) Movie night! (–5)

**11. Take 4 points off your score for each of the following words or phrases you've used in the past six months.**
a) You da man!
b) *Broseph.*
c) *Comme ci, comme ça.*
d) *Dude.* It's a whole new *Hobbit* trilogy.
e) *Cray cray.*
f) I hate to bring it up, but you still owe me two dollars.

**12. Can I trust you to hold on to the rings?**
a) Yes (5)
b) No (–5)
c) I'm offended that you had to ask. (10)
d) Trick question! I'm not your ring bearer. (–5)

**13. My niece goes missing at the reception. What do you do?**
a) Make sure no one's accusing me of losing her. (–10)
b) Mention it to her parents. (–5)
c) Check the sofas and closets; she probably just fell asleep. (5)
d) Bring her back from the dance floor, apologize, and let them be surprised when they see that the photographer got one of those cute pictures in which she's dancing by standing on your shoes. (10)

**14. Which of the following sentences are you most likely to use in your toast?**
a) I love you guys. (10)
b) If I can find someone who makes me half as happy as she makes you, I'll consider myself a lucky man. (5)
c) You sure went through a lot of candidates before settling on this one. (–10)
d) You sure went through a lot of candidates before settling for this one. (–20)
e) She should be with me. (–50)

**15. Can you be appropriate in front of older people?**
a) Yes (10)
b) No (–10)

**16. My nana will be there.**
a) Cute. (5)
b) Let it go. I apologized. (–15)

**17. We need a ride to the airport, please.**
a) Gladly. Let me get my keys. (5)
b) Me, too. (–5)

## – ANSWER KEY –

- **MORE THAN 100 TOTAL POINTS**
  You will be the best man.

- **50 TO 100 POINTS**
  You'll probably be a groomsman. That's still something.

- **FEWER THAN 50 POINTS**
  Consider yourself lucky to be invited.

## WEDDING PREP

One of these vows is not like the others.
Find it.

......................
*To HAVE*
......................
*To HOLD*
......................
*To LOVE*
......................
*To CHERISH*
......................
*To LISTEN to*
......................
*To VALUE*
......................
*To RESPECT*
......................
*To HONOR*
......................
*To MONITOR closely at all times*

## THE PEP TALK

### A Few Words for a Man on His Wedding Day

THE WORST THING that can happen at the ceremony will not happen. You will not faint. You will not flub your lines. The best man will not throw up. She will not run away from you and get on a bus. No uncle will split his suit pants bending over. Nothing that *America's Funniest Home Videos* leads you to believe may happen will happen. Because unless you've been practicing an elaborate entrance involving choreography and the bride's being carried in on a litter (which is a mistake, frankly, but you will get through it), this is not a high-pressure situation. Almost everything is scripted, prescribed, watched over, ordained by God, and decreed by the state. And everyone knows what their role is—you, your bride, the officiant, the guests, the bored waiters, everyone.

Also, you have your shit together. This is not a small thing. She has her shit together, too. And the people around you have their shit together. That's why you're all gathered on this glorious day: to celebrate having your shit together.

You know what to expect at the ceremony. It's on the program. And it includes getting married. Not *wanting* to be married. Which is not simple. Nor *being* married. Which is not simple. But *getting* married. Which is simple. Walk and smile. Say "I do." Walk and smile. Done.

The reception is also simple—if you know how to attend a party, you know how to attend your own reception—but it's not quite as simple as the ceremony. Because it involves one thing that the both of you and the both of you alone must independently express without prompting: thanks. Everyone must be thanked. Even that guy over there. This is a requirement. For efficiency's sake, do this when people are still seated at tables. As soon as the appetizer course is served, begin going around to each table (both of you) to offer thanks and bask in the good wishes. Pace yourself. Do a few tables, go eat something, do a few more tables, go drink something (not too much), do a few more tables, and you'll be done before dessert. When you've walked away from the last table, you will be seen as a grateful man. And she will be seen as lucky to have you. Easy. Congratulations. —ROSS McCAMMON

# With This Ring

Or maybe that one. A brief but illuminating look at wedding bands.

## STYLES

### DOMED
The classic choice. Simple and understated. Because they are peaked (when looked at in profile), domed rings can be slightly more susceptible to dings. PLATINUM RING BY DAVID YURMAN.

### FLAT
As simple and understated as a domed ring, but with a level surface and squared edges for a modern feel. STERLING-SILVER RING BY DAVID YURMAN.

### PATTERNED
Popular options are milgrain (textured along the edges), woven (a simple over-under pattern), and wave (you know, the ocean). WHITE-GOLD RING BY VAN CLEEF & ARPELS.

### GEMSTONE
When patterned rings just don't provide enough flash. The safest choice is diamonds, and only just a few. Try to keep them small. WHITE GOLD-AND-DIAMOND RING BY CARTIER.

## METALS

- Gold is the most traditional. It was also the most popular until a few years ago, when sterling silver took over.

- Platinum is the most expensive option. But also the shiniest! (And thus the worst at hiding scratches.) It's hypoallergenic, too, which can be beneficial for up to 15 percent of men.

- Sterling silver is a less expensive choice yet still has a high shine. It smudges easily, so be ready for frequent polishing.

- Your other two budget-friendly options are titanium—hypoallergenic, light, and durable, with a matte finish—and tungsten, which is as shiny as silver but much darker and more resistant to scratches.

## Your Wedding Photo

*It's the most lasting picture you'll ever take. Make it good.*

Never look at the camera.

Avoid the setup. A candid shot captures real emotion, from body language to hand placement.

Don't be afraid of the dress. You just married this woman, right? If you're leaning in to avoid damaging her dress, you'll leave a gap between you, which doesn't exactly convey love.

If you're wearing a jacket, try not to raise your arms, unless you want to look like you're wearing a cape.

The kiss shot: Make sure both hands are on the bride. A lot of grooms leave one arm hanging in front. Strange. Not flattering.

Put one foot slightly behind the other, directly beneath your spine. It forces you to stand up straight.

Have the photographer get on a stool. The slight downward angle and a telephoto lens flatten features and generally make everyone look more beautiful.

No mustaches.

*With thanks to Brian Dorsey of Brian Dorsey Studios in New York City.*

# The **WORST-CASE-SCENARIO** Guide to Being a Good **GROOMSMAN**

### THREE PROBLEMATIC SCENARIOS, THREE HEROIC SOLUTIONS

**ISSUE:** With all heads turned up the aisle toward the bride, no one sees Grandma struggling to get out of her chair.
**RESPONSIBILITY:** Help her. You can't be blamed for ostentatious chivalry, since no one's looking at you anyway. When she's stable (and before the bride—and the group gaze—reaches you), return to your place in the wedding party.

**ISSUE:** No one's dancing.
**RESPONSIBILITY:** Grab a (willing) mom, grandma, or child and lead her to the dance floor. (Not your date. That's not as fun or cute to watch.) People will soon follow your lead. If for whatever reason they don't, give up when the song is over. Longer than that and you risk coming off as creepy.

**ISSUE:** Cousin Tina isn't having much fun.
**RESPONSIBILITY:** Get her a drink. Ask her to tell you an embarrassing story about the bride/groom. Try to get her to dance or to watch you do so. Giving her something to focus on will make her feel less uncomfortable. But remember: You owe her 20 minutes, tops. If she's still bored at that point, she'll be that way all night.

## *So you met* SObrmEONE — *Can you act on your new feelings? Depends.*

### THEIR RELATION TO THE BRIDE OR GROOM
(YOUR RELATION TO THE BRIDE OR GROOM)

| | FRIEND | CLOSE FRIEND | RELATIVE | DISTANT RELATIVE | CO-WORKER | GUEST'S DATE | BRIDE | GROOM |
|---|---|---|---|---|---|---|---|---|
| **FRIEND** | Proceed | Proceed | Caution | Proceed | Caution | Proceed | X | X |
| **CLOSE FRIEND** | Proceed | Caution | Caution | Caution | Caution | Caution | X | X |
| **RELATIVE** | Proceed | Proceed | X | X | Proceed | Proceed | X | X |
| **DISTANT RELATIVE** | Proceed | Proceed | X | Caution | Proceed | Proceed | X | X |
| **COWORKER** | Proceed | Caution | Caution | Proceed | Caution | Proceed | X | X |
| **GUEST'S DATE** | Proceed | Proceed | Proceed | Proceed | Proceed | Proceed | X | X |
| **BRIDE** | X | X | X | X | X | X | | Proceed |
| **GROOM** | X | X | X | X | X | X | Proceed | |

**LEGEND ▶** PROCEED: 🙌 PROCEED WITH CAUTION: ⚠ UNADVISED: X

---

**THE DRINKS TIMELINE:** Activities that will seem like good ideas, depending on your level of consumption

**1 DRINK**
Talk to your date.
Whisper during the toast.
Slow dance.

**2 DRINKS**
Talk to the woman next to your date.
Fast dance.
Introduce yourself at the grandparents' table.

**3 DRINKS**
Yell to the woman at the next table.
Sing a little.
Dance with the mother of the bride.

# The [ ] *really* know how to **party**

Wedding traditions from around the world

**GREEKS** You know about the plate breaking, which brings good luck—and is just plain fun. But before that, in many villages locals roll a baby on the couple's bed, hoping to encourage fertility. One highlight of the ceremony is the *zeibekiko*, often referred to as the drunken-sailor dance, since it basically looks like a drunken sailor spinning and bouncing slowly around the dance floor. The groom and other men participate while guests throw flowers, whistle, and yell, "*Opa!*" at every opportunity.

**INDIANS** When it comes to big weddings, no one does it better. First, the bride and her friends have their hands and feet painted in henna for the *mehndi*. In the tradition of all traditions, the *baraat*, the groom rides in on an elephant or a white horse to kick off the official ceremony. There's also the elaborate, multicolored canopy, under which the families perform ceremonies around a sacred fire to signify their new union, and some pretty fantastic dancing. But really, nothing beats the elephant.

**CHINESE** It's all about the food—and messing with the betrothed. The entire ceremony centers on an extensive meal during which the bride and groom circulate among the guests. At each table the guests stack up their *hong bao*, or red envelopes, filled with money. To receive the gifts, the couple must often do whatever the table tells them to, whether it's eating a shrimp ball off a chopstick together à la *Lady and the Tramp*, moving an egg up one of the groom's pant legs and down the other while blindfolded, or whatever this is, above.

**JEWS** Traditionally it takes place beneath a *chuppah*—a tent within the venue held up by four poles, symbolizing the house within which the bride and groom will begin their lives. At the conclusion of the ceremony, the groom crushes a wineglass wrapped in cloth. A few people might yell, "Mazel tov!" Then the fun begins. At the reception, the bride and groom are each raised on a chair for the dancing of the hora. This can be a time to impress and entertain the new couple, sometimes including men doing Russian-style squat dances and flips.

*A Lesson in Archetypes:* **The Wedding Band** *With thanks to Tzo Ai Ang of Ang Weddings and Events in New York City.*

| | THE DEEJAY | THE STRING QUARTET | THE CROONER | THE COVER BAND |
|---|---|---|---|---|
| **STRENGTHS** | Doesn't have to learn a song to be able to play it. Encourages dancing. | Unobtrusive, never overpowering. Plays throughout ceremony and reception. Encourages waltzing. | Soothing, makes for excellent background music. | Energy. Lots of dancing. Fun. |
| **WEAKNESSES** | Not so good for background music during dinner. | Hard to "let loose" to. Encourages waltzing. | Not so much enjoyed by guests under 45. | "Shout!" will be fun no matter who sings it. That's not the case with a lot of other music, so choose your playlist carefully. |
| **AVERAGE COST** | $1,500 to $3,000 | $5,000 to $10,000 | $11,000 to $22,000 (including band) | $10,000 to $20,000 |

**4 DRINKS**
Help yourself to two more pieces of cake.

Ask Uncle Chuck how much his gift cost.

Dance with the father of the bride.

**5 DRINKS**
Stop talking to your date.

Complain about the bride.

Look at dark corners as possible restrooms.

**6 DRINKS**
"It's okay if I lie down here, right?"

# HOW TO:
# NAVIGATE THE **AFTERPARTY**

### THE WEDDING IS OVER. THE FUN, NOT SO MUCH.

The bride and groom may change clothes. You should not. Taking a break between the wedding and afterparty means getting a chance to sit down. Which means a chance to fall asleep. Don't preempt your second wind.

With a thinned-out crowd, the bride and groom **[A]** no longer have responsibilities—or an obligation to talk to distant relatives. This is your best chance to spend some time with them.

Make sure you have cash. Cash bar at the reception is annoying. Cash bar at the after-party is standard.

Stick with beer **[B]**. You're winding down at this point, for one thing, and it's easier to buy rounds without taking orders.

Most events will provide some sort of comfort food, but if not, you don't want to be the only person sitting down to a greasy bag of delivery. Get a few people together and order a bunch of pizzas

**[C]** for the room. Remember: You're not the only one who's drunk and hungry. You'll be a hero.

If that lonely bridesmaid **[D]** is going to make her move, now is the time. Avoid/engage accordingly.

If there's a TV **[E]**, it will be surrounded by older men. They don't want to talk. But they'd love for you to join them.

Everyone's had a bit to drink, which makes it your best time to meet new people. Just don't stay too long with one group and wear out your welcome.

Unlike at the reception, you don't have to stay to a certain point. Stay until the room starts spinning or the bride's cousin corners you to discuss his thoughts on health care.

If your sweet-talking skills are still functional, try to get the bartender **[F]** to give you a leftover bottle of booze. Somebody's gotta start the after-afterparty, right?

---

# LORD of the DANCE

### A FEW RULES FOR CUTTING A RESPECTABLE RUG

Always lead your date to the dance floor. It's a little formal, but so are weddings.

No dipping.

Spins, however, are encouraged. (Just remember that she's been drinking.)

If you know the mother of the bride or groom, ask her for a dance. It's her day, too.

Was that air drumming? Carry on.

If your efforts to start a group rendition of the Electric Slide do not find immediate group approval, move on.

Are you the only one tangoing? Stop.

Have another drink.

Relax.

Stop worrying about how you'll look in the pictures.

---

## THE GENEROSITY CALCULATOR

Check off each of the following experiences, institutions, or people you have in common with the bride or groom. Multiply the number of check marks by $20 to find out how much you should spend on the couple's gift.

☐ ALMA MATER *(including preschool, elementary, middle, high, college, or graduate)*

☐ FRATERNITY/ SORORITY

☐ PARENT/ GRANDPARENT

☐ MISTRESS

☐ CHILD

☐ EMPLOYER

☐ HOUSE OF WORSHIP

☐ TROOP *(including Cub, Boy, and Eagle Scouts, and their female equivalents)*

☐ POTTERY CLASS

☐ MEETUP GROUP

☐ ROTARY CLUB

☐ COUNTRY CLUB

☐ SUMMER CAMP

☐ MILITARY UNIT

☐ REC-LEAGUE SPORTS TEAM

☐ COMPLEMENTARY TATTOO

☐ CUL-DE-SAC

☐ CARPOOL

☐ NEIGHBORHOOD WATCH

*TOTAL: $ _____*

---

## HOW TO
## GO OFF REGISTRY

## STEP ONE:

# SEATING:
## A HOW TO

Behavioral tips for optimizing
your reception-table fun

Never try to change your table assignment. You know better than that.

It is perfectly acceptable to continue eating during the toast(s).

If only a few places at the table have been taken, don't sit as far away from them as possible. Make a new friend.

Talking, however, should be saved until the toasts are finished. Even if you all agree the toasts are boring.

Similarly, don't leave just one spot between you and another guest. Most people are here with a date.

Limit your alcohol consumption. (This will also help with the tip above.)

Introduce yourself as people sit. It's easier to remember names for a few small groups than for one large one.

No asking for seconds. Even if it was delicious. (But you can probably sneak another piece of cake.)

Stop clinking your glass. It's strange to enjoy watching other people kiss that much.

## FREQUENTLY ASKED QUESTIONS

**Q. Should I bring my gift to the wedding?**
**A.** No. Ship it to the newlyweds at home.

**Q. May I bring my kids?**
**A.** Are those kids the flower girl or ring bearer? If not, then no.

**Q. May I take my coat off to dance?**
**A.** Yes, but only after the groom or his father does so.

**Q. Is there a foolproof way to avoid a hangover?**
**A.** No. Just take a few Advil before bed, and realize you aren't alone.

**Q. When may I leave?**
**A.** When the dinner is concluded and the cake has been cut.

**Q. But I'm the groom.**
**A.** In that case, not until the last light is turned off.

**Q. Should I tip the bartender?**
**A.** Can't hurt. You know how annoying you people can be.

**Q. You people?**
**A.** That joke's a little old by now, don't you think?

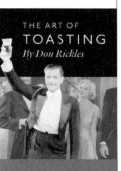

## THE ART OF TOASTING
### By Don Rickles

Prepare nothing and be confident. I have no idea what I'm going to say when I stand up to give a toast. But I do know that anything I say I find funny. If you start questioning your toast, you're in a lot of trouble. So find the right attitude and go with it. Riff on the bride or groom for most of it. Just be sure to be respectful. Be sure not to say something sappy in the middle of the toast. You put kindness in the middle and everybody will leave. Do kindness at the end. I call it my rabbi speech. It's where you let the couple know that you really care about them. That's why you're there. Because you shouldn't be toasting someone you don't like.

*Adapted from Esquire, December 2005.*

## THE ART OF BEING TOASTED

Try to keep a low profile. Don't talk to one group of people for too long—less chance of saying something stupid. Drink water. Smile. Not that much. Oh, you meant that way? Just sit and smile.

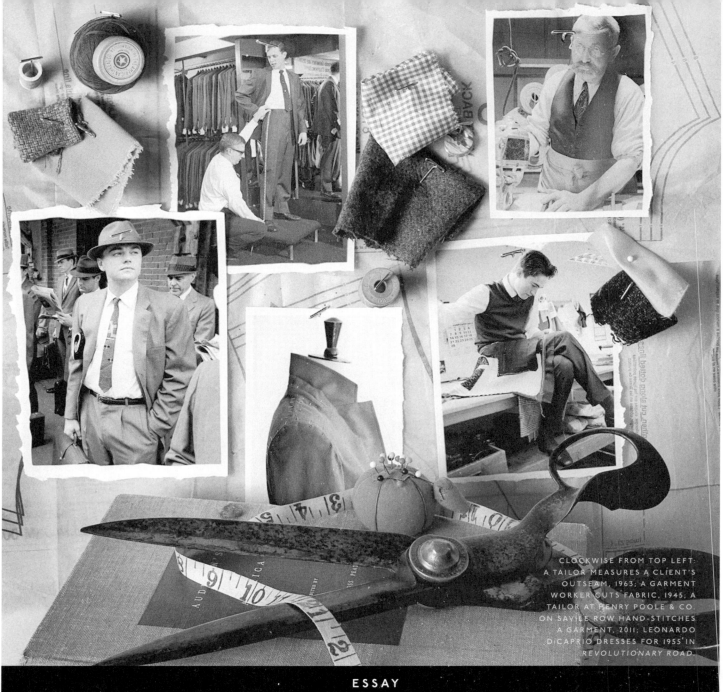

## ESSAY

# FIT
## Is a Four-Letter Word

HOW AMERICANS LEARNED TO STOP WORRYING
AND LOVE A SUIT THAT ACTUALLY (REALLY, TRULY) FITS

BY NICK SULLIVAN

ITALIANS ARE EMOTIONAL, which makes for interesting lunches. One afternoon, not too long ago, having lunch with Andrea Benedini, export manager of Luigi Bianchi Mantova—a manufacturer of tailored garments—was like watching fireworks. Amid the branzino and the costoletta, the hands thrust and the steel stabbed as he spoke about his work. He was upset, you see, about suits. Suits are his family's business: His mother is a Bianchi, and since Luigi Bianchi has been making men's clothes in Mantova for bang on a century, this matters quite a lot. The thorn in Benedini's otherwise unruffled side—and we have spoken about it many times—is fit, and the fact that in America men like to wear clothes, suits specifically, that don't fit well. "It was a culture shock when I moved to America," he says. "Big, floppy, messy suits on a professional business guy?" *Hand gestures.* "I couldn't believe that the sales staff in big stores would be pushing clothes to guys that would make them look fat"— *more agitated hand gestures*—"or at least like a clown. Honestly, it's better to stay in a T-shirt." *Hand gestures of resignation.* Benedini had to respect demand, though, if he wanted to build a market here. "I had to make a fit just for the American market, with big arms, no fit to the chest, no waist, baggy pants. It was depressing."

Sartorial claustrophobia (yes, I made the term up) has been a recurring theme in Italy—in connection with America— among higher-end labels for years, with designers and tailors alike pointing out, with varying degrees of emotion, that wearing a loose-cut jacket with low armholes, far from being comfortable, can only be more awkward, given the swaths of extra cloth. Many point out that a tailor's real artistry is about using those hundreds of individually sewn pad stitches and carefully layered canvases to coax a form of three-dimensional memory into the chest pieces of a jacket so that they perfectly overlay the torso. All of that is rather wasted if a man goes and buys a size too big. One Neapolitan designer who was trained in London cites a Savile Row tailor famed for making tight-fitting cavalry officers' uniforms, who said that if you can charge in the saddle and kill with a sword at the gallop in such close-cut tailoring, freedom of movement at the office cannot really be an issue.

It falls to the likes of Benedini and Enrico Libani, managing partner of Attolini—a Neapolitan master of handmade ready-to-wear that opens its first stand-alone store in New York this fall— to make the case to their U.S. clients. "I always say to a customer who is unaccustomed to our close fit, 'When you wear a jersey undershirt, is it uncomfortable?' No. Yet it's worn very close to the skin. The same goes for the blazer. The art is in making it super comfortable." Attolini, like other Neapolitan brands, has the advantage of a full hand make. The more hand cutting and sewing there is (especially when it's done in Italy), the less structure is needed, and the closer the fit can be to the body.

But America is not Italy, even though it's taken most of its style cues from that country since World War II. Benedini and his cohorts are fighting a tradition of looser fits that goes way back to the Brooks Brothers sack suit of the mid-20th century, something the trad contingent will not abandon easily. In the nation that invented

and propagated the idea of casualness, looser-fitting clothes are still part of the national psyche.

There's taste, too. It is a personal theory of mine that while European style takes much of its inspiration from the tight-fitting dynamic of the 1960s—i.e., the time it finally emerged from postwar poverty into modern prosperity—America has a similar nostalgia for the golden age of the 1950s, when men were men and suits were a different, bigger kettle of fish altogether and the aforementioned sack suit ruled the day.

But something major happened during the recession. Emerging from it, rather than returning to their safe old ways, men have found a new enthusiasm for expressing themselves with their clothing, through color and pattern and by putting this with that. Woe betide the retailer who has not kept pace. Benedini's personal ten-year crusade now seems to be making headway. Sales of the old American fit are flat, while sales of his closer-fitting L.B.M. 1911 brand are up. "The biggest satisfaction is speaking to our core customer, a 35-year-old guy," he says. "He has a hungry new attitude for making his own style on his own terms."

"The change" he goes on, "is not just in the American man but in the retailers, too. They knew they had to adapt their approach because the classic old-style clothes were not selling. Clothes now need to be more casual, but conversely, they have to be more elegant; to be elegant, they have to be closer-fitting." They're also typical of the high-low mood of men's fashion right now, but they don't work if they don't fit well. Sleeves should be narrow, armholes should be high. The bottom hem of the jacket barely covers the glutes.

Which brings us to Benedini's next challenge. The pants . . .

*Look for higher, smaller armholes, a narrower sleeve, and shoulders that follow your body's natural curve. The side should hug your body, but not so much that you see creases or ripples radiating from fastened buttons.*

DOUBLE-BREASTED CASHMERE SUIT AND
COTTON SHIRT BY CESARE ATTOLINI;
WOOL TIE BY DUNHILL.

*The shirt collar fits when you can just slip your index and middle fingers side by side snugly between your neck and collar.*

COTTON SHIRT BY HART SCHAFFNER MARX;
CASHMERE TIE BY BRIONI.

*Hold your arms at your sides: The bottom hem should be level with your thumb knuckle.*

WOOL JACKETS BY L.B.M. 1911.

*Only a little cloth should drape on your shoes—ask your tailor for a one-inch break in your front crease.*

WOOL FLANNEL TROUSERS
BY RALPH LAUREN BLACK LABEL.

# Suits

SINCE IT WAS INTRODUCED IN THE SEVENTEENTH CENTURY,

THE MODERN SUIT HAS BEEN ABOUT TWO THINGS: POWER AND SEX.

HERE'S HOW TO UTILIZE YOUR SUITS TO GET THE MOST OF BOTH.

# The All-Purpose Suit

### THE ONLY ONE YOU NEED FOR WORK, WEDDINGS, FUNERALS, PARTIES, AND EVERYTHING IN BETWEEN

**Deep-navy cloth**
It's dark enough to appear professional, but is also lighter and classier than rather dour black.

**Notched lapel**
A small, high notch right on the collarbone is the mark of a killer suit.

**Lightweight wool**
Stands up best to repeated wearing and can be worn year-round.

**A Fitted Waist**
The jacket should have some fit to it in the waist area to give your body a more dynamic shape

**Simplicity**
The more streamlined the details, the more widely you will be able to wear it. Avoid extra pockets and flamboyant stitch detailing.

**Trousers**
Flat-front trousers are considered more modern, but pleats will be a touch more forgiving should your waistline expand over time.

*Two-button wool suit by Dunhill; cotton shirt by Valentino; silk tie by Hickey Freeman.*

> "All it takes are a few simple outfits. And there's one secret—the simpler, the better."
> —*Cary Grant*

## FUSED VS. CANVASED:

### *HOW TO TELL*

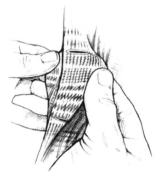

**Pinch an inch** of the jacket's fabric, preferably between the bottom two buttonholes. If you feel only two layers, that means the jacket is fused: Since the interlining has been glued to the exterior, you will feel only the exterior and the inner facing. If, however, you feel three layers, that means the jacket is canvased, and what you're sensing is the facing, the exterior, and the canvas itself floating in between. If after performing this test, you're still not sure, ask the salesman. And if he doesn't know what you're talking about, you're probably in the wrong store.

### THE HIDDEN DETAIL:
# THE CANVAS

**Inside every proper suit jacket**, between the exterior cloth and the lining, lies the secret of its shape: a layer of cloth called the canvas. A bespoke suit or a top-end ready-to-wear design features what's known as a full-hand canvas, sewn into the jacket by hand, stitch by stitch, so that it echoes the curves of the chest, gives the lapel its roll, and, in a sense, determines the very integrity of the jacket. Cheaper brands, however, use a process called fusing, in which a synthetic interlining is heated by machine until it adheres to the exterior fabric and provides the jacket with its rudimentary shape. Until you're caught in a rainstorm, that is, when the glue dissolves, leaving blisters on the chest and lapels. Although fusing has long been deemed inferior to hand canvasing, this is no longer universally so. Improvements in fusing technology have made it possible to create fused suits that fit and even feel better than some canvased ones. Never, however, offer this opinion to a tailor, unless he be of robust constitution.

---

***THE BESPOKE ADVENTURE:*** THE MAKING OF A SUIT
It can be as long as two months (and 80 hours of tailoring) between getting measured for a bespoke suit and walking out of the shop the handsomest man in the world. Here's what happens in between.

**I.** You enter the shop of your local tailor. Most likely he offers you a drink. You accept.

**2.** You select your fabric from a book of samples. Specialty materials like super180's and 200's can run up your costs to as high as $10,000. Complex plaids will increase the price as well, as the tailor will have to order extra yardage to ensure that every piece matches at the seams.

## How to Tell
# IF IT FITS

**TROUSER BOTTOMS:**
Only a little cloth should ever drape over your shoes; ask your tailor for a one-inch break in the front crease.

**THE SHIRT CUFF:**
A quarter to half an inch of shirt cuff should always be visible. Anything more, your sleeves are too long. Try rubber bands.

**THE COLLAR:**
The collar of your jacket should neither stand away from nor conceal your shirt collar at the back of the neck. When fastened, your shirt collar should not cause you to turn red or blue.

**THE SHOULDER:**
No outline of your own shoulder should appear in the sleeve (in which case the suit is too small), and the sleeve's head should never sag (in which case the suit is too big).

**THE BUTTONS:**
There should be no creases or ripples radiating from a fastened button. If there are, switch up a size. Or, better, lose weight.

**THE JACKET LENGTH:**
The bottom hem should be level with the knuckles of your hand. (Or, alternately, just long enough to cover your ass.)

# THE SIX PATTERNS
## *You Should Know*

1. **windowpane**
*Good for:* Business suits that moonlight as party wear.

2. **houndstooth**
*Good for:* Bold jackets and suits for special occasions.

3. **chalk-stripe flannel**
*Good for:* Hearty cold-weather suits that mean business.

4. **pinstripe worsted**
*Good for:* Business of any kind.

5. **bird's-eye**
*Good for:* Cocktail suits that women always seem to notice.

6. **herringbone**
*Good for:* Casual blazers and cold-weather trousers.

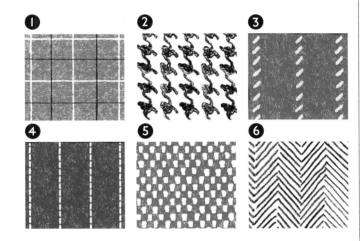

> **"A man should look as if he had bought his clothes with intelligence, put them on with care, and then forgotten all about them."** —*Hardy Amies*

# The 3 Jacket Shoulders

## natural

**It looks like:** The Roman Empire—a gradual, stately decline.
**Why you should wear it:** It shows off, rather than hides, your body shape. Tailors prefer it.

## roped

**It looks like:** The top of the sleeve is laid over a piece of rope. (It isn't.)
**Why you should wear it:** Conveys a rigorous formality and a little old-school glamour.

## padded

**It looks like:** You're a comedian from the 1980s.
**Why you should wear it:** You're slight and could use some more implied lateral bulk.

**3.** Your measurements are taken. The jacket requires an average of ten measurements, including chest circumference, arm length (be sure your tailor measures both arms, as one is usually shorter than the other), and shoulder slope. The pants require an average of eight measurements.

**4.** The cutter draws patterns for each piece of your suit on paper, then transfers those shapes to the fabric using chalk.

**5.** These pieces are cut with large fabric shears and stitched together into a temporary form called the *baste*, which is loosely held together by long white stitches. It has incomplete lapels and no buttons or buttonholes. And only one arm.

# The Way of the **Double-Breasted Jacket**

**A lean cut**
Though they cover more of your body, double-breasted jackets are way less forgiving than single-breasted ones. Seek out a lean but not severe cut, i.e., a less bulky chest, gently nipped waist, narrower sleeves, and higher armholes.

**To vent or not to vent?**
There's no halfway here: It's either no vent or two vents. (Strangely, it's never one.) Since the jacket is meant to be fastened, the vents can improve comfort, but they can also amplify the illusion of girth.

**A lighter cloth**
Thicker cloths can visually add pounds to your frame. Go with a lightweight worsted wool, and keep patterns small in scale. (See below.)

**The right lapels**
Lapels are tricky. Take time with them. They should always be peaked. Beware of lapels too narrow or too wide.

**How many buttons?**
Six in this case, though fashion has decreed two, four, and even eight to be good before. This "six over two" has six buttons on show but only two (the middle and lower ones on the wearer's right) are functional. By the way, you can leave the bottom one undone.

**How do you button?**
Left over right, always. This dates from the days when men, being in the majority right-handed, went about with swords on the left hip; the left-over-right closure prevented the hilt from being caught in the opening when the sword was drawn. Those canny tailors think of everything.

*Double-breasted wool suit, cotton shirt, and silk tie by Ermenegildo Zegna.*

---

## THE BEST CLOTHS FOR A **DOUBLE-BREASTED SUIT**

**Finest gray flannel**
Fuzzy texture is killer with plain shirt and tie.

**Glenurquhart**
Fine checks give visual interest without bulk.

**Chalk-stripe flannel**
Vertical stripes narrow and elongate the body.

**Self pattern**
A one-color herringbone has hidden depths.

---

**THE MAKING OF A SUIT (CONT'D)**

**6.** After three to four weeks of assembly, the baste is ready for you to try on.

**7.** The tailor observes you in the basted suit and marks any necessary changes with chalk or pins. If you want to change the height of the buttonholes or the width of the lapels or shoulder, now is the time to do it.

**8.** By this stage, the pants are mostly complete, except for the hemming, which will be done at the penultimate fitting.

**9.** The basted jacket is torn apart and rebuilt using the new specifications. Your paper patterns are also updated for future orders.

---

### WAR ON LINT:
# YOUR WEAPONS

**Lint Brush**
A velvet-like pad with hundreds of fine bristles to capture microscopic lint. It can clog quickly, so it's best for quick swipes across lapels and shoulders. Don't rub it the wrong way.

**Lint Roller**
This roll of sticky paper picks up everything. It's incredibly effective, though it can leave a residue on the cloth.

**Clothes Brush**
The most important tool and the only one that can get the deep-down dust out of your jacket. You add years to a suit by using one of these regularly.

---

### THE ONE-QUESTION QUIZ:
## WHAT IS A JIGGER?

A) The sail set on a boat's jiggermast.
B) On a double-breasted jacket, the important internal button that fastens the jacket's fronts neatly together.
C) A small whiskey glass that holds two ounces of delicious hellfire.
D) A variety of flea common to the southern United States.
E) All of the above.

Answer: E, though for our purposes here, we're just interested in answer B.

# *Four* UNCOMMON WEAVES

 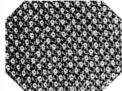  

**BARLEYCORN**
Small pattern resembling ears of barley; known as Priest's Hat in Italy.
*Common usage:* Jackets

**BIRD'S-EYE**
Fine geometric pattern using two colors to create a strong matrix of dots.
*Common usage:* Suits

**GLENURQUHART**
Bold country check first made for staff on Scottish estate of Glen Urquhart.
*Common usage:* Jackets

**SHARKSKIN**
Aka pick and pick, a fine-textured weave with a smooth surface.
*Common usage:* Suits

*Cloth samples courtesy of Holland & Sherry, New York; hollandandsherry.com.*

## The Year in Wool Suits

### JANUARY
*Ideal weight:* 16 oz
*Suggested blend:* Pure wool. Kick off the new year with a heavyweight classic that is both practical and warm.

### FEBRUARY
*Ideal weight:* 15 oz
*Suggested blend:* Pure wool flannel. In the depths of winter, it provides a cozy tactile luxury while maintaining a hardy reliability.

### MARCH
*Ideal weight:* 13 oz
*Suggested blend:* Pure wool twill. A great transition fabric that will carry you from late-winter chills through the start of spring.

### APRIL
*Ideal weight:* 11 to 12 oz
*Suggested blend:* A midweight pure wool in a classic Prince of Wales or overcheck pattern subtly ushers the winter out like a lamb.

### MAY
*Ideal weight:* 10 oz
*Suggested blend:* A midweight wool-mohair blend is ideal for spring jaunts; it travels well and is comfortable while still looking sharp.

### JUNE
*Ideal weight:* 8 oz
*Suggested blend:* A lighter-weight wool-mohair blend is cooling and is crease-resistant for the more active summer months.

### JULY
*Ideal weight:* 7.5 oz
*Suggested blend:* Ultra lightweight pure wool can help draw warmth away from the skin and help you beat the heat.

### AUGUST
*Ideal weight:* 7.5 oz
*Suggested blend:* Wool and linen. Though a pure linen suit should be a staple in every man's summer wardrobe, a wool-and-linen blend creases less than pure linen.

### SEPTEMBER
*Ideal weight:* 11 oz
*Suggested blend:* A wool-and-cashmere in a luxurious midweight blend starts fall on the right foot.

### OCTOBER
*Ideal weight:* 12 oz
*Suggested blend:* Nothing says autumn like a classic British tweed, a reliable barrier to the approaching damp and chill of fall.

### NOVEMBER
*Ideal weight:* 14 to 15 oz
*Suggested blend:* A classic mid-to-heavy pure wool cloth travels well and can hold up to the cold.

### DECEMBER
*Ideal weight:* 8 oz
*Suggested blend:* Give your heavier wool suiting a rest and try a festive wool-silk weave for holiday parties. The silk adds a touch of shine to the warmth of wool.

*With thanks to Savile Row mainstay Kilgour.*

## WOOL & CO.

*Pure wool is great, but it's not perfect—sometimes you need a blend of wool and something else to get what you need. Here's what the following materials bring to the table when paired with wool.*

**Cashmere:** Softness, warmth.

**Silk:** Smoothness, lightness.

**Mohair:** Crispness. Mohair is a harder fiber than wool, so it holds its crease well and has a natural luster.

**Cotton:** Comfort. (Plus, wool retains color better than cotton, so garments made from this blend are less likely to fade than pure-cotton items.)

**Nylon:** Wool-nylon blends often find their way into socks. Wool cushions the feet and can absorb 30 percent of its weight in moisture (i.e., sweat), so your feet don't get wet or clammy.

**10.** On the basis of the new measurements, a horsehair canvas is cut, then soaked in water and line-dried to shrink it down to the appropriate size.

**11.** Once dry, the canvas is stitched into the suit fabric.

**12.** The roll of the lapel and collar are intricately shaped—using as many as 1,000 stitches.

# A Man's Best Friend

### THE FINER POINTS OF FORGING A RELATIONSHIP WITH YOUR TAILOR

## FOLLOW HIS LEAD

A new tailor will start you off with a suit you will wear often—say, a plain navy wool—rather than something adventurous that you will wear less regularly. Do not insist on the canary-yellow shetland tweed jumpsuit.

## INSIST ON VALUE

It is against your interests—unless you have limitless cash—to have a tailor aping the latest look you saw on a runway somewhere that will be gone in months. Full bespoke is built to last and should be thought out accordingly.

## RESPECT THE MAN

Your tailor is not a servant. He is your counselor, PR executive, savior, guru, and savant. He will advise you against mistakes that will a) make you feel you did not get value for your money or b) make you look like an idiot. Listen.

## TRUST THE MAN

Ready-to-wear flatters to deceive. Some waistbands may say you're a 34, yet when your tailor measures you—which he will at every meeting—you find you're a 36. If you don't wish to know the grim truth, don't ask.

## *Should You Get a Suit* Custom Made?

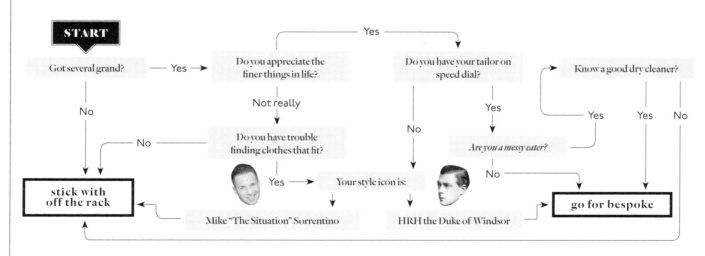

**START**

Got several grand? — Yes → Do you appreciate the finer things in life? — Yes → Do you have your tailor on speed dial? — Yes → Know a good dry cleaner?

Got several grand? — No → stick with off the rack

Do you appreciate the finer things in life? — Not really → Do you have trouble finding clothes that fit?

Do you have trouble finding clothes that fit? — No → stick with off the rack

Do you have trouble finding clothes that fit? — Yes → Your style icon is: Mike "The Situation" Sorrentino → stick with off the rack

Do you have your tailor on speed dial? — No → Your style icon is: HRH the Duke of Windsor → go for bespoke

Are you a messy eater? — Yes → Know a good dry cleaner?

Are you a messy eater? — No → go for bespoke

Know a good dry cleaner? — Yes / Yes → go for bespoke

Know a good dry cleaner? — No → stick with off the rack

---

**THE MAKING OF A SUIT (CONT'D)**

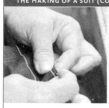

**13.** The lining is stitched in. Pick stitching—the small decorative threads along the lapel and edges of the suit—is added.

**14.** Buttonholes are added. Buttons, too.

**15.** You are brought back for a second fitting. Some basting stitches remain, but the suit is much closer to being complete.

**16.** Your tailor judges the suit and marks any necessary alterations.

# THE DIY DANDY

HOW YOU (OR, MORE LIKELY, YOUR FAVORITE TAILOR) CAN CUSTOMIZE AN OFF-THE-RACK BLAZER

**BUTTONS:**
Trade out the original plain for brass, steel, or white.

**BUTTONHOLES:**
A tailor can easily turn the strip of nonfunctional buttons on the sleeves into functional buttonholes for a more bespoke look.

**SUEDE ELBOW PATCHES:**
Added to protect the part of the sleeve that wears most easily, or to give life to an older jacket.

**SUEDE CUFF PATCHES:**
Protects any fraying on the sleeve of a well-worn blazer.

**SUEDE PIPING:**
Piping can be added along the pockets, sleeves, lapels, or almost any seam in the jacket, to protect any edges that might fray over time.

**FABRIC UNDER THE COLLAR:**
Colored suede or silk under the collar gives an understated personal touch—and a great excuse to pop your collar.

**THE LINING:**
Trade the navy silk lining for a brighter color or printed pattern.

**A CREST:**
If you have a family crest or club patch, you can stitch it on. Just be prepared to be mocked, unless you are royalty. And even then.

## So Your Pants Split

### *A few questions to ask yourself:*

**1.** Am I at home? If so, change your pants.

**2.** Okay, so I'm not at home, but did I think ahead and leave an emergency stash of Stitch Witchery and maybe even an iron in my desk drawer? Impressive. You'll be fine.

**3.** Okay, so that is not an option, but do I have a safety pin lying around, or even a piece of regular tape? You will get by. Barely.

**4.** I have neither. What am I going to do? If it's an event you can miss, miss it. If not, stay seated as long as possible. And stick close to walls.

**17.** Those alterations are made.

**18.** As many as eight to ten weeks after your initial appointment, you are brought back in for what will hopefully be your final fitting.

**19.** The tailor approves. You approve.

**20.** Payment is made.

**21.** You walk out more confident than you've ever been.

*With thanks to Keli Roberson at Oxxford Clothes in Chicago and Betty Wilcox at Lord Willy's in New York.*

# JOSEPH TING

### Tailor, New York City

**I've been working more than 30 years.** Being a tailor has its challenges. No one has a perfect shape, so it's something different each time. It's fun to tackle each person as an individual.

**With some celebrities**—I don't want to mention their names—today everything's okay, the next day nothing is right. Fashion people, they know how the construction works, how the concept works, stuff like that. It's much easier dealing with them.

**The toughest thing** to work with is leather, which requires a lot of hand-stitching because you can't really put it on a machine. Some suits might take a little more attention, too—wool, if you press it too hard, will shrink or shine, things like that. But when you have the experience, you can handle any kind of fabric.

**Justin Timberlake** has a concert tour that I worked on with the stylist. It's a lot of coats because there's the band, the background singers, the dancers. We're talking about 45 to 55 garments. It was all nine of my people working six days a week. But you gotta get the job done.

**I'm definitely** on the more modern side of tailoring, not the old-school trade. But I don't wear a suit myself. I wear jeans, I wear T-shirts.

**When people have** a nice suit they paid thousands of dollars for, they don't want to beat it up, yet they've dropped five, ten pounds, so we have to cut the whole suit. We can do anything.

**Good hand-tailoring,** good handwork. That's my signature.

**There was a custom jacket** that required hand-stitching on the outside and topstitching. It was three and a half, almost four days. That's the longest time I ever spent on a single garment.

**The deadline thing.** People are always in a rush. But you get used to it. I've been doing this all this time, I know what they want. You just have to put in the hours for it.

**I never** turn down work.

**I don't really alter** anything for myself—just pick it up from the store and wear it.

---

## HOW TO SEW A BUTTON

1. Stitch an X where you want the button to be.

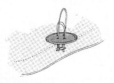

2. Thread the needle up one button-hole and down the diagonally opposite hole. Do the same with the other holes. Repeat four times.

3. Wrap the thread around to make a shank below the button.

4. Push the needle through the shank a few times and cut the thread.

---

## Great Moments in Tailoring

**1200s:** The word *tailor* first enters the English lexicon.

**1730s:** Savile Row is constructed in London. The street becomes a hotbed of tailor shops by the beginning of the 19th century.

**1789:** With the French Revolution, the elaborate, foppish dress favored by the aristocracy gives way to more practical fashion styles.

**1800s:** Beau Brummell popularizes trousers, a longer version of riding breeches.

**1860s:** The Prince of Wales commissions Savile Row tailor Henry Poole to make the first version of a tuxedo.

**1883:** The Journeymen Tailors' Union of America is founded.

**1938:** The Disney film *Brave Little Tailor,* in which Mickey Mouse uses a needle and thread to defeat a giant in a fight, is nominated for an Academy Award.

**1977:** Martin Greenfield, a Buchenwald survivor, founds his own tailoring company in Brooklyn. His clients will later include three presidents, a vice-president, and, reportedly, President Obama.

**1995:** Chandler learns the difference between a good touch and a bad touch from Joey's tailor on *Friends.*

**2001:** Geoffrey Rush plays the titular character in the movie version of John le Carré's spy novel *The Tailor of Panama.*

**Circa 2006:** Swedish shirt-maker Eton incorporates convertible cuffs into all its shirts.

---

## An Easier Way
### TO SEW A BUTTON

1. Put your shirt in the car and drive it to the tailor.
2. Pull out $3.
3. Pay him.

THE HURRIED MAN'S GUIDE
# TO REGIONAL STYLE, SUIT EDITION

  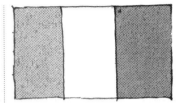

**UNITED STATES:** Often called a sack suit. Single vent, very little padding, a fuller cut, and a natural shoulder that mimics your body's shape. Trousers will often be cuffed.

**BRITISH:** Double vented, with more padding in the often roped shoulders, higher armholes, and a tighter silhouette, to give the wearer more of a V-shape. Often made of heavier cloth. Trousers are uncuffed.

**ITALIAN:** The Continental style. A simple modern silhouette and a shorter jacket length. Armholes are generally high, but with Neapolitan shoulders for comfort. Trousers are often cuffed.

## What to Look for in Suit Fabric

Nicholas Antongiavanni, author of *The Suit: A Machiavellian Approach to Men's Style*, offers a short primer

**fabric:** Suits are made of wool. Mostly. At the upper end, you see wool blended with cashmere. You might even see 100 percent cashmere. For hot weather, linen and cotton and silk are available, but most suits are still made of wool. Stick with that.

**fineness:** It's usually reflected in the so-called "super number." You know, "super 150's" and the like. Two things: First, the super number denotes the fineness of the individual fibers. The higher the number, the thinner the fiber and the smoother and silkier the cloth. Second, wool gets rarer the finer it is, so very high supers—180's and above—are expensive. But that doesn't make them better, necessarily. They can be wrinkle-prone, and they show signs of wear—such as shininess—early.

**weight:** It varies widely. Cloth that weighs seven ounces per yard will be thin and cool. Thirteen and above will feel quite warm. You'll have a hard time finding anything heavier than 12 ounces off the rack, but going custom can take you to 16 and beyond. It's best to get the heaviest cloth you can comfortably wear; the beefy stuff lies cleanly on the body and lasts longer.

**strength:** Take a bunch of the cloth and squeeze it. Does it bounce back to life quickly, with little to no visible wrinkling? Does it feel like there's something to it, some structure—what tailors call "guts"? That's a good sign. It's nearly ineffable, but play around with cloth long enough and you'll come to know it.

**variety:** What you will see on most store racks is plain weave or worsted (the smooth, tightly woven stuff)—basic business cloth. But there's more to cloth than worsted. The most common alternatives are flannel (spongy, fuzzy stuff) and tweed. Flannel is a classic cool-weather cloth. And we all know what tweed is.

---

## BUTTONS AND YOU:
### *A Handy Guide*

ᵛ

### The Short Guy
Lengthen your silhouette by choosing a one-button jacket with natural shoulders. The deep V will give length to your torso.

ᵛ

### The Skinny Guy
A double-breasted jacket gives more width to a slim torso. The button stance and the extra cloth add bulk.

ᵛ

### The Broad Guy
A two-button jacket gives a slimming effect similar to a one-button jacket, with a deep V between the lapels to lengthen the torso.

ᵛ

### The Big and Tall Guy
A three-button suit has the shortest V of all. Its fit should be close and comfortable.

---

# QUESTIONS YOU SHOULD NOT ASK YOUR TAILOR

**DO YOU SELL FEDORAS THAT MATCH THIS?**

*Are all of your clients this ticklish?*

*Which side do YOU dress to?*

DO THESE PANTS MAKE MY BUTT LOOK BIG?

*How long is this going to take?*

I CAN PEG THESE PANTS, RIGHT?

THAT MUSSOLINI WAS A SHARP DRESSER, DON'T YOU THINK?

SERIOUSLY. JUST TELL ME. WHAT IF I PROMISE NOT TO GET MAD?

WHAT ARE MY OPTIONS IN FLANNEL?

HOW GREAT WOULD THIS BLAZER LOOK WITH FIVE BUTTONS?

CAN YOU TELL I'M FLEXING?

*When is Ed Hardy going to start making suits?*

## A GUIDE TO CLOTHS

### What to wear and when

**COTTON:**
Light and breathable, cotton is ideal for summer wear. Although perfectly acceptable in the workplace, a quality cotton suit lends itself to more casual settings.

•

**WOOL:**
Wool can be blended with other materials for wear in nearly any season or situation. A light 100-percent-wool suit will be comfortable in the summer, while a heavier wool flannel is good for winter use.

•

**LINEN:**
Intended for summer wear, though some suits blend it with cotton, silk, cashmere, or other materials. Linen is very breathable but wrinkles easily, so it may not be ideal for wearing to work.

•

**MOHAIR:**
Mohair is cool enough for summer use, but is frequently blended with wool in high-end winter suits. The material, which comes from Angora goats, is fine and lustrous.

# The Bespoke Revolution

*The three entities most responsible for taking the stuffiness out of English tailoring in the late 19th and early 20th centuries*

### PRIME MOVER #1
### *VINCENZO ATTOLINI*

Although an admirer of British tailoring traditions, Vincenzo Attolini had the then-radical idea to do away with what he considered to be nonessential elements of a suit, which not only bulked up a suit's silhouette but also, in the Neapolitan heat, substantially increased the discomfort of anyone wearing it. Attolini set about a total deconstruction—removing every extraneous bit of lining, softening the shoulders, and shortening jacket length.

### PRIME MOVER #2
### *FREDERICK SCHOLTE*

This Dutch tailor is widely credited with inventing the concept of drape—extra fabric just in front of a jacket's armholes that modified the rigidity of traditional English tailoring. The Duke of Windsor was his most famous client.

### PRIME MOVER #3
### *ANDERSON & SHEPPARD*

If Scholte invented draping, this Savile Row shop (now actually just off Savile Row, but it still counts) gave it scale. Trained by Scholte, founding tailor Per Anderson expanded his ideas to create the natural, fluid tailoring for which Anderson & Sheppard came to be known.

---

### A BRIEF HISTORY OF **THE TWO-PIECE SUIT**

Matching jacket and trouser ensembles that bear some resemblance to the suits we know today began to take shape in the 1700s. But it wasn't until the early 19th century that the closely tailored look of modern suiting (with pants that extended past the knees) was popularized among the British gentry by fashion arbiter Beau Brummel. The look found wider acceptance as industrial economies developed, providing a more presentable alternative to dress shirts—and something to wear to church in the American South. And while the proportions have changed considerably over time—we're looking directly at you, 1983—the basic structure has remained largely the same ever since.

*With thanks to Mark-Evan Blackman at Fashion Institute of Technology.*

---

### THE BROTHERHOOD OF
# *The Traveling Pants*

The Duke of Windsor made bold choices that still influence men's fashion today. Not only did he popularize large-scale patterns, he also was one of the first to wear pants with a decidedly un-British cuff. In addition, the Duke had the traditional button flies in his suits changed to zip flies (a newish invention at the time). But perhaps the most interesting and peculiar of his habits was one the rest of us didn't follow: Long a client of renowned tailor Frederick Scholte (see above), the Duke was quite fond of the relaxed cut of Scholte's suit coats. But he never liked the way Scholte made trousers—to be worn high above the waist, held up by suspenders—so he had pants that could be worn with a belt made by other tailors. When he was governor of the Bahamas during World War II, he asked New York tailor H. Harris to replicate his beloved trousers. The replacements were made so well that, from then on, the Duke had his jackets tailored in the United Kingdom and his pants tailored in the United States.

## HOW TO BUY *For Your Body Type*

| YOU ARE | YOU WANT | AVOID |
|---|---|---|
| Big and tall (e.g., Andre the Giant) | Pants with cuffs to break up your seemingly endless inseam; pants with slimming, shallow pleats; a dark-navy suit. | Anything with horizontal lines, which accentuate your girth; anything with vertical lines, which make you look taller. |
| Long and lean (e.g., Barack Obama) | Anything with horizontal lines to help you look broader; three-button jackets that match the scale of your torso. | Anything with vertical lines, which only make you look taller; tight suits and jackets that advertise your thin limbs. |
| Short and stocky (e.g., Danny DeVito) | Single-button suits that have a deep V at the chest to make the torso look longer; V-neck sweaters that do the same. | Anything with horizontal stripes or busy plaids, which break up the body's vertical lines; wide pants with cuffs. |
| Short and lean (e.g., Tom Cruise) | Two-button suit jackets that work in proportion to your torso; thicker fabrics (like corduroy), which offer the illusion of heft. | Anything baggy or loose, which draws attention to your size; anything that's all black. |

## *First, Apprentice.* Then Master.

Traditional tailoring was never taught in schools. It was taught at the hand of a master. For years. In Naples, this classic method of instruction is as strong as ever. Here, a few thoughts from former apprentices, now masters themselves, on the experience that turned them into the craftsmen they've become.

"OUR CRAFT ISN'T TAUGHT IN SCHOOL, IT'S A CRAFT OF PASSION."
—CIRO PALERMO

"[VINCENZO] ATTOLINI WAS A MAN WHO TAUGHT SIMPLICITY TO MANY OF US. HE COULD HAVE THOUGHT HIMSELF SUPERIOR, BECAUSE HE WAS ONE OF THE GREATS, BUT HE WAS EVERYONE'S FRIEND. HE RAISED HIS WORKERS, THEY ATE TOGETHER. NO ARROGANCE. THAT WAS ATTOLINI."—PALERMO

"WE'D LEAVE OUR VILLAGES IN THE EARLY MORNING AND GET BACK LATE IN THE EVENING. IT WAS TOUGH FOR A KID OF TWELVE. WE WORKED SATURDAYS, TOO. FOR FREE, OF COURSE. YOU NEEDED INFLUENCE TO GET INTO THOSE WORKSHOPS. WHY WAS THE IMPORTANT WORKSHOP SO DESIRED BY ALL THE KIDS? BECAUSE THERE THEY TAUGHT YOU TO MAKE TUXEDOS, TAILS, CAPES, CLOAKS. YOU'D COME OUT KNOWING EVERYTHING."—PASQUALE SABINO

"PAY? WHAT? IT DIDN'T EXIST. WHEN I WAS WITH BLASI IN 1954, I GOT 150 LIRE A WEEK. EVERY DAY I'D SPEND 25 LIRE FOR THE STREETCAR, PLUS 50 TO GET TO MY VILLAGE. SO 75 LIRE TRAVEL MONEY. FORTUNATELY, MY FOLKS DIDN'T NEED MY MONEY. BUT THOSE THINGS STAY WITH YOU."—ANTONIO PANICO

"I BEGAN WHEN I WAS 7. I DID 10, 15 YEARS OF APPRENTICESHIP. BUT I DID THEM WITH ENTHUSIASM. . . . AS KIDS, WE'D MAKE BETS ON WHO COULD SEW THE LONGEST WITH HIS EYES CLOSED. . . . WHEN YOU PUT 30 KIDS TOGETHER IN A WORKSHOP, KIDS FROM 9 TO 15, THAT WAS OUR YOUTH. IT WAS A CONTINUOUS CHALLENGE. LET'S SEE WHO'LL BE FIRST TO FINISH THIS PAIR OF SLEEVES. WE LOVED THAT COMPETITION. WE WERE JUST KIDS—WE HAD TO BE KIDS IN SOME WAY."—SABINO

Excerpted from *O'Mast*, the most informative documentary on Neapolitan tailoring we've seen.

The Gregory Peck, aka the Kansas Highway

----

The Montana, aka the Royal Flush

----

The Gibraltar, aka the Schooner

----

The Tuck and Go, aka the Drunken Uncle

----

The JFK, aka the Little Cheops

----

# CHAPTER NINE

# Shirts

THE OTHER, TOO-OFTEN-OVERLOOKED STAPLE THAT MAKES A MAN'S OUTFIT COMPLETE.

BE IT WHITE OR PATTERNED, TUCKED OR UN-TUCKED, THE SHIRT IS ESSENTIAL.

# Can It Be Saved?

**RING AROUND THE COLLAR?** Yes. Use hair shampoo to pre-treat the collar, then wash. To prevent it from happening again, don't wear the same shirt twice between washes, and wash your neck more often.

**FRAYED COLLAR?** Yes. A good tailor can remove the collar, flip it over, and sew it back on, thereby hiding the frayed part. It's short-term only, and make sure you've got a good tailor.

**UNDERARM STAINS?** Yes. Use OxiClean sparingly, or try denture-cleansing tablets dissolved in a bowl of warm water.

**FRAYED CUFFS?** Yes. Go to a custom shirtmaker and have him sew new cuffs on in plain white cotton; ask him to do the collar at the same time. Or, hey, buy a new shirt: It will cost just as much.

**MISSING BUTTONS?** Yes. Required tools include needle, thread, and *The Biggest Black Book Ever.*

**FADED COLOR?** Nope—but that's usually a good thing.

---

## A Field Guide to **Mixing Patterns**

*Because a man cannot survive on solid colors alone*

**Patterned tie, striped shirt:**
The pairing looks best with plain jackets or mélange flannels.

**Striped tie, striped shirt:**
The tie's stripes should always be bolder than the shirt's.

**Checked shirt, striped jacket:**
The shirt's checks should be as big in scale as the jacket's stripes.

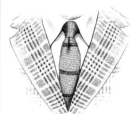

**Checked jacket, knit tie:**
Match a visual texture (a check) with a tactile texture (knitted silk).

**Striped jacket, striped shirt:**
The shirt's stripes should always appear bolder than the suit's.

**Bold-check jacket, plain shirt:**
The bolder the check, the plainer the shirt.

**Patterned jacket, striped shirt:**
Contrast the shirt's stripes with a fine-patterned suit.

**Flannel jacket, checked shirt:**
The bolder the shirt check, the plainer the suit cloth.

---

### WHEN TO
## Tuck Your Shirt In

For some, the only answer to this question is "always." For others, a few kinds of shirts can be worn untucked with impunity. These include a casual shirt with a bottom hem that cuts straight across (as opposed to one with a shirt-tail) and doesn't hang below the hip-bone, anything knitted (e.g., piqué or plain-knit polo shirts), and, of course, fitted T-shirts. For the rest of your shirts, tuck them in, and don't even think about doing that half-tucked, one-in-one-out business. That only works if you're 24 and dating an actress, and even then it doesn't look good.

# WHAT IT LOOKS LIKE: THE FOUR BEST TIE KNOTS

### the windsor
*What it looks like:*
Chunky, big, plutocratic

*What to wear it with:*
Spread collars

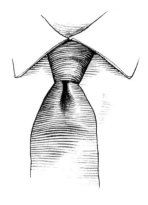

### the half windsor
*What it looks like:*
Solid, balanced, sober

*What to wear it with:*
Medium-spread collars

### the four-in-hand
*What it looks like:*
Asymmetrical, long, tight

*What to wear it with:*
Point collars and button-downs

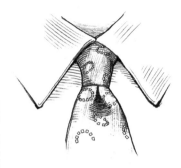

### the pratt
*What it looks like:*
A smaller, more economical Windsor

*What to wear it with:*
Smaller-collared shirts

---

## *Four Shirt Cloths* for Every Closet

**OXFORD COTTON**
Dense piqué weave popularized by Brooks Brothers. Crisp.

**MATTRESS STRIPE**
Gray stripes of varying thicknesses against white. Serious.

**BUTCHER'S STRIPE**
Bold, fat stripes of color (often blue) against white. Jaunty.

**GINGHAM**
Simple two-color check that puts life into a sober ensemble. Fun.

## THE MONOGRAM

### HOW TO MAKE YOUR MARK ON YOUR INFORMAL SHIRTS

John Forbes Kerry, Jack French Kemp, John Fitzgerald Kennedy: Three men with three approaches to monogramming. Kerry, an ambitious kid at college, was said to have worn his initials loudly and proudly. Kemp, on the stump with Old Man Dole, positioned his discreetly on his cuffs. And then there was Kennedy, stamping away at anything that didn't move (shirts, briefcases, showgirls), which was as much about self-promotion as it was about keeping tabs on his stuff. (It's how the help at Hyannis Port distinguished Jack's shirts from Bobby's, and further back, how British officers could tell their horses apart.)

#### HERE, A FEW SIMPLE RULES THAT SHOULD BE FOLLOWED.

- Two or three letters has always been the standard, no larger than a quarter inch in size.
- The simpler the font, the better. Curlicue at your own peril.
- Where you choose to place it is up to you—prominently (Kerry), discreetly (Kemp), indiscriminately (Kennedy)—but remember that the monogram should draw attention to the man, not his possessions.

# The Marks of a *Well-Made Dress Shirt*

**THE BUTTONS**
Mother-of-pearl buttons are harder than the more ubiquitous plastic. Insist on them—they last.

**COLLAR STAYS**
A dress shirt isn't dressy without them. They should be removable, but they're essential for giving the collar some body.

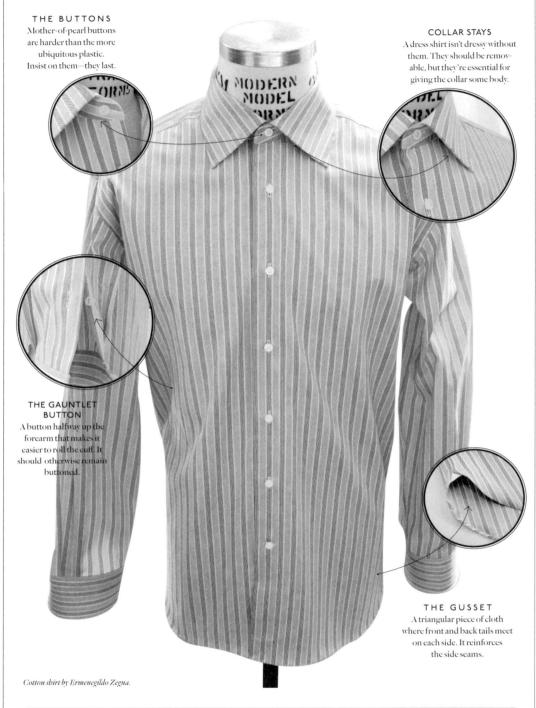

**THE GAUNTLET BUTTON**
A button halfway up the forearm that makes it easier to roll the cuff. It should otherwise remain buttoned.

**THE GUSSET**
A triangular piece of cloth where front and back tails meet on each side. It reinforces the side seams.

*Cotton shirt by Ermenegildo Zegna.*

**THE BEST (SHIRT) ACCESSORIES**

**COLLAR STAYS:**
Thin tabs that, when inserted under the collar, keep it straight and ensure its tips don't curl.

**COLLAR PINS:**
It sits under the tie and holds the collar ends together. An acquired taste that has recently resurfaced as a trend.

**TIE CLIP:**
A thin bar that holds the necktie to the shirt's placket. Also trendy right now, if you like that sort of thing.

*How to iron the tricky parts of your dress shirts*

**The collar:** Unfold the collar and lay it flat on the ironing board. Starting at the left tip with a high-steam iron, work your way to the center using firm, consistent pressure. Then press from the right tip and work your way to the center until there are no wrinkles. Fold down the collar and proceed to . . .

**The cuffs:** Pull the cuff as taut as posible and lay it on the ironing board. (If it's a French cuff, unfold it.) Starting at the left with a high-steam iron, work your way to the center using firm, consistent pressure. Repeat from the right side until you reach the center. Then move on to . . .

**The sleeves:** Lay the sleeve flat on the ironing board and work downward from the shoulder with a high-steam iron. Press the cloth at the center of the sleeve without applying pressure to the edges. When the center of the sleeve is free of wrinkles, rotate the sleeve so the cloth that was at the edge is now at the center, and begin pressing the center without putting pressure on the edges. Continue until you have a rounded, uncreased, and well-pressed sleeve.

*With thanks to John and Charles at Madame Paulette in New York City (madamepaulette.com).*

The following pieces all go together to make an oxford shirt. Do you know which is which?

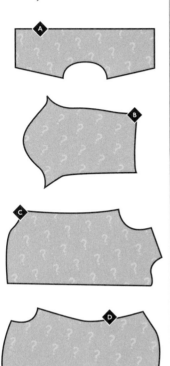

**A.** Yoke (the part on your shoulders) **B.** Sleeve **C.** Front **D.** Back **E.** Collar (the part that spreads out beneath your chin) **F.** Inner collar (the part that holds the other part up) **G.** Sleeve placket **H.** Cuff

*With thanks to Simone Olibet at Bellucci Napoli in New York City.*

# THE GREAT UNDERSHIRT QUESTION:

## A ONCE-AND-FOR-ALL HIGHLY SCIENTIFIC DICTATE ON WHETHER TO WEAR ONE

ON MAY 17, 1881, *The New York Times* estimated that several thousand New York City deaths had resulted from the switch from winter to spring undershirts. This is a serious matter. We've all been there, too, contemplating the hot-man-in-summer dilemma: Will I sweat more, or will it show through my dress shirt less, if I wear an undershirt? After consulting with experts, our conclusion is thus: A thin cotton undershirt will, in fact, keep you cooler in warm weather while protecting your dress shirts from your body. First, it wicks moisture away from the body, which in turn stabilizes your body temperature and maximizes comfort. Second, cotton is an inherently airy material: The fibers that make up the yarn in cotton are hollow, and this creates an additional layer of cooling air.

# Four Breeds of Undershirt

## AND A FEW THOUGHTS ON EACH ONE

| white crewneck | gray crewneck | white v-neck | white tank top |
|---|---|---|---|
| **The good:** When chosen well, covers your entire torso. **The bad:** Neckline will show with an open collar. Very bad indeed. | **The good:** Unlike white, won't show through lightly colored dress shirts. **The bad:** We got nothin'. | **The good:** Wear your polo or dress shirt unbuttoned with ease. **The bad:** Excessive chest-hair exposure. | **The good:** Covers the high-sweat areas of the torso. **The bad:** Does nothing for your armpits. |

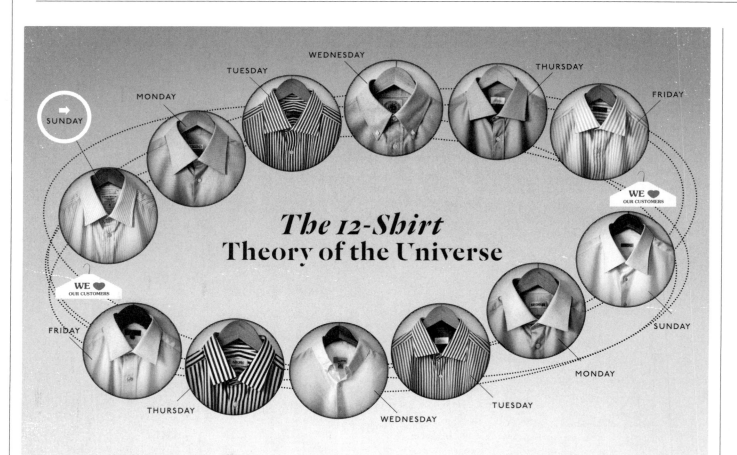

# The *12-Shirt*
# Theory of the Universe

**How many dress shirts does a man really need?** We've tested it out. We've done the math. And assuming you don't have someone at home cleaning and ironing for you, we've arrived at a nice round number—12—that maximizes your shirting options and minimizes your trips to the dry cleaner or laundry. Beginning on any given Sunday, wear a clean shirt every day; on Saturday, take those six used shirts to the cleaner and give yourself a day free of dress shirts. Then, the next day, begin wearing a clean shirt every day for the rest of the week, and come the following Saturday, head back to your cleaner to drop off the six shirts you just wore and to pick up your newly clean shirts. With this system, you'll always have six dress shirts at the cleaner's and enough in your closet to get you through your week. Choose your shirts accordingly and have fun.

*Clockwise from left: Cotton shirts by Emma Willis, Zilli, Hickey Freeman, J. Press, Brioni, Hamilton, Zilli, Ascot Chang, Brioni, Jack Spade, Ascot Chang, and Hamilton.*

---

## *What Country* IS YOUR COLLAR FROM?

### THE BUTTON-DOWN

The least formal collar is quintessentially *American.* Wear it with nothing dressier than a sport coat.

### THE STRAIGHT POINT

The *British* stalwart has depth and a certain solidity ideal for the man of serious affairs.

### THE SPREAD

Sitting low, flat, and wide, this favorite of the *Italians* is the perfect canvas for a big fat Windsor knot.

---

### THE D.I.Y. GUIDE TO
## SHIRT MEASUREMENTS

REQUIREMENTS: A MIRROR, A FLEXIBLE CLOTH OR PLASTIC TAPE MEASURE, AN EXTRA SET OF HANDS, TWO MINUTES.

---

**NECK:** Measure just below your Adam's apple, and place two fingers between your neck and the tape measure to ensure a comfortable fit. Your size is the number of inches on the measuring tape, and if it's not an exact number (e.g., 16 or 16.5), round up. (Better your collar be a little too roomy than a little too tight.)

**ARM:** With your arm out straight at a 45-degree angle from your body, ask your wife or friend to measure from the base of your neck down to the top of your wrist. The number of inches is your sleeve length.

**CHEST:** Not usually necessary, but good to have just in case. Measure just under the armpits around the fullest part of chest and shoulder blades.

# RIPPED! HOW TO GET ANYTHING MENDED

**THE PROBLEM:** Tear in your suit jacket.
**THE SOLUTION:** Take it to a tailor. If the hole is along a seam, he'll open the lining and mend it from the inside. If it's small, he might be able to iron in mesh interfacing that will prevent further tearing and disguise the hole. Larger holes will require more expensive reweaving.

**THE PROBLEM:** Frayed shirt cuff.
**THE SOLUTION:** You have options. A custom shirtmaker can remove the frayed cuff and sew on new cuffs in plain white cotton. Or you can take it to a reweaver, who can take fabric from inside the shoulder area (where it's often doubled up) and reweave it over the frayed section.

**THE PROBLEM:** Tweed weave is coming undone.
**THE SOLUTION:** A reweaver will assign it to a French weaver (i.e., a specialist who works with small holes). Then they'll open up the seams, pull out individual threads, and reweave them back in. With a standard tweed, you shouldn't see a difference once it's done.

**THE PROBLEM:** Ripped coat lining.
**THE SOLUTION:** A tailor can patch up a small tear in just five minutes, but for more substantial problems, you'll have to get a new lining, which can cost between $40 and $80.

**THE PROBLEM:** Pants hem is coming undone.
**THE SOLUTION:** Depends on how handy you are. If you're feeling enterprising, you should iron down the hem and gently stitch up the undone portion with your average hotel sewing kit or a strip of Dritz Stitch Witchery. If you're not, take it to a tailor.

**THE PROBLEM:** Cigarette burns.
**THE SOLUTION:** N/A. There's generally no going back after a cigarette burn. You can try to patch the hole with a darning needle, but it's best to replace the garment.

## The Semiotics of CUFF LINKS

"YOU CAN TRUST ME WITH YOUR DAUGHTER."
*Cuff links by Bulgari.*

"GO AHEAD AND ASK ME WHAT IT STANDS FOR."
*Cuff links by Hermès.*

"YES, THIS IS A GATOR. AND YES, IT IS A METAPHOR."
*Cuff links by Jan Leslie.*

"CAN'T TALK, EN ROUTE TO THE GALA."
*Cuff links by David Yurman.*

"I CAN MAKE YOU DISAPPEAR."
*Cuff links by Montblanc.*

"GRAB ME ANOTHER G&T, WOULDYA?"
*Cuff links by Thomas Pink.*

## THE D.I.Y. EMERGENCY MENDING KIT

You've edited your travel wardrobe down to the wire, and then you pop a button minutes before a meeting. It happens. What you need is an emergency mending kit, and here it is. Keep it all in a small tin in your suitcase, and while you're at it, learn to sew a button. (Find out how on Esquire.com.) Clockwise from top left:

• **Fine scissors** for cutting loose threads. (FAA rules state the blade must be less than four inches long for carry-on.)

• **Safety pins** in two sizes.

• **The sewing kit** from your last hotel trip.

• **Spare shoelaces.**

• **Silk knots** for when you forget your proper cuff links.

• **Collar stiffeners.**

• **Stitch Witchery** for controlling wayward trouser hems.

• **Straight pins.**

• **Suit buttons, suit-cuff buttons, shirt buttons.** (You know it's going to happen.)

## How Formal Is Your Cuff?

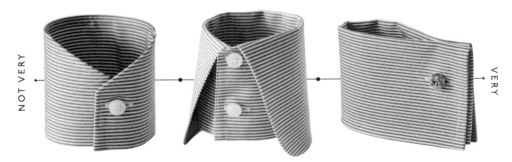

NOT VERY

VERY

### THE BARREL
The basic anywhere, anytime cuff. No cuff links necessary. Not too dressy, and well suited for the average workday.

### THE COCKTAIL
The best of both worlds: It combines the elegance of a double cuff with the ease of buttons, the perfect multitasker.

### THE FRENCH
The most dressed-up version, the double—or French— for the man who always shows a quarter inch of cuff.

| HANGER | SHOULDER COVER | GARMENT BAG |
|---|---|---|

A suit should hang in a closet the way it hangs on your body. Use something thick and about as wide as you are. Too wide and the ends poke into the sleeves; too narrow and the shoulders hang off the ends, creating dimples.
*By the Hanger Project.*

When hanging a suit in the closet that you don't wear often but want easy access to, cover it with a shoulder cover instead of a garment bag to protect the top third from dust.
*By the Hanger Project.*

Avoid plastic. It can lead to mildew. Instead, find a heavy canvas garment bag (to let the suit breathe) with a small plastic window (to let you see which suit you put inside).
*By the Hanger Project.*

| MOTHBALLS | LINT REMOVER | STEAMER |
|---|---|---|

Mothballs help keep moisture out of your clothes. And, you know, they stop moths from eating the things you care about.

Peelable rolls of tape are a good, convenient option, but they can leave an adhesive residue on your suit. Even better is a stiff-bristled garment brush, which lifts dirt out and can even remove some food stains. Use it after every wearing.

A steamer saves you money by helping you avoid the dry cleaner, and it's less harmful to fabric. (Suits should be dry cleaned only once per season— less for a fused suit. The heat from the pressing can cause the glue to bubble.)

**COFFEE, TEA:**
Rinse with peroxide, white vinegar, or club soda.

**GREASE, OIL:**
Blot excess oil with a napkin. Work baking soda or cornstarch into stain to draw it out. Launder with a heavy-duty detergent. Pray.

**INK:**
Douse with aerosol hairspray or rubbing alcohol and blot. Sponge detergent on the stain before washing.

**LIPSTICK:**
Remove as much as possible with a dull knife. Dab with baby wipes, then rinse with hot water to dissolve oils.

**TOMATO SAUCE:**
Scrape off excess, then apply a mixture of cool water and liquid dish soap. Blot stubborn stains with white vinegar.

**WINE:**
Blot with club soda. The salt helps prevent permanent staining while the carbonation lifts the stain out.

**BLOOD:**
Rub fabric against itself under cold water. Avoid hot water; it will set the stain.

## The Rules:

**Amost always blot rather than rub.**
Rubbing damages the fibers, removes dyes, and can spread or set the stain.

**Act quickly.**
The less time the stain sits, the better your odds of saving your shirt. Know your limits. You might do more harm than good with oil-based stains. Find a dry cleaner.

HOW IT WORKS:
# DRY CLEANING

# WE ♥ OUR CUSTOMERS

**FIRST THINGS FIRST:** There's nothing dry about it. So called because no water is used in the process, it supposedly picked up the name in the 19th century when a Frenchman, Jean-Baptiste Jolly, spilled an oil lamp on his greasy tablecloth and noticed that it started to look cleaner. (Thankfully, he was klutzy, slobby, and keenly observant all at the same time.) Today the chemical of choice is perchloroethylene, or perc, a liquid solvent used by almost 80 percent of all dry cleaners. Perc works by saturating the fabric and breaking up the molecular bonds that make up stains. Unlike water, it doesn't warp or twist delicate fabrics and usually won't lead to shrinking, bleeding, or other tragedies that can befall a man's wardrobe. The clothes are dried, then pressed or steamed and returned to you to soil and spill on all over again. It's a miracle, right? But there's a catch. The same properties in perc that dissolve stains in your clothes also (over many visits) break down the natural fibers in the clothing itself, potentially shortening its life span. And another thing. Long-term exposure to perc fumes might cause cancer. The National Institute for Occupational Safety and Health has designated it a "potential occupational carcinogen." So while it's harmless to wear clothes cleaned with perc, working with it can be hazardous to a person's health. Remember that the next time your dry cleaner loses a button on your shirt.

# An *Illustrated* **Guide to Folding**

| THE T-SHIRT | THE SWEATER | A STACK OF SHIRTS |
|---|---|---|

**{1}**
Lay shirt faceup. Pinch shoulder with your left hand and chest with your right.

**{1}**
Lay sweater facedown with arms spread. Smooth out any wrinkles.

**{1}**
Stack shirts faceup on top of one another, with arms spread.

**{2}**
Crossing left hand over right, pinch the shoulder and the bottom hem together.

**{2}**
Touch the left sleeve to the bottom of the right hem.

**{2}**
Fold the bottom half of the stack under the top half.

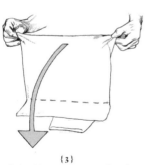

**{3}**
Lift the shirt, uncross your hands, and pull the shirt taut. Shake it and fold over.

**{3}**
Touch the right sleeve to the bottom of the left hem, making a neat rectangle.

**{3}**
Place one set of sleeves across the chest and fold the other across it.

**{4}**
Lay the shirt down faceup, and smooth and straighten accordingly.

**{4}**
Fold the top half over the lower half and neaten accordingly.

**{4}**
Place stack of shirts directly in suitcase. Remove upon arrival and hang in closet.

# CHAPTER TEN

# Coats
# & Sweaters

NO MATTER WHERE YOU ARE IN THE WORLD, YOU WILL AT SOME POINT BE A LITTLE CHILLY.

LAYERING WITH STYLE, FROM V-NECK TO PARKA, ENSURES YOU'LL KEEP WARM WHILE LOOKING GOOD.

# THE BEST BREEDS BAAA NONE*

THESE ARE A FEW OF OUR FAVORITE SOURCES FOR WOOL. COLLECT AND TRADE ALL EIGHT!

## Hampshire

Defining characteristics:
Black-faced, woolly-legged
Average micron count:
25-33
Frequently found in:
Woven outerwear, socks

## Merino

Defining characteristics:
White-faced, smooth-bodied
Average micron count:
17–26
Frequently found in:
Fine suit cloths

## Targhee

Defining characteristics:
Large size, woolly-legged
Average micron count:
21-25
Frequently found in:
Socks

## Cheviot

Defining characteristics:
Small size, bare legs
Average micron count:
27–33
Frequently found in:
Tweed tailoring

## Corriedale

Defining characteristics:
Medium size, hardy wool
Average micron count:
25–31
Frequently found in:
Thick, burly sweaters

## Romney

Defining characteristics:
Medium size, coarse fleece
Average micron count:
32–39
Frequently found in:
Carpets and such

## Columbia

Defining characteristics:
Hardy, white-faced, friendly
Average micron count:
23–30
Frequently found in:
Heavy wool coats

## Rambouillet

Defining characteristics:
Large size, fine fleece
Average micron count:
19-24
Frequently found in:
Underwear

* Sorry. With thanks to the American Sheep Industry Association (sheepusa.org).

# The Others  BECAUSE THERE'S MORE THAN ONE SOURCE FOR WOOL, YOU KNOW

**VICUÑA**
These animals provide just about the finest, softest wool out there. They're also rare and can be shorn only every three years, which makes their wool extremely expensive.

**GOAT**
Responsible for the suave sheen of mohair (often used in tuxedos) and the softness of cashmere (woven or knit).

**TIBETAN CHIRU ANTELOPE**
The fiber is known as shahtoosh, and it's soft, warm, and incredibly lightweight. It is also incredibly pricey.

**ARCTIC MUSK OX**
The undercoat of the arctic musk ox is eight times warmer than sheep's wool and finer than cashmere. The material is also known as qiviut.

**YAK**
Each yak yields two to three pounds of underhair a year, and it's as soft and fine as merino but warmer and stronger. Hypoallergenic, too.

**CAMEL**
Camel hair is gathered in spring from the molting undercoats of Bactrian camels. Soft, plush cloth most famously used for the classic camel-hair polo coat.

---

## THE *Black Sheep*

**Shrek:** A renegade ram in New Zealand who evaded shearers for more than six years. When he was finally captured, shearers removed 60 pounds of wool, enough for 20 large men's suits.

**Bemya:** A Botswanan sheep-goat who mounted so many unwilling females that he had to be castrated well before his time.

**George W. Bush:** The family screw-up who made good. And then made bad.

# WHAT'S SO GREAT ABOUT WOOL, ANYWAY?

Sheep may not look clever, but they have a lot to offer, particularly in the warming department. All effective insulation—whether it's for your house or for you—requires the trapping of air as a barrier between different temperatures (inside and out). Wool is particularly warm because of the natural crimp of the individual fibers, which tend to mesh and entangle

*{A fiber of wool, magnified. A lot.}*

themselves, trapping air and forming a layer of insulation from the cold. Since fewer fibers touch the skin compared with other fabrics, less heat is conducted away from the skin. The scales on each fiber also have microscopic pores that actually suck in moisture, absorbing it chemically. In this way, wool can absorb 30 percent of its own weight in water while still holding in the heat.

## *Key Moments in the* **History of Wool**

**715 B.C.:** Wool dyeing is established as a craft in Rome.

•

**13th century A.D.:** The spinning wheel is invented.

•

**1589:** Development of the first modern knitting machine.

•

**1733:** The flying shuttle is introduced in England, doubling the existing weaving capacity.

•

**1882:** German scientist Otto Braun develops a method for removing lanolin (material used in many cosmetic products) from wool using a centrifuge.

•

**1996:** Dolly the Sheep, the world's first cloned mammal, is born. Currently stuffed and on display in the Royal Museum of Scotland.

## THE *Lightning Round*

**Why does wool shrink?**
Actually, wool doesn't shrink—it felts. It has to do with the scales on the fiber's surface, which, in their natural state—i.e., sticking out of a sheep—all point in the same direction. When wool fiber is woven or knitted, the scales end up all pointing in different directions. Add moisture and some agitation (like a washing machine) and the scales slide past one another

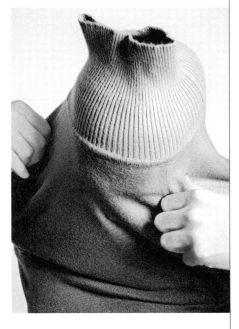

and lock into place, tangling tightly and shrinking the space between fibers. Remember this equation: wool + heat + water + mechanical action = felt.

**Do sheep go bald?**
Only if something goes very, very wrong. Like mange. Otherwise those lucky bastards just keep sprouting their downy manes till they bah out to that great pasture in the sky.

**Why does wool itch?**
It has to do with the length of the individual wool fibers: Shorter-staple fibers tend to stick out of the yarn more readily than combed, long-staple fibers, and when they do stick out, they prick or irritate the skin. That's why woolens tend to itch more than finer worsteds.

**Why does wet wool smell bad?**
Sheep themselves can be a pretty rank bunch, but the oils that cause that ripe scent generally get removed during scouring before the wool is woven. More likely, though, it's you. Wool naturally absorbs odors—the kimchi you spilled on your blazer, sweat from that crowded bar, smoke from when you snuck a cigarette outside—and all those smells come back to bite you when moisture releases the odors from the fabric.

**What is virgin wool?**
This is wool from those good Midwestern ewes that are saving themselves for the right ram. Or: wool that's processed for the first time.

**Isn't most wool processed for the first time?**
Yes, actually. But not so long ago, a large industry existed that recycled wool cloth, or rags, which were shredded, respun, and rewoven into cloth called shoddy. Reused wool is never as strong as new wool.

# THE EXPLAINER:

### The Staple
When a wool fiber is sheared from a sheep, its fate is determined by how long it is. This measurement is known as the wool's staple, and when used in reference to articles of clothing, it refers to the average length of the constituent fibers. Longer fibers can be twisted into thinner, smoother yarn, the kind that can be woven into fine-gauge sweaters

and worsted suits. Shorter staples are rowdier and tend to show up in rougher sweaters and gloves.

### The Damn Pills
Anyone who's ever owned a sweater knows about the pesky pills that tend to form around high-friction areas like the elbows. These are a result of shorter fibers, or

short-staple fibers, that break and bunch up after a few wears. (Wool or cashmere with shorter fibers is cheaper for the designer to buy, meaning more profit.) You can remove them with sweater shavers and stones, but it's only a temporary fix: Another day out in the world will only yield more pilling. Better to invest in long-staple wool sweaters (like merino) that will hold up better under duress.

# The Buyer's Guide to ... Cashmere

Choosing a cashmere sweater is like choosing a melon: It's all about feel. The first rule? Softer is not always better. Extreme cuddliness can be a sign of short fibers, which can cause the sweater to wear out quickly. You need to hit the sweet spot between softness and durability. Rub your palm against the surface of the garment and see if it starts to pill. Stretch the garment side to side to see if it snaps back into shape. If it doesn't, you could have low-quality fiber or a poorly knitted garment on your hands. Now you can get down to technical questions. Is the garment made of one- or two-ply yarn? Two-ply construction keeps things soft and reliably strong. Do you want pure cashmere or a cashmere blend? A cashmere-silk mixture will save you some cash, but it also won't be as soft. Cotton blends can create a cooler (and, yes, cheaper) garment while still retaining some of the softness of cashmere. Make the investment, care for it well, and a cashmere sweater or jacket should last a lifetime.

*Cashmere sweaters by Canali.*

# THE JOY OF SWEATERS

| THE CREWNECK | THE V-NECK | THE CARDIGAN | THE TURTLENECK |
|---|---|---|---|
| **TYPICALLY WORN WITH** | | | |
| A T-shirt underneath; you can wear it with a collared shirt, too, but it can look a little square. | Collared shirts, including polo shirts (with the shirt's collar tucked into—yes, into—the sweater). | Anything from a T-shirt to a dress shirt and tie. A good cardigan is often a suitable way to add warmth on chilly fall days. | A tweed blazer or a sport coat. You should also feel free to wear it on its own. |
| **POSITIVELY ASSOCIATED WITH** | | | |
| Athletes | Laid-back weekends | Mr. Rogers | Steve McQueen in *Bullitt* |
| **NEGATIVELY ASSOCIATED WITH** | | | |
| Yuppies | Casual Fridays | Fusty English professors | Steve Jobs (His were cotton. But still.) |
| **BEWARE OF** | | | |
| Thinking you can wear it without a collared shirt under a jacket. You can't. | A plunging neckline. Never show more than the top two shirt buttons. | Losing a button. And never tuck a cardigan into anything. | Anything too tight or fitted. Or too loose and long, for that matter. |

## THE WOOL ENTHUSIAST'S GUIDE TO
# STAIN REMOVAL

**STEP ONE:** Act fast. Wool is naturally soil-resistant because its fibers have a thin, protective, waxlike film that enables it to shed droplets of liquid without absorbing them. For a while, anyway. In other words, spill a liquid on a wool surface and you may have time to mop it up. If you don't act quickly enough, proceed as follows:

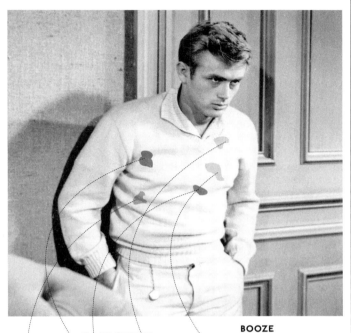

### BLACK COFFEE
**The savior:**
Rubbing alcohol and white vinegar in equal parts.
**The fix:** Soak a clean cloth in the solution and lightly dab stain. Press gently with a second cloth.

### BOOZE
**The savior:**
Rubbing alcohol.
**The fix:** Remove as much liquor as possible with an absorbent cloth and sponge the area with a mixture of warm water and rubbing alcohol. Then refill your drink. Repeat as needed.

### MUD
**The savior:**
Soap and water.
**The fix:** Wait till the mud dries, then scrape it off before sponging from the back with cold, soapy water. Or: Leave it. Mud builds character.

### BLOOD
**The savior:**
A paste made from cornstarch and water.
**The fix:** Blot with the paste and rinse from the back with soapy water.

### LIPSTICK
**The savior:**
White bread.
**The fix:** Buy a loaf of Wonder bread, rub a slice firmly but gently over the stain. Or: Leave it.

### THE PROS AND CONS:
# The Unscoured Wool Sweater

The unscoured wool sweater has a lot going for it: Because its fibers are still coated with the lanolin that is normally stripped away during scouring, it is highly resistant to water. (Lanolin is the sheep's natural oil, and it helps protect the sheep from the elements.) Fishermen, the Royal Navy, and nautical types in general know that unscoured sweaters are a positive advantage at sea. They tend not to get waterlogged, and even when wet, they dry more quickly. But there's a catch: An unscoured wool sweater tends to whiff. Not because of the sea dog wearing it (although that could contribute), but rather because the lanolin gives off an unmissable farmyard aroma. It's not offensive. If you like the country, it's positively attractive. It's just a little . . . ooff.

*North Sea Clothing in London makes an authentic replica of the submariner's unscoured wool sweater issued to Royal Navy seamen during World War II. Complete with smell.*

---

# Super Furry Animals

### THE SHEEP
*Locale:* Pretty much everywhere.
*Eating habits:* Broad-leaved plants, weeds, and grass.
*Hair-procurement method:* Shorn.
*Micron measurement:* Generally 16 to 40 (the thinner, the better; the average human hair is 60 microns).
*Cost per pound:* $21
*Thank them for:* Everything from your favorite sweater to your best business suit.

### THE ALPACA
*Locale:* Native to the Altiplano; predominant in Peru, Ecuador, Chile.
*Eating habits:* Low brush.
*Hair-procurement method:* Shorn.
*Micron measurement:* 18 to 22.
*Cost per pound:* $32
*Thank them for:* Sweaters, socks, scarves.

### THE CASHMERE GOAT
*Locale:* Native to the Himalayas.
*Eating habits:* Anything from branches to tussock grass.
*Hair-procurement method:* Combed.
*Micron measurement:* 14 to 19.
*Cost per pound:* $225
*Thank them for:* Cashmere everything.

### THE ANGORA GOAT
*Locale:* Found in Turkey, South Africa, United States.
*Eating habits:* Sparse vegetation.
*Hair-procurement method:* Shorn.
*Micron measurement:* 23 to 38.
*Cost per pound:* $55
*Thank them for:* Your mohair suit.

### THE TWO-HUMPED BACTRIAN CAMEL
*Locale:* Native to eastern and central Asia.
*Eating habits:* Sparse vegetation.
*Hair-procurement method:* Clipped.
*Micron measurement:* 17 to 21.
*Cost per pound:* $170
*Thank them for:* Your camel-hair coat.

*No animals were harmed in the making of this article.*

# THE WARMEST COAT IN THE WORLD
## BUY THIS ONE—OR ONE JUST LIKE IT—AND THANK US LATER

**The hood**
The detachable, down-filled hood closes up to shield the lower part of the face from wind and cold.

**The shell**
It's made from ripstop nylon, a tear-resistant, lightweight fabric that's been coated with a wind- and water-repelling laminate. The manufacturer says its shell is five times more durable than conventional shells. We believe it.

**The down**
The filling is 650-loft down (i.e., a very good loft), which traps body warmth and insulates from exterior temperatures.

**The construction**
Made with what's called baffle construction, the shell is not stitched directly to the lining but rather to pieces of cloth, or baffles, in order to create down-filled pockets throughout the jacket. When down is clustered this way, its warming potential rises dramatically.

**The zippers**
The multiple zippers are covered by plackets that shield them from water and wind.

**The pockets**
They're lined with fleece to maximize hand warmth.

**The cuffs**
Adjustable with Velcro to expand and contract as needed.

*Goose-down Sub Zero SL parka by Mountain Hardwear.*

## . . . AND WHAT TO WEAR UNDERNEATH IT
### *The pros and cons of cold-weather clothing*

| | PROS | CONS | BEST FOR |
|---|---|---|---|
| COTTON | Inexpensive and comfortable; wicks moisture easily. | Slow to dry, not the greatest insulator. | Base or middle layers. |
| SILK | Warms and wicks moisture easily. | Fragile, usually not machine washable, and often more expensive. | Base layers; also good for neckties, though that's got nothing to do with warmth. |
| WOOL | Traps warmth and, if finely knit, repels wind and water. | Can be scratchy on the skin; weighs a ton when wet. | Middle or top layers. |

## *How Does* Layering Work?

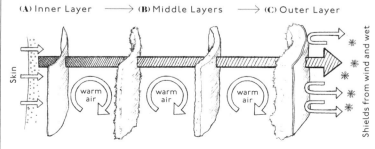

**(A)** Inner Layer ⟶ **(B)** Middle Layers ⟶ **(C)** Outer Layer

Skin

warm air · warm air · warm air

Shields from wind and wet

**(A)** Silk, polyester, or other non-absorbent material draws moisture away from the skin and transfers it to the next layer.

**(B)** Wool, fleece, cotton, or another insulating material traps warm air and transfers moisture to the next layer.

**(C)** Gore-Tex, gabardine, or another wind- and water-resistant material lets body moisture escape.

## MEN WHO KNEW FROM COLD

**Eriksson, L.** First European to reach North America.

**Peary, R.** First man to reach the North Pole. (Or so he claimed.)

**Amundsen, R.** First man to reach both the North and South Poles.

**Hillary, E.** First man to reach the summit of Mount Everest.

**of the North, N.** First Inuit to reach movie screens.

## *The Four Coats* Every Man Should Own

**casual**
Travelmaster jacket by Belstaff.

**sharp**
Polyester coat by Nautica.

**formal**
Cashmere coat by Bottega Veneta.

**functional**
Anorak by Hawke & Co.

> *IQ/A:*
> *Why do winter coats have fur trim?*
>
> In the Arctic, the fur around the hood of a jacket will keep moisture from sticking—and freezing—to your face. In your backyard, it'll inhibit snow, sleet, or rain from running onto your exposed skin, which is also nice.

## What We Owe the INUIT

HINT: IT'S MORE THAN JUST THE ESKIMO KISS

**SNOW GOGGLES**
Well aware that the reflected light from snow and ice could impair vision, the Inuit fashioned winter goggles from wood, leather, or bone that used small slits instead of darkened lenses to cut down considerably on the amount of rays hitting the eyes.

**WATERPROOF SHELLS** Inuits used the intestines or esophagi of various animals and the skins of fish to create tightly stitched parkas or anoraks (the design of which is something else we owe them) that were breathable and nearly waterproof.

**WICKING SOCKS**
Socks woven from grass were durable enough to last a season. They drew moisture away from the foot and absorbed any that made its way through boots without becoming too waterlogged.

**DOWN OUTERWEAR** Coats painstakingly sewn from the feathered skin of as many as 60 small seabirds and soaked in tannin or urine for preservation were lightweight but extremely warm. And not as smelly as you'd think.

# The Secrets *of Cold-Weather People*

**THE INUIT:** To anticipate winter storms, the Inuit observed the clouds: Elongated clouds indicate strong winds are coming and people should stay indoors.

**HOW YOU CAN USE IT:** Call out of work, citing seriously elongated clouds on the horizon.

**THE VIKINGS:** They would keep their farm animals—pigs, cows, sheep—inside their longhouses so that their body warmth could act as central heating.

**HOW YOU CAN USE IT:** Use this as a reason to buy the large dog you've always wanted.

**THE TIBETANS:** The women of Tibetan villages could often be found collecting yak dung in a basket. They would then take said yak dung and smear it either on the ground or on a stone wall to act as insulation.

**HOW YOU CAN USE IT:** N/A.

# THE WIDE WORLD OF ETHNIC SWEATERS

**Cowichan**

*Provenance:* Cowichan Valley, Vancouver Island
*It's the kind with:* Two-tone animal patterns all over the body, with the collar sewn into a folded yoke around the neck. *Wool sweater by Filson.*

**Aran**

*Provenance:* The three Aran Islands off the west coast of Ireland—Inishmore, Inishmaan, and Inisheer.
*It's the kind with:* Cables and patterns, with each knit one color—usually cream, the color of sheep. *Wool sweater by L.L. Bean.*

**Norwegian**

*Provenance:* Norway (the country, not the town in Maine).
*It's the kind with:* A simple two-tone pattern in the sleeves and torso, offset by single-color cuffs and collar. *Wool sweater by L.L. Bean.*

**Fair Isle**

*Provenance:* An island off the northern tip of Scotland.
*It's the kind with:* Complex, small-scale patterns in a variety of colors that evoke flowers, crosses, and stars. *Wool sweater, Polo by Ralph Lauren.*

# *Know Your Enemy:* MOTHS

The casemaking clothes moth (*Tinea pellionella*) and the common webbing clothes moth (*Tineola bisselliella*) are probably already living in your home, hungrily eyeing your wool suits and sweaters. Instinct suggests that killing them will take care of the problem. But it's the moth larvae, not the adults, that do the actual damage. They feed on keratin, a natural protein found in wool, cashmere, mohair, silk, and even leather. They're also virtually invisible—so even if you see no adult moths

in your closet, that doesn't mean you don't have a problem. How best to solve it?

Keeping your clothes pristine is paramount; both washing and dry cleaning destroy moth eggs and larvae. Emptying and airing the contents of your wardrobe regularly is also advisable. And vacuuming prime moth hideouts—along baseboards, in closets, under furniture, and along carpet edges—will help rid your home of adults.

Sensible storage is another crucial defense. If possible, dry-clean or wash all wool items before you put them away (in a snug drawer or closet, of course). For long-term storage—sweaters in summer, lightweight suits in winter—Space Bags (spacebag.com) or other tight-sealing containers are ideal. (Natural moth repellents like cedar are, regrettably, only temporarily effective, as their power disappears as soon as they lose their scent.)

But if you still suffer the misfortune

of a full-blown infestation, your only option is all-out war. Begin with a thorough inspection and vacuuming of all clothing, carpets, and other keratin-rich materials. Isolate as-yet-undamaged clothes and toss the rest. For the survivors, dry cleaning or a couple days in a bag in the freezer are the most effective ways to kill off any undiscovered larvae and unhatched eggs. And a resolution to strictly follow the prevention regimen is the most effective way to avoid the moths' return.

## FOUR SUREFIRE WAYS TO
# *Keep Yourself Dry*

### Storm System coat

*History:* Loro Piana's patented fabric technology, first intro-duced in 1995, has all the warmth and comfort of Italian finery while keeping out wind and rain.

### Barbour jacket

*History:* The product of rural British pursuits, it has its most powerful impact on city streets, where the roomy pockets, designed for a brace of pheasant, work equally well for the WSJ.

### Duster

*History:* Full-length oilskin-cotton coat with a capelike flap to protect the shoulders. Favored by cowboy types in the Old West, which is why the best dusters, like this from Driza-Bone, come from Australia.

### Mackintosh

*History:* Prehistoric performance clothing at its best, the mackintosh, even in this version from Jay Kos, remains a simple sandwich of two layers of cotton and a layer of rubber, with taped seams.

---

### How to Wear a Turtleneck
# Without Looking Like Bert

- Choose a dark, neutral shade. It's more slimming, and you won't look like you're on your way to the ski slope.

- Don't roll the neck down.

- Go with wool, not cotton. Wool is more luxurious and will hold its color longer, and it's also less clingy and more forgiving.

- Forget mock, or faux, turtlenecks, a.k.a. the ones that have short necks. Erase them from your mind forever.

- No tucking, not ever.

---

# *How to* Wash Wool Sweaters

1. Wash in lukewarm or cold water using a mild, bleach-free soap or liquid detergent like Woolite according to directions. In a pinch, you could also use gentle hair shampoo; just make sure it's not too fragrant.

2. Let soak for three to five minutes, gently squeezing suds through without twisting or wringing the garment.

3. Rinse twice in clean water that is the same temperature as the wash water.

4. Gently squeeze out excess water and roll the garment in a towel to absorb excess water.

5. For knits, lay the garment on a dry towel and smooth it out so that it resembles its original shape.

6. Dry flat away from sunlight and direct heat.

---

### HOW TO *Store Wool*

**Keep it clean:** Moths and carpet beetles in the larva stage will feed on the keratin protein present only in animal fibers. Both washing and dry-cleaning destroy moth eggs and larvae.

**Store it well:** Have your sweaters et al. dry-cleaned before packing them away in a snug drawer or closet—it'll kill the larvae. For longer-term storage—sweaters in summer, lightweight suits in winter—look for air-tight garment bags (like Space Bags, spacebag.com) or boxes and trunks with secure airtight lids.

---

## FOUR WAYS TO TIE A SCARF

**❶ the loophole**

*What you're telling people:* "A French girlfriend of mine taught me how to do this right before she dumped me."

**❷ the whiplash**

*What you're telling people:* "G-g-g-g-god, it's f-f-f-fucking freezing. I'm g-g-g-glad I've g-g-g-got this scarf."

**❸ the jedi**

*What you're telling people:* "I know it's far too warm to actually wear a scarf, but I won't let that stop me. My scarf is my statement."

**❹ the novice**

*What you're telling people: :* "How do I tie this thing again?"

# THE UPDATED ADVENTURER

What Ernest Shackleton might wear, were he around today

## 1908

## 2012

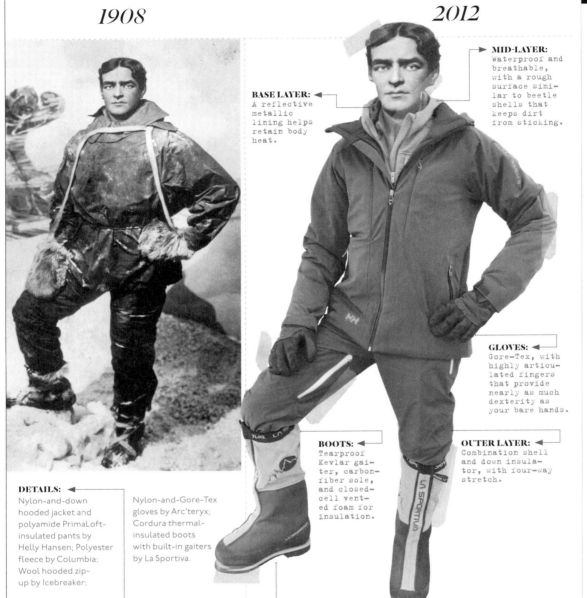

**BASE LAYER:** A reflective metallic lining helps retain body heat.

**MID-LAYER:** Waterproof and breathable, with a rough surface similar to beetle shells that keeps dirt from sticking.

**GLOVES:** Gore-Tex, with highly articulated fingers that provide nearly as much dexterity as your bare hands.

**BOOTS:** Tearproof Kevlar gaiter, carbon-fiber sole, and closed-cell vented foam for insulation.

**OUTER LAYER:** Combination shell and down insulator, with four-way stretch.

**DETAILS:**
Nylon-and-down hooded jacket and polyamide PrimaLoft-insulated pants by Helly Hansen; Polyester fleece by Columbia; Wool hooded zip-up by Icebreaker;

Nylon-and-Gore-Tex gloves by Arc'teryx; Cordura thermal-insulated boots with built-in gaiters by La Sportiva.

## HOW TO GET A NEW OLD JACKET

JACKETS ARE A LOT LIKE SHOES: You invest in a good one, break it in until it's perfect, and then start worrying about what you'll do if it ever falls apart. Luckily, like shoes, jackets can be repaired. Especially if they were made by Barbour. Like a sartorial cobbler, Barbour has started replacing worn or damaged components of its clothing. But instead of using new zippers, pockets, and cuffs—things that would stand out in a well-loved coat—Barbour's team of tailors takes advantage of an inventory of thousands of pieces, finding items with similar wear patterns so that replacement parts don't disrupt the aesthetic. They've received clothing from as far back as the 1920s that has suffered the effects of everything from dogs to motorcycle accidents to firearms. Barbour also offers a range of customizations, from tailoring the fit to adding details like ticket pockets or cuff linings. Because a favorite jacket should never be retired. Just refreshed.

*For more information, go to barbour.com/us/repairs-reproofing-us.*

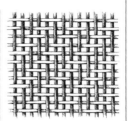

## HOW TO
# Dress for Any Situation

### Climbing K2

You'll want lighter layers when you're moving, but at base camp you'll be glad for the warmth of a good down jacket. Especially if your porter, not you, is the one carrying the extra weight.

Nylon-and-down parka by Canada Goose. Wool-and-polypropylene pullover by Helly Hansen. Polyester shirt by Patagonia. Polyester pants by Columbia. Cortura thermo-lined boots by Scarpa.

### At the Game

For early fall games, a vest will keep your torso warm—and keep your arms unencumbered for all that clapping.

Nylon-and-down vest by Canada Goose. Cotton shirt by Victorinox Swiss Army. Cotton henley, cotton corduroy trousers, and canvas-and-shearling boots by L. L. Bean Signature. Wool-and-sheepskin cap by Filson.

### Clearing the Gutters

Soft shells are typically flexible. Hard shells are typically waterproof. The Marmot Zion is both.

Polyester-and-polyurethane hooded jacket by Marmot. Cotton shirt by Eddie Bauer. Cotton jeans by Levi's. Rubber boots by LaCrosse Footwear.

### By the Fire

It's all about the slippers. Look for something warm but not too bulky. Something you don't mind another person seeing you wear.

Wool-and-cashmere Fair Isle sweater by Brunello Cucinelli. Cotton shirt by Hamilton 1883. Wool trousers by Burberry Prorsum. Suede-and-wool slippers by Sorel.

## TWILL: The Gore-Tex of Weaves

Before there was an industry for performance clothing—before Gore-Tex and ripstop nylon, before megastores like REI and Kittery Trading Post became tourist destinations—there was twill. For hundreds of years, twill brought more than just a distinctive stair-step pattern to clothing. It increased durability, for one thing; twill's interrupted flow of threads is much less likely to tear. The rough, uneven structure also adds wrinkle and stain resistance—or at least the appearance of such, since the textured surface minimizes a stain's visibility. Perhaps most important, with its heavier fibers and tightened weave, twill can be extremely warm and waterproof without a special coating. The twill weave is used for everything from outerwear to denim, and is appropriate for fox hunts or cocktail parties. While twill may not have changed your life, it certainly changed your clothing.

# Kill Your IDOLS

NOTES ON THE NEW ANXIETY OF (STYLE) INFLUENCE BY JOSH PESKOWITZ

ESSAY

CLOCKWISE FROM TOP LEFT: TOM WAITS, 1976; LEONARD COHEN, 1980; JACQUES COUSTEAU, 1975; MALCOLM MCLAREN, 1983; PETER SELLERS WITH BRITT EKLAND, 1966; LAPO ELKANN, 2004.

And don't get me wrong: It's wonderful that things like fit, cloth, and provenance are part of the conversation now, and there's nothing wrong with having a style idol, especially one of those guys. Every man, at one point or another, learns to dress himself by dressing like somebody else. For most of us it starts with our dads; from there it moves on to musicians and movie stars, and from there we develop, over the course of a lifetime, a sense of style we can call our own. The only trouble is when you get stuck. When you become so enamored of one figure that you're no longer getting inspiration from him—you're aping him. You're no longer simply wearing the same kinds of clothes; you're wearing the full costume, as if you're trying to be someone you're not, a character in a movie or everyone else at the local coffee shop. And if that's your idea of style, it doesn't allow any room for authenticity or self-expression— or any of the other things that style is really all about.

A FEW YEARS BACK, around the time that this whole Americana craze started to really take off, you may have noticed a lot of men dressing like Steve McQueen circa The Great Escape, or a young Paul Newman or Marlon Brando. These guys favored women, booze, and fast cars. Their comfort in their own skin and their own clothes defined masculinity for a whole generation. In both their real lives and their most famous movies, they made it okay for men to care about clothes—and for your friends and neighbors who've lately taken to wearing shawl-collar cardigans, close-cut chinos, and chambray shirts, McQueen and friends are nothing short of style idols.

And so it falls to me to say that enough is enough. Too many of us are stuck in a McQueen-Newman-Brando rut—and don't even get me started on *Mad Men*. The key to getting unstuck isn't to throw out everything you own. The solution is to be creative in your hero worship, to seek out new idols who aren't distinguished by a singular style of dress but rather a singular approach. Anti-idols, if you're so inclined, who took risks, developed their own style, and didn't care two licks what other people had to say about it. Take, for starters, Tom Waits: Nobody would call Waits inauthentic. His hats, soul patch, and adventures in footwear might not be what you'd choose, but he

wore them because they say a lot about who he is. (In a word: a badass.) Leonard Cohen, too, has a signature—a collared shirt buttoned at the throat, a double-breasted suit, and a fedora. Now, is a fedora for everybody? Certainly not. But Cohen, still a moody, magnificent son of a bitch at 76, doesn't really care. He puts it on day after day, night after night, because that's just how he rolls. Jacques Cousteau's red knit cap, Gore Vidal's patch-pocket suits, Malcolm McLaren's way with a scarf, Peter Sellers's way with eyewear: all great examples of men defining themselves as individuals through the simple act of wearing clothes. For them, it's not so much what you wear but how you wear it. And if anybody gave them shit about it, well, who cares?

And then there's Lapo Elkann, the Fiat scion and grandson of Gianni Agnelli, whose appropriation and reinterpretation of his grandfather's wardrobe lands him on every best-dressed list in the world. Elkann has become nearly synonymous with the vibrant double-breasted suit jacket, and he wears it with everything from bright-orange trousers to rumpled camouflage pants. He's taken the ideal of Italian men's dress and made it his own. He's not afraid to take risks, personally or sartorially, and he never dresses like anybody but himself.

These are just a few of the unlikely idols worth a Google image search, and you can take some individual cues from them—more on that to the right—or, you know, not. The most important thing is developing a style that's your own. Even Steve McQueen didn't always dress like Steve McQueen. He was a creature of his times, and as the world changed around him, he progressed through race-car leathers and three-piece suits all the way to shearling and cowboy boots. Mimicking the man from *The Great Escape* or *Bullitt* doesn't do him, or you, justice.

# Taking a Cue
## STYLE SIGNPOSTS FROM THE ROAD LESS TRAVELED

**The Waits Way**
Denim jacket and 505 jeans by Levi's. Cotton shirt by Gitman Vintage. Leather boots by John Varvatos.

**A Little Bit of Gore Vidal**
Two-button cotton-and-polyamide jacket by L. B. M. 1911.

**Throw in Some Elkann**
Double-breasted cotton-cashmere-and-silk jacket by Kiton.

**Make Like McLaren**
Linen scarf by Etro.

# CHAPTER ELEVEN

# The Extra Ten Percent

SOMETIMES IT'S THE LITTLEST THINGS THAT MAKE THE BIGGEST DIFFERENCE.

EVEN IF YOUR SUIT FITS GREAT, YOUR PANTS BREAK PERFECTLY, AND YOU CAN CHARM YOUR WAY THROUGH

ANY SITUATION, JUST A TOUCH MORE EFFORT CAN TIP THE SCALES OF LIFE AND STYLE IN YOUR FAVOR.

# *The Tools Every Man Needs* In His Wardrobe

**The shoe-cleaning kit**
A buffing cloth, some polish, and a couple of brushes.

**Lint remover**
The quick self-adhesive solution to visible fluff, pet hair, and dandruff.

**Drawers or shelves for knitwear**
Because they'll last much longer folded flat and laid on a shelf than stuck on a hanger.

**The clothes brush**
A friend to your suits. Removes stuff you didn't even know was there.

**The shoehorn**
Your shoes will be much better off in the long run.

**Shoe trees**
Maintain the shape of your shoes. Will triple their life span.

**The belt-hole punch**
You need it only once before it's paid for itself.

**Stitch Witchery**
A white-tape wonder that you iron under your trouser hems for short-term take-up solutions.

**Hangers**
The right shape for the right garment.

**Space Bags**
Something you can use to seal against the elements and bugs.

**Suit bags**
For hanging your more expensive clothing when it's not being worn. Obsessive? No, sensible.

**A sleeve board**
A mini ironing board to get those shirtsleeves looking immaculate.

**A good steam iron**
Invest in the best: lots of temperature settings, a steam release, and water-spray buttons for problem areas.

**An ironing board**
Because you need something to use the steam iron on.

**The seam ripper**
Use this ingenious tool to remove troublesome labels and unpick pocket-basting thread.

**Collar stays**
Save the spare collar stiffeners you get when you buy a shirt in a small box. Collar stays get bent out of shape in the wash and often need replacing.

**The clothes shaver**
Used sparingly, an effective way to remove annoying pilling from expensive sweaters.

**The professional steamer**
The best investment you can make. Save yourself a fortune in dry-cleaning bills .

**Metal polish**
Dip your favorite cuff links in this cleansing solution.

**A small box in a drawer for bits and pieces**
Stores cuff links, studs, and watches safely in one place.

### 5 THINGS NO MAN NEEDS

1.
Sleeve garters

2.
Sword baldric

3.
Sweater chain

4.
Spats

5.
Opera cape

---

# THE ULTIMATE CLOSET

### HOW A MAN SHOULD ORGANIZE HIS WARDROBE

{1} **Suits and overcoats:** Hang three inches apart to minimize crushing.
{2} **Extra shirts:** If you're not planning on wearing them soon, fold and store on a shelf.
{3} **Primary shirts and trousers:** Hang two inches apart to reduce creases.
{4} **Sweaters:** Fold in piles, and in the off-seasons, store in sealed containers.
{5,6,7} **Socks, underwear, T-shirts:** Fold neatly.

{8} **Ties:** Fold in half and then roll them up and place along with pocket squares and other accessories.
{9} **Athletic clothing:** All in one place.
{10} **Thick knits and sweatshirts:** Store in deep drawers.
{11} **Shoes:** Keep them on shoe trees and place on sloping shelves.

NOTE: if your closet doesn't look like this, call California Closets (800-274-6754) or another organizing powerhouse immediately.

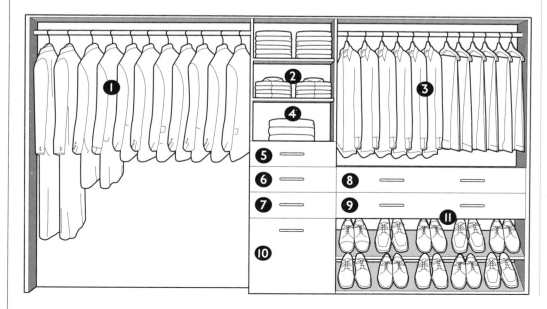

## A FIELD GUIDE TO
# HANGERS

General purpose, dependable support.

For sport coats only.

For trousers only, by the hem.

For suits.

For breaking into your car.

## THE
# *Troubleshooting Guide*
### TO EYEGLASSES

**The problem:** You lost the screw that attaches the eye wire (the front part of the frame) to the temple.
**Can it be saved?** Yes.
**The solution:** Temporarily stick a toothpick in the hole (or a paper clip) and break off the excess. As soon as you can manage, take it to an optical store, where it can be replaced with the proper-sized screw. Don't use superglue.

**The problem:** The bridge is broken, right above your nose.
**Can it be saved?** No.
**The solution:** You can try Krazy Glue or even white tape, but you'll look like an idiot and it still won't look right. (See above.) Get a new pair.

**The problem:** Your lens popped out.
**Can it be saved?** Yes.
**The solution:** Don't try popping it back in at home. If it's a metal frame, you're likely missing the tiny screw that holds the lens in place; if it's a plastic frame, the lens probably popped out because the frame is warped. An optician can fix it, screw and all.

**The problem:** Your lens cracked.
**Can it be saved?** Maybe.
**The solution:** All depends on the lens. Some manufacturers don't offer an exact replacement, but an optician may be able to obtain one that's close enough.

# *SUNGLASS LENSES 101*

## HOW A GOOD PAIR OF SHADES PROTECTS YOUR EYEBALLS

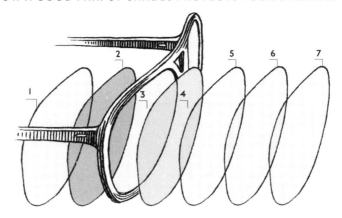

**1. Antireflective back:** A couple layers of coating on the concave surface of the lens's back that protect the eye from the glare of light that's behind you.
**2. Tinting layer:** Gray is best for viewing true colors. Yellow is a contrast enhancer and best for outdoor activities in low light. Vermilion (a rosy-peach color) is best for overcast days and sports like skiing. Green and brown are soothing colors that work well in both low and bright light.
**3. The lens:** Generally made of either glass, plastic, or polycarbonate. Glass provides the least amount of UV protection but is the most scratch resistant of the three. Plastic is naturally more effective at filtering UV and is the cheapest option, but it's the least durable. Polycarbonate is the lightest and most durable, and it is fully UV protective.

**4. Polarization layer:** Multiple waferlike sheets that block horizontal rays (i.e., rays reflected off other surfaces, like a body of water) to prevent glare. Interesting note: If both horizontal and vertical forms of light were blocked, you wouldn't be able to see at all.
**5. UV coating:** A coating that typically filters out two types of ultraviolet rays: A and B.
**6. Antireflective coating:** Multiple layers of various metal oxides that reduce glare and, in some cases, even repel water.
**7. Scratch-resistant coating:** Usually made from an ultrathin Teflon polymer, a durable type of plastic that prevents scratches on the surface of the lens.

*With thanks to Dr. Harvey Moscot, O.D., and Moscot Eyewear and Eyecare in New York City.*

## HOW TO PICK **the Best Sunglasses for Your Face**

**Round**
Angular frames add structure and definition to a round face. Try a rectangular pair of sunglasses to counterbalance the roundness and to make your face appear thinner and longer. Avoid circular frames, which just look wrong.

**Oval**
If you have an oval face, you can actually wear any shape as long as you follow the rule of keeping the frame in proportion to your face and to you. Go for what's really happening right now, which is a retro-inspired shape.

**Square**
Get a frame that's more rounded and oval to soften the angular jaw line. Try an oversized metal-wrap frame, which is broader in the horizontal direction and has a nice, soft edge to it. Stay away from harder-angled frames.

**Egg**
This face shape is characterized by a narrow forehead and a broad chin. To bring more attention to the upper part of your face, try aviators, which are broader across the top and softer at the bottom. Stick with lighter metal frames.

## THE GREAT MEN **MEN OF SHADES**

| 1942 | 1946 | 1950 | 1953 | 1963 | 1966 | 1968 | 1975 |
| --- | --- | --- | --- | --- | --- | --- | --- |
| Faulkner, W. | Monk, T. | MacArthur, D. | Baker, C. | Mastroianni, M. | Dylan, B. | McQueen, S. | Onassis, A. |

# The Well-Dressed Face

*Three styles of sunglasses, their origins, and their possible relationship to Tom Cruise*

### Aviator

Aviators' wide lenses were made to cover and protect a pilot's full range of vision. General MacArthur popularized the style during World War II, but Tom Cruise and *Top Gun* made them famous. We suggest: Randolph Engineering, Tom Ford, and Ray-Ban.

### Wayfarer

Wayfarers were among the first sunglasses to use molded plastic over metal. They were released in 1952 and owe much of their fame to none other than Tom Cruise in *Risky Business*. We suggest: Ray-Ban, Moscot, Warby Parker, and Oliver Peoples.

### Wraparound

Meaning: glasses that curve slightly around the head to offer peripheral protection, and their popularity, as far as we can tell, has nothing to do with Tom Cruise. That was all Oakley. And NASCAR. We suggest: Oakley, Smith Optics. (Never mirrored.)

---

## HOW TO MAKE NEW JEANS LOOK OLD

1. Start with a 14-ounce pair of raw denim jeans with a classic ringspun weave. (These work best as your blank canvas.)

2. Without washing them, wear the jeans around for a week. This will create a natural crease pattern.

3. Once the creases become apparent, take a piece of 240-grit sandpaper and lightly rub against areas you want to distress—most likely the pockets, the hems, and the seams.

4. Try overstuffing your wallet and putting it in your back pocket, then rubbing with sandpaper for effect.

5. Don't wash too soon or too often. When you do, wash the jeans in cold water and hang to dry. The signs of abrasion won't really show until after you wash them.

6. Pretend as if you've worn them forever.

*14-ounce raw rigid denim jeans by J Brand.*

*With thanks to Sean Hornbeak, director of men's jeans at J Brand.*

### A CELEBRATION OF UTTER UTILITY:

## THE SWISS ARMY KNIFE

When Victorinox delivered its first shipment of "soldier knives" to the Swiss army in 1891, it figured that a man needed only a few tools: a screwdriver to disassemble his rifle for cleaning, a can opener to open a tin of food, a punch to puncture things, and a blade to cut things. That, more or less, was it. Swiss Army knives have since grown more complicated, but you still won't find a better marriage of form and function.

*125th Anniversary Heritage Knife by Victorinox Swiss Army.*

---

## Pick Your Jacket Pocket!

**BESOM**
Pocket set into the jacket. Sharper, more formal.

**PATCH**
Pocket sewn directly onto the the jacket. Elegant but casual.

**FLAP**
Pocket covered by a piece of cloth, i.e., a flap. Conceals sag.

**TICKET**
Small pocket set above the main hip pocket.

# COWBOY BOOTS: A BUYER'S GUIDE

### BY BARRY SONNENFELD

COWBOY BOOTS ARE COMFORTABLE, they make you an inch taller, and they embrace affectation. I've got boots made of boa, distressed sheep (the boot maker's description, not mine), leather, and ostrich. The most indestructible ones I own are made of stingray. I also have a pair of Vibram-soled kickers for the big winter snows.

Focus on the lower half of the boot. It's a shame to have cool cactuses and longhorns fashioned out of fur on the upper half. You find yourself wondering if you can tuck your pants inside the boot. You can't. My advice for your first pair is to go with the textured pearlescent stingray. They're distinctive, and they make an excellent conversation piece. I've owned three pairs of Billy Martin's stingrays (black, blue, and green) for close to 20 years. With the exception of having replaced soles and heels, they haven't been pampered at all, not even a shine. (You don't shine stingray; it's part of the appeal.) The front end of the Billy Martin's comes to a point a good half inch beyond the end of the sole—very similar to a Formula One race car. One warning about the rays: You really need them to fit perfectly. The skin is so tough that they can't be stretched.

I can't tell you how many compliments I've received wearing my white cowboy hat, pinstripe Etro suit, and a pair of distressed-sheep-and-boa boots. Well, maybe not so much compliments as comments. Embracing your inner cowboy is not for sissies.

ADAPTED FROM ESQUIRE, MARCH 2008.

## *Peacock* HALL OF FAME

Overdressed? Nah. It's all a matter of perspective.

*Clockwise from top left:* 3000, A.; Hockney, D.; Bentley, F.; Wolfe, T.; Talese, G.; Ferry, B.

### SUN-PROOF YOUR SHIRTS

As long as it's on, your shirt protects you from the sun. But it can do better. Depending on the weave and the color, most fabrics offer the equivalent of an SPF of 7 to 10, which, if you're fair-skinned, can still mean getting burned. Fortunately, there's a solution, and it's as easy as doing laundry. Before your next trip to the Caymans—or the golf course—add a product like Sun Guard to your wash. For the next 20 washes your T-shirt will have a UV coating that provides almost the same protection as slathering on SPF 30 sunscreen. And you don't have to ask anyone to get your back.

## TRUE or FALSE?

### The claim

You can wear white only between Memorial Day and Labor Day.

### The reality

**False.** Mostly. No one's certain how this rule came about, but most experts in this kind of thing believe it stems from the late 1800s, when social arbiters developed rules by which the upwardly mobile lower classes could learn how to dress appropriately. The dates were approximate at best, and meant only that white is best worn when it's hot. Today, in parts of the world where the sun continues to burn long after Labor Day, it only makes sense to continue wearing the cooling shade of white. White shoes—which are less functional and more aesthetic—are more difficult to pull off than pants or a jacket.

## CAN I BESPOKE THAT?

YOU SURE CAN. HERE'S WHAT YOU NEED TO KNOW.

### Suit

*Typical number of measurements:* 25–30
*Typical production time:* 8–12 weeks
*Obscure detail you've never thought of:* Whether your shoulders are even.

### Shirt

*Typical number of measurements:* 12–15
*Typical production time:* 4–6 weeks
*Obscure detail you've never thought of:* If you want the cuff on your dedicated watch wrist to be a little wider.

### Shoes

*Typical number of measurements:* 14
*Typical production time:* 8 weeks
*Obscure detail you've never thought of:* The height of your arch.

### Jeans

*Typical number of measurements:* 10
*Typical production time:* 4–6 weeks
*Obscure detail you've never thought of:* How deep you want your pockets.

### THE *All-Business Socks*

IN AMERICA, WE GIVE LITTLE thought to the socks we wear for work. We know they should be dark enough to match the suit, but we don't get bogged down in detail. In Italy, however, midcalf-length cotton dress socks—the norm for the American workingman—are considered the attire of bus drivers, and any sock that affords even a glimpse of hairy calf when a man crosses his legs relegates him to caveman status. Nothing less than an almost knee-length sock in navy merino wool will do, with a percentage of nylon for longevity.

# The Extravagant Man's
## *Guide to Clothing Maintenance*

FIG. A

FIG. B

FIG. C

FIG. D

FIG. E

|  | **VELVET** [FIG. A] | **SILK** [FIG. B] | **SATIN** [FIG. C] | **SUEDE** [FIG. D] | **MOHAIR** [FIG. E] |
|---|---|---|---|---|---|
| WHAT TO LOOK FOR | A silk weave that feels almost like a carpet. The denser the feel, the better the quality. | Italian silk. It is said to last longer than most Asian fabric. | Can be woven from silk, nylon, or wool, but you want 100 percent Italian silk. | Something that's not too hairy. Rough-textured suede isn't high-quality. You want smooth, tight grain. | A blend with wool will have added durability. |
| BEST WORN AS | A blazer. | A tie. | Adornment on a tux lapel. Or as a bow tie or pocket square. | Shoes. | A suit. |
| HOW TO STORE | Hung up, in a garment bag. | Always roll or hang. Never fold. | Loosely folded. | On a shoe tree in a dust bag. | With cedarwood blocks to keep away moths. |
| HOW TO CLEAN | Don't. Take it to the dry cleaner. | You can spot-treat liquid stains with peroxide, but it's better to take it to a professional. | See a professional. | Take to a leather specialist. | Hand directly to your dry cleaner. |
| PROS | Soft, sporty, and warm. | It's soft. And some women find it sexy. | Shiny! | Develops a fine patina that only gets better with age. | Holds a crease well and looks more elegant than wool. |
| CONS | Too warm for spring and summer. Can also make you look like Hugh Hefner. | Highly susceptible to wrinkles. | Doesn't have much function outside of decorating garments or upholstery. | Rain is its arch-nemesis. | Pricey and sometimes itchy. |

## THE **DIFFERENCES**

### SATIN VS. SATEEN
Both are woven materials with similar structure. Whereas satin is most often woven from silk, sateen is woven only from cotton, then treated to add sheen. Sateen is stronger than satin but will lose its sheen faster.

### VELVET VS. VELOUR
Velvet is woven; velour, however, is knitted, which gives it more stretch and makes it stronger. It also makes it a more desirable material for tracksuits, but the less said about that the better.

### SUEDE VS. NUBUCK
Both are buffed leather, but suede is made from the inner side of the hide, whereas nubuck comes from the stronger outer layer. Suede is softer; nubuck is more durable.

WITH THANKS TO GUILLERMO MOLINA OF GUILLERMO COUTURE, NEW YORK

## A GUIDE TO USING IMPORTANT PEOPLE

| | DEFINING VIRTUE | REASONABLE / UNREASONABLE EXPECTATION | TIP |
|---|---|---|---|
| Tailor | A good eye | Compensating for your body's natural shortcomings / Performing miracles | Nope. It's part of the fee. |
| Barber | Reliability | Quietly adjusting your regular cut to fit your receding hairline / Making that receding hairline go away | Fifteen to 20 percent of the bill, or three to five bucks if it's just a trim. |
| Caddie | Prescience | Knowing which club you need at the exact moment you need it without your having to ask for it / Grabbing you a beer from the snack shack | Twenty bucks for 18 holes with a young caddie, $50 to $100 with an experienced one. |
| Personal Trainer | Motivation | Recognizing your limits and pushing you slightly beyond them / A six-pack | A hundred at the holidays. Or some good wine. |
| Shoe Shiner | Affability | A good shine, a sunny disposition, rapid brush skills / Making cheap shoes look like anything more than cheap shoes | Two dollars on a five-dollar shine. |
| Bartender | Wisdom | The occasional buyback / Listening to your drunk rambling all night long | If you're running up a tab, 15 to 20 percent of the bill. If you're paying by the drink, one or two bucks per drink. |
| Personal Assistant | Discretion | Lying to your boss or wife about your availability / Lying to a grand jury | Cash at the end of the year. |

### OTHER PEOPLE YOU SHOULD TIP

Valet: $5.
Car-wash guy: $3.
Coat check: $2 an item.
Hotel porter: $3 a bag.
Barista: $1 or $2, if she smiles.
Housekeeping staff: $5 a day.
Skycaps: $5.
(Note: if you tip them $20, they might upgrade your luggage to first-class status to ensure your bag comes out of the belt first.)

### PEOPLE YOU SHOULD NEVER TIP

Cops. Doctors. Teachers. Wives. Mall Santas.

---

## Things Every Man *Should Really Do for Himself*

Trim his own nails. ● Light his own cigarette. ● Change his own oil. ● Procure his own drugs. ● Open his own mail.
Fight his own fights (metaphorical only). ● Mow his own lawn (less than a quarter acre). ● Bait his own hook. ● Impregnate his own wife.

---

# THE PERSONALIZED MAN

*Because you can get just about anything custom made these days*

[ MOST COMMON ] — [ LEAST COMMON ]

**Suits**
*Suggested providers:*
Hayward,
Norton & Sons,
Brioni

**Shoes**
*Suggested providers:*
John Lobb,
Salvatore Ferragamo,
G. J. Cleverley

**Briefcases**
*Suggested provider:*
Louis Vuitton

**Belts**
*Suggested provider:*
Brioni

**Shirts**
*Suggested providers:*
Turnbull & Asser,
Charvet,
Kiton

**Cashmere sweaters**
*Suggested provider:*
Loro Piana

**Ties**
*Suggested provider:*
Ermenegildo Zegna

**Sunglasses**
*Suggested provider:*
Oliver Goldsmith

# CHAPTER TWELVE

# Shoes

THE WELL-SHOD MAN IS A MAN WHO CAN GO ANYWHERE. FOLLOWING IS A COMPLETE GUIDE

TO THE FORM, FUNCTION, AND MAINTENANCE OF FINE FOOTWEAR.

## THE *Anatomy of the Shoe*

1. **Quarter:** The rear of the shoe, from the laces to the heel on both sides.

2. **Counter:** A half-moon-shaped piece of leather that reinforces the heel.

3. **Throat:** The opening of the shoe, into which the foot is placed.

4. **Facings:** The parts of the quarters through which the shoelaces pass.

5. **Tongue:** A strip of leather running under the laces of the shoe.

6. **Vamp:** The front part of the shoe, including the toe cap and apron.

7. **Welt:** A strip of leather running all around the shoe to which both sole and upper are attached, making a waterproof seal.

8. **Brogueing:** The distinctive patterning of small holes on a wing tip.

9. **Gimping:** The zigzag cut edges of the parts of a wing tip's uppers.

10. **Wing cap:** The distinctively shaped toe cap of a wing tip that, with wings reaching back either side, gives the shoe its name.

*Shoes by Salvatore Ferragamo.*

## THE PERIODIC TABLE OF IMPORTANT SHOES

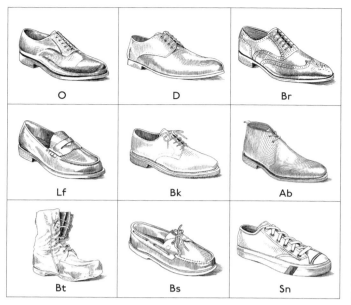

**Oxford (O):** Classic dress shoe with closed lacing. The tongue is cut separately from the vamp and anchored along with the facings under its edge.

**Derby (D):** Classic (slightly less formal) dress shoe with open lacing. The tongue and vamp are made in one piece, and the facings are laid on top.

**Brogue (Br):** Country shoe of Celtic origin with a distinctive pattern of perforations throughout. Also known in the U. S. as a wing tip.

**Loafer (Lf):** Slip-on shoe worn as a semiformal shoe in America. The practice of slipping pennies into the diamond-shaped cutout on the strap across the vamp of some loafers led to the term "penny loafer."

**Bucks (Bk):** Casual derby-style shoe with nubuck upper. Typically comes in white with a comfortable red crepe-rubber sole.

**Ankle boot (Ab):** Casual lace-up boot in a derby construction in which the throat is about one to two inches higher than a normal dress shoe's. Variations include the Chelsea boot and the desert boot.

**Boot (Bt):** A general term for functional footwear that covers the foot well above the ankle. Variations include the hiking boot, the cowboy boot, and the motorcycle boot.

**Boat shoe (Bs):** Laced moccasin shoe with a nonslip sole meant for wet boat decks. Also known as the deck shoe or Top-Sider, after its most popular iteration, the Sperry Top-Sider.

**Sneaker (Sn):** Sports footwear with crepe or rubber sole. Upper is made of two or three pieces of canvas, suede, or leather. Also known as running shoes, tennis shoes, or kicks.

## *. . . but the ones* A MAN TRULY NEEDS

**Black oxfords**
The bedrock of the grown man's shoe collection, provided you keep them shiny.

**Brown wing tips**
Look for robust construction and a rich color, but nothing too casual.

**Loafers**
The ultimate all-purpose shoe. Formal enough for offices and casual enough for weekends.

**Brown bucks**
Worn with khakis or jeans. Consider them a semi-dress-up alternative to sneakers.

**Off-white canvas sneakers**
You need a pair in your closet. And we don't mean running sneakers. We mean sneakers.

*From left: Shoes by J.M. Weston, A. Testoni, Allen Edmonds, Johnston & Murphy, and PF Flyers.*

### FIELD TO CLOSET

## THE ODYSSEY OF A LEATHER SHOE

IT CAN TAKE WELL OVER THREE MONTHS FOR LEATHER TO GO FROM AN ANIMAL'S BACK TO YOUR FOOT. HERE'S HOW THE TRANSFORMATION HAPPENS.

1. Animals raised for the food industry are slaughtered and skinned. (Most hides are actually a by-product.)

2. The insides of the hides are scraped clean of any unsavory bits left over from the butchering process. Hides are washed in a salt solution or hand-salted until they're partially cured and preserved well enough to withstand the journey to the tannery without decaying.

# The Jargon

What shoemakers talk about when they talk about making shoes

**AGLETS:**
The tiny plastic or metal sheaths placed on each end of a shoelace.

**CHANNEL KNIFE:**
An old-fashioned hand tool used to cut the grooves when constructing a shoe's sole.

**LAST:**
The solid form that a shoe is molded upon and that determines the shoe's exact shape and size.

**LASTING PINCERS:**
A metal tool with curved jaws meant for pulling the uppers tightly around the shoe last.

**PIG:**
A term used by London shoemakers for a bespoke shoe that, for whatever reason, has gone irredeemably wrong. (Also known as "N.F.G.," i.e., No Fking Good.)

**SKIVING:**
Tapering edges of the uppers and liners to prevent lumpy seams.

*With thanks to George Glasgow Jr. of G.J. Cleverley.*

## AROUND THE WORLD IN
# HIGH-QUALITY FOOTWEAR

### ITALY
TRADEMARK:
Sleek architecture.

MAJOR PLAYERS:
A. Testoni, Salvatore Ferragamo, Fratelli Rossetti.

LOCAL CULTURE:
Leaving a shoe upside down means the owner will quarrel with someone.

WHAT TO WEAR WITH THEM:
Kiton suit, Truzzi shirt, Ermenegildo Zegna tie.

### FRANCE
TRADEMARK:
Rich, deep patina.

MAJOR PLAYERS:
J.M. Weston, Berluti.

LOCAL CULTURE:
Berluti's Swann Club members meet semiregularly to celebrate the brand ... and polish their shoes.

WHAT TO WEAR WITH THEM:
Hermès navy cashmere blazer, Dior Homme charcoal flannels.

### ENGLAND
TRADEMARK:
Robustness.

MAJOR PLAYERS:
G.J. Cleverley, John Lobb, Church's, Grenson, Crockett & Jones.

LOCAL CULTURE:
Shoes that creak have not yet been paid for.

WHAT TO WEAR WITH THEM:
Cordings tweed hacking jacket, Hackett moleskin trousers.

### UNITED STATES
TRADEMARK:
Rounder toe.

MAJOR PLAYERS:
Alden, Allen Edmonds, Johnston & Murphy.

LOCAL CULTURE:
The term "white shoe" is used to describe elite law firms and companies.

WHAT TO WEAR WITH THEM:
Ralph Lauren herringbone jacket, Bills cotton khakis.

## THE HOLY REGISTER OF
# BESPOKE SHOEMAKERS

*The best places to go for extraordinary shoes*

Edward Green
(London; edwardgreen.com)

Vincent & Edgar
(New York; 212-753-3461)

G.J. Cleverley
(London; gjcleverley.co.uk)

Oliver Moore
(New York; olivermoorebootmakers.com)

Stefano Bemer
(Florence; stefanobemer.it)

John Lobb Ltd.
(London; johnlobbltd.co.uk)

Gaziano & Girling
(London; gazianogirling.com)

Perry Ercolino
(Doylestown, Penn.; perryercolino.com)

Calzoleria Gatto
(Rome; 011-39-06-474-1450)

László Vass
(Budapest; vass-cipu.hu)

Silvano Lattanzi
(Rome, Milan, New York; silvanolattanzi.com)

Lajos Bálint
(Vienna; balint.at)

**BESPOKE SHOES**

## *By the Numbers*

### 14
The total number of measurements typically taken during the bespoke process, including (for each foot) the length of the foot, the width of the toes, the height of the arch, and the circumference of the ankles.

### 12
The amount of leather, in square feet, typically required to make one pair of shoes.

### 8
The number of weeks it typically takes to create a pair of bespoke shoes.

### 0
The number of pairs of shoes that are exactly like yours.

# The Secret Life *of Shoes*

THE TOWN OF NORTHAMPTON is the historic epicenter of British shoemaking and is still home to Edward Green, Crockett & Jones, Grenson, and Church's, among others. The Northampton Museum, naturally enough, has a lot of shoes, and one of its more esoteric studies is the Concealed Shoe Index. It logs the discoveries of shoes hidden as long ago as the 16th century in purpose-built ledges and nooks in chimneys, wall spaces, and under floorboards in old houses all over the country. Shoes—it was long believed—were lucky and therefore effective talismans against evil spirits, witches, and general bad luck. It's an ancient practice that survived well into the 20th century. See the shoes at northampton.gov.uk/museums.

**3. HIDES ARRIVE** at the tannery, where they are either cut to the half hide or left whole. Thirty percent or less of any given load is premium leather.

**4. SOAK ...:** Hides are soaked in large vats to remove the salt and any other impurities trapped in the skin and hair.

**5. ...AND BURN:** A depilatory akin to industrial-strength Nair is added to dissolve and remove all the hair down to the follicles.

**6. BATING:** A pretanning process whereby the hide goes through an enzyme wash to flush out the natural, perishable fats and oils.

# BUYING SHOES

**Wear the right socks.** If you wear a thick pair of white crew socks when trying on a dress shoe, you'll only buy a pair that's too big.

**Get sized.** By a professional, using the indispensable Brannock Device, and taking into consideration your foot width. Your shoe size can change over the course of your life, so it's always best to be accurate.

**Buy in the afternoon.** Your feet swell to their largest as the day progresses, and it's better to buy a pair of shoes that are a little too big than a little too small.

**Check the inside.** If the inside of the shoe has no lining and the grain of the leather is exposed, the shoes won't last as long.

**Walk around the store when trying them on.** Don't settle for sitting down and checking the tips of your toes; you need to see how they function with your arch flattened and while exerting yourself.

**Don't wear them outside.** Take a night or two to wear your new shoes around the house. As long as the soles haven't been worn away by walking outdoors, many shoe stores will allow you to return them in the event that you change your mind. (Ask about the return policy.)

*With thanks to Jim McFarland and McFarland's Shoe Repair.*

---

## NOTABLE YEAR IN HISTORY
### 1822

The first left and right shoes were introduced in America. People sent them back to the manufacturer, complaining they were crooked.

---

### THE APPRECIATION:
## THE BRANNOCK DEVICE

When you were a kid, the shoe salesman at Stride Rite or Footaction would grab the thing off its nail on the wall, and then he would ease your heels—first one, then the other—into the little backstops at either end. The jolt of the cold aluminum against your foot added to the suspense that was part of the ritual. The instrument is called the Brannock Device. Every one you ever stepped on was manufactured by the Brannock Device Company, Inc., on Luther Avenue in Syracuse, New York. It's the company's only product, and it's the only thing shoe salesman Charles Brannock ever invented. The device he came up with is disarmingly simple and highly accurate. And very cool.

---

## The Other **Windsor Knot**
### A quick-release, nonslip knot for your shoelaces

As a young woman, Olga Berluti, the guru behind the luxury brand, would sometimes fit custom-made Berluti shoes on the Duke of Windsor, aka ex-Edward VIII. She noticed he tied his shoes in a particular way, and he explained that he'd been taught the knot by his grandmother Queen Alexandra to ensure he was never embarrassed by trailing laces. This is it.

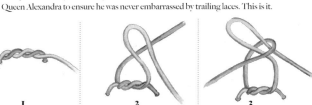

**1**
Instead of the usual over-and-under start, wrap one lace under for a second time.

**2**
Make a loop with the right-hand lace and bring the left lace behind as in a usual knot.

**3**
Wrap the left lace around the loop you made in the right end.

**4**
Make a loop in the left lace in the usual way and begin to tighten.

**5**
Before fully closing the knot, take the left-hand loop and loop it through once more.

**6**
Tighten the knot by pulling as usual on the two bows. Ta-da!

---

## *Consider* the Refurb

**BEFORE**

THINK OF ALL THE SHOES you've worn to death. That lived-in pair of loafers from your college graduation. Those shiny oxfords that killed on job interviews. The handy lace-ups that carried you through three promotions. RIP, the lot of them, and the worst part is, you could've saved your shoes (and the money you spent to replace them) with a good old-fashioned refurb. Most good shoemakers and repairers offer refurbishing services, replacing the soles, heels, welting, foot beds, and laces before conditioning and hand polishing the leather. While they're not always miracle workers—if your leather's cracked, you're out of luck—they'll usually take what's old and make it look brand-new again.

**AFTER**

---

>>> THE ODYSSEY OF A LEATHER SHOE, CONTINUED

**7. PICKLING:** The hides are soaked in a salty, acidic solution to achieve a particular pH and temperature, based on the desired feel of the final leather.

**8. TANNING:** Most leathers are tanned in one of three ways: chrome, vegetable, or some combination of the two. Chrome tanning results in a more durable hide. A chromium-salt solution is added that binds the proteins in the hide for strength and flexibility. Up to 48 hours later, the process is finished, and the hide has a bluish tint.

Vegetable tanning, which uses vegetable extracts and tannins, often takes much longer: ten days to bate and pickle and anywhere from 24 hours to one year to tan. But it's much more environmentally friendly. It results in a darker, taupe-colored hide with less durability than a chrome hide but better patina and malleability.

# HOW TO WHITEN YOUR SHOES

### Leather sneaker

For scuff marks, try swabbing with nail-polish remover and then wiping clean. If the whole shoe starts yellowing or darkening, spray with a 50/50 mixture of water and lemon juice and let sit in the sun for a full day. Sneakers by Adidas Originals.

### Canvas sneaker

The 50/50 mixture of water and lemon juice works for canvas, too, but for more serious stains, mix a tablespoon of baking soda with a touch of water and rub the sticky paste onto the offending spots. Wipe dry. Or try a whitening polish like Hollywood Sani-White (pictured above). Sneakers by Converse.

### Leather shoe

For lighter scuff marks, lightly rub a pencil eraser against the area. Still dirty? Hollywood Sani-White and similar polishes work, too. But if the shoes were never white to begin with, try slapping on a fresh coat of matte white latex paint. Shoes by Tommy Bahama.

# Goodyear VS. Blake

## A BATTLE FOR YOUR SOLE

### Goodyear welt

The most common construction. The sole and the upper are each stitched to a welt or strip of leather running around the whole shoe, with a layer of cork or filler between the insole and the outsole. It's incredibly strong and lends itself to resoling many times over.

**VS.**

### Blake construction

A common alternative to Goodyear, Blake construction stitches the sole directly to the upper without a welt. It is simpler and generally results in a lighter shoe, but it's nearly impossible to do by hand. It is named after the inventor of the machine that does the sewing.

## A USER'S GUIDE TO Casual SHOES

From the most formal to the least, five ways to dress down from the ankle down

**Penny loafers**
*Good for:* casual cocktail party

**Desert boots**
*Good for:* a walk in the park

**Suede bucks**
*Good for:* saturday lunch

**Driving shoes**
*Good for:* driving, walking to car

**Sneakers**
*Good for:* exercising, hangin'

FROM LEFT: SHOES BY TOD'S, CLARKS, JOHNSTON & MURPHY, TOD'S, AND CONVERSE.

**9. RETANNING:** To replenish the softness that was lost when the hides' natural oils were removed, and to change the color of newly tanned leather, blends of vegetable extracts, oils, and fats are forced into the leather in a process called hot stuffing. Depending on the desired use for the leather, hides can be as much as 30 percent oil. Higher oil content is better for garment leather, as it will be softer and stretchier. Lower-oil-content leather is used as a protective layer, like the sole of a shoe.

**10.** If desired, dyes are added to give the leather a particular color.

**11.** Retanned leathers are air-dried for five to ten days.

**12. FINISHING:** Leathers are surface-stained for desired color and shading. Softness, feel, and shine are also tweaked by buffing, polishing, and plating.

**13.** Leathers receive a final check for quality (grain, thickness, and color) and are shipped to the shoe factory.

# WARM-WEATHER *FOOTWEAR*

The stylish man's guide to summer shoes. Even flip-flops.

## THE *Loafer*

**Why they're built for summer:** No laces, which is nice. And loafers are soft, light, and flexible.
**What to look for:** Something unlined. It molds better to the shape of your foot for improved comfort. This is especially important because you'll be going sockless.
**What to wear with them:** Shorts, light-colored chinos. Just be sure the pants aren't too baggy.
**Care:** Get shoe trees. And be sure to treat them with a leather protector like Scotchgard.
BY GUCCI.

## THE *Derby*

**Why they're built for summer:** Derbies are casual, but still dressy enough to wear to the office. Plus, they'll look almost as comfortable as they'll feel.
**What to look for:** A light, neutral shade. If you're feeling particularly brash, you can opt for a colorful sole.
**What to wear with them:** Chinos, jeans, or a light suit.
**Care:** Same as the loafer.
BY ERMENEGILDO ZEGNA.

## THE *Sneaker*

**Why they're built for summer:** Sneakers fit in whether you're at the beach or on the street. Plus, the canvas allows for maximum breathability while fully protecting your toes.
**What to look for:** Simple colors like black, gray, navy, and white.
**What to wear with them:** Anything. Except a suit.
**Care:** Treat stains with a 50/50 mix of water and lemon juice. Throw them in the washer when they start to stink.
BY CONVERSE.

## THE *Flip-Flop*

**Why they're built for summer:** Flip-flops are the least you can wear without going barefoot.
**What to look for:** Something comfortable. If the rubber is too hard and inflexible, the pegs can pinch the skin on your toes.
**What to wear with them:** Swim trunks. And only when you're at the beach or pool.
**Care:** Wash them off in the sink every once in a while. Dish soap is fine.
BY SEAVEES.

**SHOE TREES:** Allen Edmonds combination cedar shoe trees help shoes retain their shape, but they also give them a chance to dry out by absorbing any accumulated sweat into the wood. (For this reason, always choose a porous wood, never varnished.) Germs thrive in moisture, so when you reduce moisture, you reduce germs. And when you reduce germs, you reduce odor. Which lets you take your shoes off without apologizing.

**DEODORIZERS:** They're not a permanent solution, as they don't actually do anything to reduce all that festering, but deodorizers do cover smells with a pleasant alternative. New Balance's convenient Gear Bombs twist open and can be put in shoes or a gym bag—or anywhere else in need of an olfactory boost. Maybe in the kitchen after your next batch of signature pork and sauerkraut.

**DEODORANT:** It works on your feet just like it does under your arms. Roll on a deodorant to add a better scent, or an antiperspirant to block the sweat glands entirely. Degree is nice. But so is whatever you already have in your medicine cabinet.

**TEA:** That's right, tea. The tannins kill bacteria. Just remember to let it cool first.

>>> THE ODYSSEY OF A LEATHER SHOE, CONTINUED

**14.** At the factory, hides are laid out, measured, and cut into the patterns that will become the upper of the shoe.

**15.** Eyelets and guide holes are punched in preparation for sewing.

**16.** The inside lining, a softer leather that will mold to the foot, is matched to the upper and cut.

**17.** Individual components the upper are stitched an sewn together. What you recognize as a shoe begins take shape in preparation lasting.

# What I've Learned

RICKEY THORNTON, 45, SHOE SHINER, DALLAS

## FIVE SHOES, FIVE FINISHES

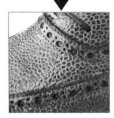

**PEBBLE GRAIN**
Di Bianco

**CROSS GRAIN**
Grenson

**PLAIN CALF**
Cole Haan

**SPAZZOLATO**
Canali

**PATENT**
J. M. Weston

IT'S JUST ME OUT THERE. I'm like the Lone Ranger.

THE GUY I LEARNED FROM, we used to call him the Shine King. He said, "Man, sit down. I'm going to show you how to do this." I told him he was going to have a problem with me, and he said, "Well, I'm not gonna leave until *you* show *me* how to do this the right way." And he did. And I never looked back.

IT STARTS AT EIGHT BUCKS. And that can increase based on how dirty the shoes are or the person's attitude.

WHEN I FIRST STARTED, I had a real bad habit. Everyone who walked by, I'm looking at their shoes. It was constant. Everywhere I go, I'm looking at shoes. I'd be in the grocery store—I'm looking at shoes.

YOUR SHOES TAKE A BEATING. And not only that, but hey, however many times you may go to the restroom—always be careful, because of the splash.

YOU GOTTA BE APPROACHABLE, and you gotta be a good listener, too. We need to be psychologists, man. You know, because a lot of times guys may leave that office and they'll just dump everything on us.

IT WAS A RATHER BUSY DAY. This guy began telling me something personal. He was really contemplating doing something to himself, like suicide. This turned from a normal 6-to-8-minute shoeshine into a 30-to-45-minute shoeshine. And this guy began to start weeping, just crying, you know. I enjoyed just being able to impart something to his life, something positive.

ONCE HE GOT in the chair, it seemed like everything just stopped. No one else came up, no one asked me for service or anything like that.

I HAD A CLIENT one time—I saw this guy from a distance, getting his shoes shined. He came back four or five days later. I was right in the middle of shining his shoes, and I stopped. I said, "Wait a minute." I grabbed his shoes and I said, "You've been cheating on me." He said, "Rick, what are you talking about?" I said, "Man, you've been letting somebody else shine your shoes. I don't appreciate that at all." This guy, for about ten minutes, didn't say a word. And I said, "I'm just teasing with you, man."

ALLEN EDMONDS, they have a very distinctive heel. Anytime I see a heel like that, I tell the guy, "You got a nice pair of Allen Edmonds shoes on." They're like, "Whoa, man, how did you know that?" I never tell them my secret, though. I just told you my secret, so it ain't no secret no more.

I SPENT ALL THIS TIME going to school, getting certified [in air-conditioning repair], and now, you know, I can't get away from the shoe business. It's just the love that I have for it. It's a passion, it really is.

I DON'T THINK I can do anything else.

I CAN GET TIRED, you know, because I may have a long workday. And there are times where, hey, there's nothing but elbows and shoe polish, my friend. But I enjoy doing it.

WHEN I CAN make a difference in somebody's life, man, even in their shoes, it's really important.

## THE PERFECT SHINE

Leather is going to give you only so much. Softer leathers, you're not going to get a high-gloss shine, so I like to always use creams and leather balms. It's more of a moisturizer. Coarser leather will get you a brighter sheen. Here's how:

**1.**
Always clean the shoe first. I use the analogy of taking a shower: If you get in the shower and don't use soap, guess what? You're still gonna be dirty.

**2.**
Using my two fingers, I'll dab the soft side of a T-shirt in water, then I'll dab it in the polish itself, just a little bit.

**3.**
Rub the shoe in a circular motion. The rag closes the pores of the leather a little, creating a slight friction. With that friction the shine starts coming up, and it's unbelievable.

**4.**
Product is essential. I wish I could keep the cover over Saphir products (hangerproject.com) and call it Brand X to keep it a secret, but I can't.

—RICKEY THORNTON

**18. LASTING:** The upper, lining, and insole are nailed into place around the last, the wooden form that will ultimately determine the shoe's shape and size.

**19.** The shoe's inner linings and upper are stapled into place, and the nails are removed from the last.

**20.** The toe of the shoe is shaped around the last.

## Emergency Measures and Long-Term Care for Shoes

**SHOE TREES:** Shoe trees are crucial. They allow your recently worn shoes to contract and dry out to their ideal shape—but only if you choose the less decorative unvarnished ones. Varnished trees look posh, but they don't properly draw moisture—i.e., sweat—out of the leather. Top marks go to unfinished cedar models with a split toe and a fully shaped heel: These ensure the closest possible fit between shoe and tree. Also, there's no need to own a pair of trees for each pair of shoes. The vital time for using them is the hour or two after you have removed the shoes from your feet. After that, the shoes will have returned to their natural architecture and the trees can be removed.

**REPAIR WORK:** Invest as much care in choosing a cobbler to resole or reheel your shoes as you did in purchasing them. And to prevent permanent damage (or, at the least, outrageous repair costs), have all work done before it's absolutely necessary.

**SUEDE:** Suede shoes are in a category of their own, since you cannot polish away any scuff marks. Use a suede eraser (basically a brick of crumbly rubber) to rub away small blemishes. Then use a suede brush to restore the nap, or fuzz, of the leather.

**WET SHOES:** Stuff soaking-wet shoes with newspaper and dry them away from direct heat. Direct heat can dry the leather too fast, causing it to crack—and once that happens, nothing can save your shoes.

**SALT STAINS:** The traditional remedy for road-salt stains is a little vinegar and water, applied sparingly.

## The Ugly Weapons of SHOE CARE

THE PROTECTION AIN'T PRETTY. THE RESULTS ARE.

**Taps:**
Small pieces of metal or plastic that minimize wear and tear on the sole. Tread lightly, as you may sound like Bojangles.

**Overshoes:**
Rubber slip-ons that cover your shoes and protect from rain. They do not protect from silent ridicule.

**Snow cleats:**
Stretchy meshes with teeth that give you traction on ice. The downside? They protect your butt, not your shoes.

---

## SHOES AS *Investments*

**Cheap shoes are a false bargain.** They're made of glue, rubber, and low-grade leather, which often bears scars from shrubs, trees, and barbed wire (the normal hazards of bovine life), and which is rejected out of hand by reputable shoemakers. Good shoes begin with great leather, period. Be prepared to pay for it. Of course, once you have invested your hard-earned cash in a quality pair, you're going to want to hang on to them. Put a little time and effort into looking after them and they'll last longer than any three pairs of cheap clodhoppers.

---

## THE JOY OF BOOTS

### Chukka Boot
*Brief history:*
A descendant of the classic polo boot.
*Positively associated with:*
Off-duty polo players.
*Negatively associated with:*
Off-duty polo players.
*Beware of:*
Clompy soles that make them unwearable with suits.
*Boots by Grenson.*

### Chelsea Boot
*Brief history:*
A riding boot that defined 1960s footwear.
*Positively associated with:*
The Beatles.
*Negatively associated with:*
Imperial Stormtroopers. (They wore black ones painted white.)
*Beware of:*
Wearing them with baggy clothes.
*Boots by Moreschi.*

### Motorcycle Boot
*Brief history:*
Shorter than the cowboy boot, it came of age during World War II.
*Positively associated with:*
Marlon Brando.
*Negatively associated with:*
Hells Angels.
*Beware of:*
Wearing with anything but jeans.
*Boots by the Frye Company.*

### Cowboy Boot
*Brief history:*
A derivation of the vaquero boot, imported as early as the 1500s to the New World from Spain.
*Positively associated with:*
Johnny Cash.
*Negatively associated with:*
Jessica Simpson.
*Beware of:*
Tucking into jeans.
*Boots by Justin Western Collection.*

---

>>> THE ODYSSEY OF A LEATHER SHOE, CONTINUED

**21.** Any wrinkles in the upper are tapped and pushed out of the leather.

**22.** Excess lining and upper are trimmed and discarded.

**23.** The welt—the piece of leather that will connect the upper to the sole—is sewn to the upper.

**24.** A cork-and-glue mixture is added to the space between the welt and the sole, giving the shoe breathability and allowing the insole to shape to the wearer's foot over time.

**25.** The sole is applied, sewn to the welt, and shaped to match the upper.

# HOW TO GO SOCKLESS WITHOUT STINKING UP YOUR SHOES

**STAY CLEAN:** Wash your feet more often and arduously than you're used to, with antibacterial soap.

**USE A SHOE TREE:** Yes, for the reasons outlined on the right, but also because an unvarnished cedar shoe tree, properly inserted, will absorb perspiration, help prevent bacterial growth, and deodorize the shoes.

**USE AN ANTIPERSPIRANT:** A foot antiperspirant like Gold Bond Foot Spray can help fight sweat and bacteria.

## Three Shoe Accessories
Every Man Should Own

### a shoe tree
It's the easiest way to increase your shoes' life expectancy. It maintains their shape by mimicking the last, i.e., the carved wooden block on which your shoes were built. The vital time for using them is the hour or two after you've removed the shoes from your feet.

### a polishing kit
Because you can keep your shoes looking new even between professional shines. Go for wax-based polish in black and a chestnut or darker brown, with middling or neutral polish for your light-colored shoes.

### a shoehorn
Because every time you jam your heel into a shoe, an old Italian cobbler dies. Made of either metal, wood, or horn, a shoehorn makes slipping into a shoe easy—and it prevents the damage you can inflict by crushing the counter.

## *OTHER USES* FOR SHOES

**As a political weapon**
*See:* Khrushchev, N., at the United Nations.

**As a hiding place**
*See:* Bond, J., homing device in *Goldfinger*.

**As a lyric**
*See:* Presley, E., and "Shoes, Blue Suede."

**As a home**
*See:* Who Lived in a Shoe, the Old Woman.

## A USER'S GUIDE TO *Formal SHOES*

From the most formal to the least, five ways to put your best foot forward

**Black oxford**
*Good for:* a day in court

**Brown wing tip**
*Good for:* a day in the office

**Black monk strap**
*Good for:* a night on the town

**Split-toe blucher**
*Good for:* dinner with your wife

**Brown Loafer**
*Good for:* weekend cocktail party

FROM LEFT: SHOES BY J. M. WESTON, SERGIO ROSSI, MORESCHI, BROOKS BROTHERS, AND TOD'S.

THE END

**26. FINISHING:** Polishes and creams are applied to the welt for a seamless look between the sole and the upper.

**27.** Creams and waxes are applied to the overall finish of the shoe.

**28.** Laces, buckles, or cute little tassels are added.

**29.** Shoes are bagged, boxed, and shipped.

**30.** Shoes are tried on, paid for, and then worn.

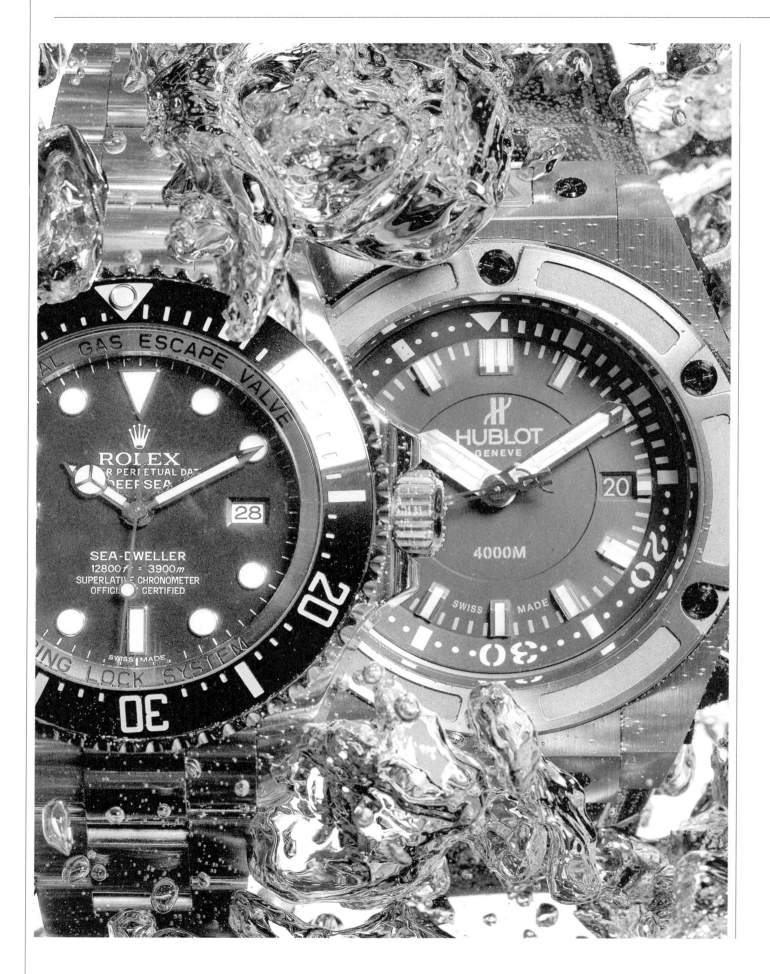

# CHAPTER THIRTEEN

# Watches

THERE'S A WHOLE WONDERFUL WORLD TICKING AWAY ON YOUR WRIST.

HERE ARE THE HOWS AND WHYS OF THE WAYS WE KEEP TIME.

# THE ANATOMY

## A THREE-MINUTE GUIDE TO WATCHMAKING JARGON

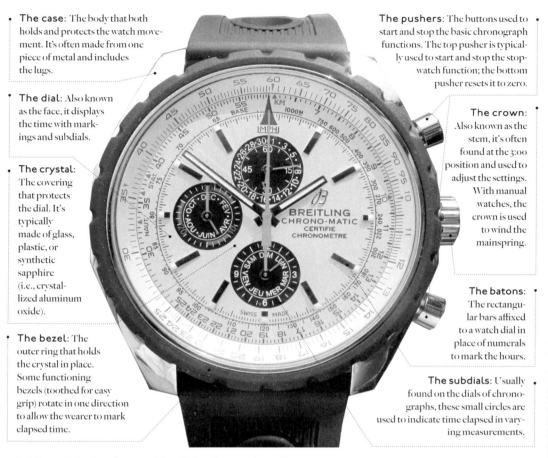

**The case:** The body that both holds and protects the watch movement. It's often made from one piece of metal and includes the lugs.

**The dial:** Also known as the face, it displays the time with markings and subdials.

**The crystal:** The covering that protects the dial. It's typically made of glass, plastic, or synthetic sapphire (i.e., crystallized aluminum oxide).

**The bezel:** The outer ring that holds the crystal in place. Some functioning bezels (toothed for easy grip) rotate in one direction to allow the wearer to mark elapsed time.

**The pushers:** The buttons used to start and stop the basic chronograph functions. The top pusher is typically used to start and stop the stopwatch function; the bottom pusher resets it to zero.

**The crown:** Also known as the stem, it's often found at the 3:00 position and used to adjust the settings. With manual watches, the crown is used to wind the mainspring.

**The batons:** The rectangular bars affixed to a watch dial in place of numerals to mark the hours.

**The subdials:** Usually found on the dials of chronographs, these small circles are used to indicate time elapsed in varying measurements.

*Steel Chrono-Matic 1461 watch (not actual size) with Ocean Racer strap by Breitling.*

---

# The Semiotics of Watch Wearing

> "What is time? Swiss manufacture it. French hoard it. Italians want it. Americans say it is money. Hindus say it does not exist."
>
> —Peter Lorre, *Beat the Devil*

**Under the wrist**
You're saying: "I wear a watch backward because I think it looks cool." *Alain Delon with a Cartier Tank.*

**Snug**
You're saying: "I wear a watch snug because I'm a very serious person." *Paul Newman with a Rolex Daytona.*

**Over a shirt**
You're saying: "I wear a watch like this because its my shtick. Capito? Bene." *Gianni Agnelli with a vintage Cartier.*

**With a space suit**
You're saying: "I wear a watch in case the shuttle computer goes FUBAR." *Buzz Aldrin with an Omega Speedmaster.*

# CAN YOU PULL OFF A POCKET WATCH?

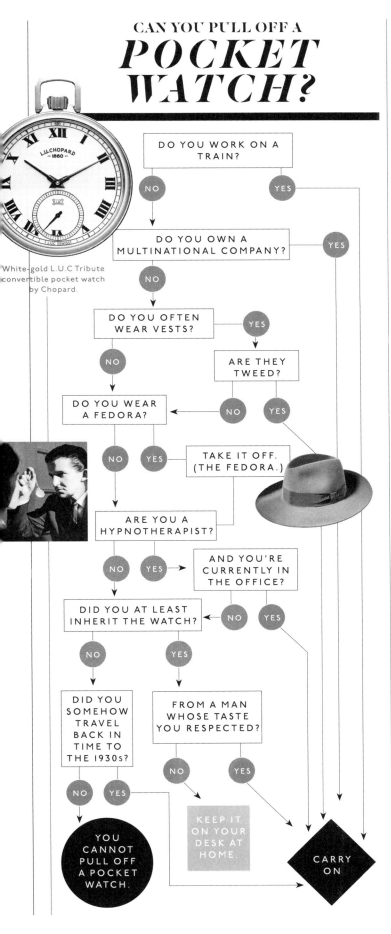

White-gold L.U.C Tribute convertible pocket watch by Chopard.

**DO YOU WORK ON A TRAIN?** — NO / YES

**DO YOU OWN A MULTINATIONAL COMPANY?** — NO / YES

**DO YOU OFTEN WEAR VESTS?** — NO / YES

**ARE THEY TWEED?** — NO / YES

**DO YOU WEAR A FEDORA?** — NO / YES

**TAKE IT OFF. (THE FEDORA.)**

**ARE YOU A HYPNOTHERAPIST?** — NO / YES

**AND YOU'RE CURRENTLY IN THE OFFICE?** — NO / YES

**DID YOU AT LEAST INHERIT THE WATCH?** — NO / YES

**DID YOU SOMEHOW TRAVEL BACK IN TIME TO THE 1930s?** — NO / YES

**FROM A MAN WHOSE TASTE YOU RESPECTED?** — NO / YES

**YOU CANNOT PULL OFF A POCKET WATCH.**

**KEEP IT ON YOUR DESK AT HOME.**

**CARRY ON**

---

## THE TOOLS

### Watch Winder:
Nobody really *needs* a watch winder, but as it keeps your automatic watch accurately ticking while you're not wearing it, it's useful. To avoid wear on the winding mechanism, most winders should run only 30 minutes a day. BY WOLF DESIGNS.

### Travel Pouch:
Connoisseurs' leather travel carrier will keep your watch safe in transit. Then again, so will a tube sock. BY VENLO.

### Watch Roll:
If you are lucky enough to have a watch collection, congratulations. You might also want a place to house them all for storage and travel. BY SMYTHSON.

---

## The Fixers

When your watch breaks, you have three main options: send it back to the watchmaker, to its U. S. headquarters, or to your local watch repairman. Here's what you can expect from each.

### To Switzerland!
The utmost care will be taken if your watch is dispatched all the way back to Geneva. Expect to be away from your watch for at least two months, maybe more, but know that it's getting treated better than you ever will.

### To the U.S. outpost!
One of the main benefits of having your watch repaired at a brand's U. S. headquarters is that, in the eyes of many collectors, repairs done there (versus a local dealer) are less likely to affect the value. If your watch is still under warranty, repair is completely free. Otherwise, you'll be treated to an estimate charge, a service charge, and a shipping charge. Plus the cost of any repairs. And your watch will still be gone for two to three weeks.

### To the shop!
Your local repairman will often get your watch back to you in less than a week. As long as you're working with an authorized dealer, you can expect the same level of care and retention of value you would get by shipping it directly to the maker. Go to an unlicensed dealer, however, and you're putting your watch—and its value—in God's hands.

# YOU *and* YOUR MOVEMENT
## THE LITTLE THINGS THAT PUT THE TICK IN THE TICKTOCK

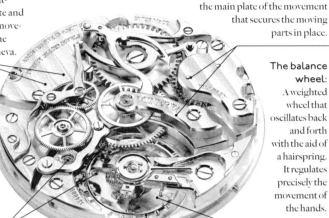

**The Côtes de Genève:**
An undulating stripe pattern etched into the plate and bridges of a fine watch movement. It originated in the top-level ateliers of Geneva.

**The jewels:**
Tiny doughnut-shaped bearings—usually synthetic garnets, rubies, or sapphires—in which all the pinions of rotating parts are set to minimize friction.

**The serial number:**
A maker's code to identify a specific movement used in a watch, in this case the Minerva 16-18.

**The bridges:**
The superstructure attached to the main plate of the movement that secures the moving parts in place.

**The balance wheel:**
A weighted wheel that oscillates back and forth with the aid of a hairspring. It regulates precisely the movement of the hands.

**Timing screws:**
Minute, threaded-metal weights set into the balance wheel that ensure it's in balance.

*Movement 16-18 for a Collection Villeret 1858 watch by Montblanc.*

### THE LONELIEST COMPLICATION:
# THE MINUTE REPEATER

BY NOW YOU'VE READ ALL ABOUT the grand complications that make up many a special watch. What you haven't read about, however, is the minute repeater, an increasingly rare complication first created in the 17th century to relay time during hours of pitch darkness. Powered by a mechanical slider on one side of the case, it sounds the time using tiny hammers and gongs, with different tones distinguishing the hours, quarters, and minutes. The hours are usually signified by a low tone (bong!), the quarters by a sequence of high and low tones together (bing-bong!), and the minutes by a high tone (bing!). For example, if the time is 4:39, then the minute repeater will sound four low tones representing four hours (bong! bong! bong! bong!), two dual tones representing 30 minutes (bing-bong! bing-bong!), and nine high tones representing the nine minutes (bing! bing! bing! bing! bing! bing! bing! bing! bing!). Next time you're asked the time, try the bing-bong system yourself. Rose-gold Portuguese watch by IWC.

---

## THINGS A MAN SHOULD TIME WITH A CHRONOGRAPH . . .

• His morning commute. • **The duration between coffee breaks.** • How long it takes to run a mile. • **How long it takes to soft-boil an egg.** • The guitar solo in "Free Bird."

## . . . AND THINGS A MAN SHOULD NEVER TIME WITH A CHRONOGRAPH

• An interview for a job. • **A talking to from his wife's mother.** • His performance in the bedroom. • **Religious ceremonies.** • Brunch.

---

### THE ONE-QUESTION QUIZ:
## WHAT IS THE GENEVA SEAL?

A) An aquatic mammal that resides in alpine lakes.
B) A secret treaty signed by Toblerone, Lindt, and other top Swiss chocolatiers in 1963.
C) A sexual maneuver particularly popular in the western part of Switzerland.
D) None of the above.

Answer: D. It's the coat of arms of Geneva, Switzerland, adopted in 1886 to mark watches made and finished in the Canton of Geneva that meet a particularly stringent set of standards of finish and decoration. Ask about it before buying your next watch.

---

# AN INCOMPLETE *History of Time*

**1500 B.C.:** The earliest sundials are used by the Egyptians. People stop being late for work.

**45 B.C.:** Julius Caesar introduces the Julian calendar to align the civic calendar with the solar cycle.

**A.D. 149:** The earliest reported hourglasses are used in Alexandria.

**1502:** Peter Henlein creates a watch with an hour hand, the Nuremberg Egg, believed to be the first watch.

**1600:** Joost Bürgi creates the first clock with minute and second hands.

**1773:** John Harrison's marine chronometer allows sailors to accurately calculate longitude, revolutionizing navigation.

**1795:** Abraham-Louis Breguet invents the tourbillon, a gyroscopic regulator, to negate the effects of gravity on the accuracy of pocket watches.

**1844:** Adolphe Nicole patents the first true chronograph; people start timing *everything.*

## *Technically* **Speaking**

On the subject of time, one should never mince words

**ACCURACY VERSUS PRECISION:**
Accuracy refers to how well a watch tells time over a set period (e.g., a watch that loses a second every month is more accurate than one that loses a second every day). Precision is the degree to which a watch measures the time (a watch that measures time to the second is less precise than one that measures time to the millisecond).

**CHRONOMETER VERSUS CHRONOGRAPH:**
A chronometer is a watch whose movement has been certified for its accuracy by the Contrôle Officiel Suisse des Chronomètres (COSC) in Switzerland after stringent testing. A chronograph is any watch with push buttons and the capability to measure elapsed time like a stopwatch.

**WATERPROOF VERSUS WATER-RESISTANT:**
Waterproof implies that you can take a watch to any depth, under any pressure, and it'll be completely impervious to water. In reality, this doesn't exist. Water-resistant watches can be taken into the water at varying depths (e.g., a watch can be water-resistant to a quick swim but not a deep dive).

**MECHANICAL VERSUS QUARTZ:**
A mechanical watch is powered by a mainspring that is either manually wound or automatic. A quartz watch is powered by a battery instead of a mainspring, and its time is regulated by the natural oscillations of a quartz crystal. Most quartz oscillators vibrate at a rate of 32,786 times per second. These vibrations go through an integrated circuit and are converted to pulses that drive a motor to move the wheels and hands.

---

### THE BACKSTORY
## STEVE MCQUEEN'S MONACO

**TRUE STORY:** When Steve McQueen set about researching his role as a race-car driver in the 1971 classic *Le Mans*, he modeled his character after a Formula One speed demon (and product ambassador for Heuer timepieces) named Jo Siffert. McQueen immersed himself in Siffert's life and, for the film, opted to wear an exact copy of Siffert's uniform: a white racing suit emblazoned with "Chronograph Heuer." And because Siffert wore Heuer watches on and off the track, McQueen sported the brand's latest creation, the square-case Monaco, during the racing sequences. The watch has since been known colloquially as the "McQueen Monaco," and though TAG Heuer recently reissued the watch with "In Tribute to Steve McQueen" engraved on the back, the original still exists. The Heuer Monaco that McQueen wore in the film recently sold at auction for $87,600.

**What You Call It**

LEAST FORMAL
↑
Bling
Ticker
Watch
Wristwatch
Timepiece
Immortal Beloved
↓
MOST FORMAL

### THE GEEK-WATCH
## *HALL OF FAME*

*Weird-looking, but that's why geeks love 'em*

---

SIX WAYS TO ASK **WHAT TIME IS IT?**

**Portuguese:** Que horas são? (Ky-OH-rash SOW?) **German:** Wie spät ist es? (Vee shpayt ist ehs?)
**Dutch:** Hoe laat is het? (Hoo laat is heht?) **Icelandic:** Hvað er klukkan? (Kvaa er kluk-ahn?)
**Indonesian:** Jam berapa sekarang? (Jam BRA-pa Sk-A-rang?) **Swahili:** Ni saa ngapi? (Nee-saa-ngapi?)

---

**1847:** Cartier, a future leader in watch innovation, is founded by Louis François Cartier.

**1884:** Greenwich mean time is adopted as the international standard, except by France. It holds off adopting GMT for another 27 years.

**1905:** Albert Einstein describes the special theory of relativity, thus defining time as we know it today.

**1908:** Rolex founded by Hans Wilsdorf; wealthy men everywhere smile.

**1927:** Creation of the first quartz-regulated clock by scientists at Bell Laboratories in New Jersey.

**1967:** The period of time we know as one second is conclusively defined.

**1969:** The Omega Speedmaster lands on the moon. A man goes with it.

**1994:** *Pulp Fiction's* Christopher Walken explains the lengths we go to for a special watch.

# Watch Commerce

### HOW TO BUY:

Though there are occasionally bargains and even great finds online, the prevalence of dodgy watches and dubious practitioners means your best bet is to go to an authorized dealer or a retailer like Tourneau that's licensed to sell multiple brands as well as its own. Come in with a budget, and if the watch you like is outside that budget, consider a few options that will help lower the price—a stainless-steel (or even leather) bracelet over white gold, a watch you wind over an automatic—or simply opt for a lesser-known brand that is still high quality. And don't expect to do much negotiating. If you do happen to find a dealer who is willing to offer a discount, it's rarely more than 5 or 10 percent. (Some brands, like Rolex and Cartier, don't allow any leeway at all on their pricing.)

### HOW TO SELL:

Don't. Think of your children.

---

**Water-Resistant:**
If nothing can get inside the watch (which is the case for most high-end timepieces), it's as simple as lightly scrubbing the exterior with a toothbrush and a little dish soap. Rinse it clean and dry with a soft cloth.

**Non-Water-Resistant:**
Run a moist (but not wet) cloth over the case. Then take a dry toothbrush to the corners and crevices where dirt has built up. Rewipe with the moist cloth and once with a dry cloth. For any harder-to-clean spots, apply a little Shout on a Q-tip.

---

### THE
# "OH, SHIT"
### guide to watch care

SOLUTIONS FOR COMMON CONUNDRUMS

**Your leather band stinks:** You can't do much to clean it without ruining the leather. Try wiping the band with a little soap and water. But if the smell doesn't go away, it's time to replace the band.

**You've scratched or cracked the crystal:** A crack or scratch in crystal can't be polished out, but you can get a new one for around $50. If the crystal is actually Lucite, a scratch can be polished out, but a crack will still require replacement.

**You got your watch wet:** Don't fret. If you paid more than $500 for it, there's a good chance it's water resistant.

---

### The
# WATCH BUDGET

KNOWING HOW MUCH TO SPEND ON A WATCH IS EASY. JUST FOLLOW THE EQUATION BELOW.

$$\frac{\left(\text{Monthly income} - \text{Fixed monthly expenses}\right)\pi^* \times \left(75.7^{**} - \text{Your age}\right)}{\text{Your age}} - \text{Outstanding creditcard debt}^{***} = \text{Your watch budget}$$

**KEY**

\* 3.14. Obviously.

\*\* Average life expectancy.

\*\*\* If this brings you into negative territory, now is not the time to be buying a watch.

**SOME EXAMPLES**

**SEIKO AUTOMATIC DIVE WATCH**
$

**RAYMOND WEIL MEN'S MAESTRO**
$$

**OMEGA SEAMASTER DIVER 300M**
$$$

**IWC PORTUGUESE AUTOMATIC**
$$$$

# The ICONS

*The stories behind some watches' most distinguishing features*

**CARTIER'S JEWEL CROWN:**
Since 1904, most Cartier watches have used a sapphire "cabochon" in the crown to reflect the brand's history in jewelry.

**IWC PILOT'S CROWN:**
This onion crown was made extra large so that pilots could adjust their watches without taking off their gloves.

**PANERAI LOCKING CROWN:**
Since the watch was originally designed for divers in the 1950s, the arm clamps the crown into the watch, sealing it against any leaks.

**BREGUET HANDS:**
Introduced around 1783, Breguet hands are longer and narrower than watch hands of that era were, in order to make the watch easier to read.

**AUDEMARS ROYAL OAK CASE:**
The distinctive octagonal shape was modeled after the portholes on the HMS *Royal Oak*.

# Three Wrists, Three Kinds of Watches

**HAIRY:**

Avoid metallic bracelets with links, which can catch and pull your arm hair. Opt instead for a watch with a leather band, like the Hermès Cape Cod.

**LARGE:**

If your huge forearms dwarf traditional watch faces, look for something with a diameter of at least 50mm. The U-Boat U-42 Chrono should stand up to the biggest wrist, since it's only slightly smaller than a dinner plate.

**THIN:**

A big watch face on a small wrist looks as bad as an oversized suit on a skinny man. You'll want a narrower watch face, like the 38.5mm Jaeger-LeCoultre Reverso Classique.

## OTHER THINGS YOU CAN WEAR ON YOUR WRIST

SILLY BANDZ*

RUBBER BAND*

SLAP BRACELET*

HOLIDAY RIBBON*

HOSPITAL ID

*NOT RECOMMENDED

# How Big Can You Go?

To get a sense of the watch diameter that's right for you, cut out the examples below and try them out on your wrist.

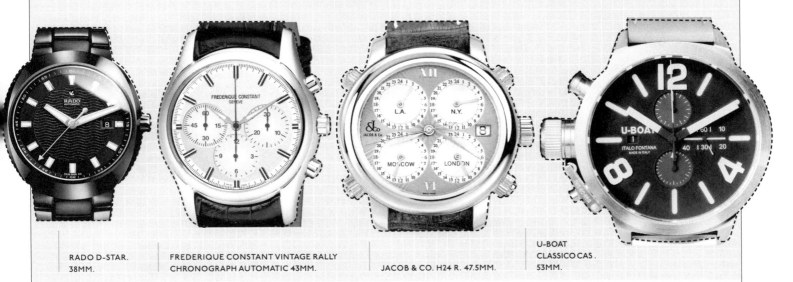

RADO D-STAR. 38MM.

FREDERIQUE CONSTANT VINTAGE RALLY CHRONOGRAPH AUTOMATIC 43MM.

JACOB & CO. H24 R. 47.5MM.

U-BOAT CLASSICO CAS. 53MM.

### Quartz

A battery makes a tiny quartz crystal vibrate; these vibrations regulate the transmission of power from the battery, which moves the hands of the watch.

**PROS:** Considerably more accurate than a mechanical watch.

**CONS:** The battery will have to be replaced.

### Mechanical Automatic

Every time you move your hand, it propels an internal rotor in the watch, which winds the mainspring in the movement to store potential energy that is used to power the watch.

**PROS:** Much more valuable, thanks to the craftsmanship required.

**CONS:** If you don't wear it often, you'll need to wind it.

### Kinetic

As with a mechanical automatic, the movement of your wrist drives a rotor. Instead of winding the mainspring, however, the movement of the rotor is converted into electrical energy, which is stored in a rechargeable battery.

**PROS:** The best of both worlds—no winding or battery replacement needed.

**CONS:** If you don't wear the watch for a long period of time—say, three months—it will eventually stop keeping time.

# The Grandest Complications

## A FEW OF THE FEATURES THAT MAKE SPECIAL WATCHES SPECIAL

*Watch movements by Piaget (A), Patek Philippe (B), A. Lange & Söhne (C), Blancpain (D), Montblanc (E).*

FIG. A

FIG. B

FIG. E

FIG. C

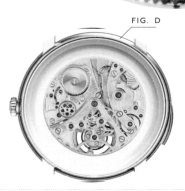
FIG. D

### FIG. A
## PERPETUAL CALENDAR:
*Correctly tracks the time, day, date, even accounting for leap years (if kept wound) until March 1, 2100.*
**First appeared:** 1925.
**How it's done:** The mechanism ticks off the full 1,461 days in four years.

### FIG. B
## MOON PHASE:
*Displays the phases of the moon via a rotating disk in the watch face.*
**First appeared:** 1500s.
**How it's done:** A dedicated gear rotates with the 29.5-day lunar cycle.

### FIG. C
## FLYBACK:
*The second hand returns to the 12 o'clock position with the push of a single button and starts counting immediately.*
**First appeared:** 1844 in London.

How it's done: Pushing that button releases a lever connected to the timing hands, which causes them to "fly back" to the original 12 o'clock position.

### FIG. D
## MINUTE REPEATER:
*The watch chimes to denote the hour and minute.*
**First appeared:** 1750, created for King Ferdinand VI of Spain.
**How it's done:** Two small hammers linked to small gongs are connected to a complex system of feelers, which read off the cogs of the hour, quarter hour, and minute.

### FIG. E
## CHRONO-GRAPH:
*Measures intervals of elapsed time.*
**First appeared:** 1822, created by the clockmaker to King Louis XVIII.
**How it's done:** The movement drives a column wheel that starts and stops a second hand when the side button is pushed.

## POWER RESERVE:
*Shows how long the watch will run.*
**First appeared:** As far as we can tell, 1948, in the Jaeger-LeCoultre Powermatic Caliber 481.
**How it's done:** The barrel, which rotates with the unwinding of the mainspring, moves the hands of the indicator.

> *"It's a gorgeous gold pocket watch—I'm proud of it. My grandfather, on his deathbed, sold me this watch."* —WOODY ALLEN

# The Swiss Connection

## NO MATTER WHERE THE WATCHMAKER IS BASED, IT ALL COMES BACK TO SWITZERLAND

**Bozeman:** Designed in the U.S., assembled in Germany, movements manufactured in Switzerland. *Stainless-steel SnowMaster Telemetric watch.*

**Cuervo y Sobrinos:** Originated in Cuba, always made in Switzerland. *Stainless-steel Torpedo Pulsómetro chronograph.*

**Bremont:** Designed in England, finished in England, movements manufactured in Switzerland. *Stainless-steel MB2 watch.*

**A. Lange & Söhne:** Designed and produced in Germany, owned by the Swiss Richemont Group. *White-gold 1815 watch.*

---

# FIVE WAYS OF THE
## *Vintage Watch*

*Steve Kivel of New York City's Central Watch on buying and caring for old-timers*

· Any watch made before the 1960s won't have what's called an "Incabloc" system, or shock-resistance. Without it, a watch is much more fragile.

· Look for the "triple signs": when the movement, the dial, and the case are individually signed. If you don't see all three, the watch may have been messed with and some parts may not be original.

· If it hasn't been recently serviced, go to a professional for maintenance. Everything is dismantled, checked under a microscope, oiled, and polished.

· Leave the polishing to the pros. At-home solutions contain chemicals that can eat away at your watch.

· No hot tub, not ever.

*For more knowledge and advice: centralwatch.com.*

---

Le Sentier, Vallée de Joux

# Greetings
## *from the* Vallée de Joux

OF ALL THE PLACES IN SWITZERLAND that make complicated movements, few are as storied as the Vallée de Joux. The valley was settled in the 17th century by farmers seeking greener pastures, but farming was a tough way to make a living year-round. While stuck inside during the winters, the farmers learned other trades—among them, watchmaking. They grew more and more specialized in creating the parts for movements, and today the area is still home to brands like Audemars Piguet, Breguet, Patek Philippe, and Jaeger-LeCoultre. Drop in sometime and pick up a postcard like the one above. Or, you know, a watch.

### THE LIMITED-EDITION WATCH

RICHARD MILLE, a brand launched in only 2001, is one of those Swiss watchmakers seemingly created with the intention of making as few watches as possible. Take Mille's RM008: Its movement, a split-second tourbillon chronograph, is composed of 444 pieces (plus another 77 for the tourbillon), and, as is often the case with such limited-production brands, the technical expertise with which it's made (rather than simple old-school bling) is what attracts its customers. The latest sale price of the titanium version of the RM008 is $530,000 (and limited to 30 pieces), but with such rarefied watches, the price is meaningless.

---

### calf leather

*Advantages:* Pliable and lighter than metal bands. *Disadvantages:* Perspiration can make the leather smell. *Care:* Wipe off excess sweat with a paper towel and let dry. Do not oil.

### stainless steel

*Advantages:* Hypoallergenic, easy to replace, dressy-looking. *Disadvantages:* Scratches easily. *Care:* Remove grime with a mixture of one part ammonia to ten parts water and massage with a toothbrush.

### nylon

*Advantages:* Inexpensive, easy to change. *Disadvantages:* Wears down easily, a little too casual for dressier watches. *Care:* Throw in a dishwasher. Seriously. Cleans up good as new. Just be sure to remove the watch first.

### rubber

*Advantages:* Waterproof and flexible. *Disadvantages:* Activity tends to wear the rubber down over time. Also, a little too casual for dressier watches. *Care:* Replace as needed.

### crocodile leather

*Advantages:* Pliable, with shiny texture. *Disadvantages:* Expensive, and can start to smell with frequent wearing. *Care:* Wipe off excess sweat with a paper towel and let dry. Wear sparingly.

............................................

# CHAPTER FOURTEEN

# The Resources

A CITY-BY-CITY LISTING OF THE FINEST COBBLERS, TAILORS, DRY CLEANERS,

AND ALL-PURPOSE NECK SAVERS AROUND THE WORLD.

# The Best Men's Stores *in the World*

## UNITED STATES

**1 BERGDORF GOODMAN MEN'S**
745 Fifth Avenue, New York
bergdorfgoodman.com

**2 BARNEYS NEW YORK**
660 Madison Avenue, New York
barneys.com

**3 PAUL STUART**
10 East 45th Street, New York
paulstuart.com

**4 MARTIN GREENFIELD CLOTHIERS**
239 Varet Street, Brooklyn
greenfieldclothiers.com (by appointment only)

**5 RICHARDS**
359 Greenwich Avenue, Greenwich, Connecticut
mitchellstores.com

**6 BOYDS**
1818 Chestnut Street, Philadelphia
boydsphila.com

**7 SID MASHBURN**
1198 Howell Mill Road, Atlanta
sidmashburn.com

**8 SYD JEROME**
2 North La Salle Street, Chicago
sydjerome.com

**9 HABERDASH**
607 North State Street, Chicago
haberdashmen.com

**10 WILKES BASHFORD**
375 Sutter Street, San Francisco
wilkesbashford.com

**11 MARIO'S**
1513 Sixth Avenue, Seattle
marios.com

**12 MAXFIELD**
8825 Melrose Avenue, Los Angeles
maxfieldla.com

**13 UNION**
110 South La Brea Avenue, Los Angeles
unionlosangeles.com

**14 TOM FORD**
346 North Rodeo Drive, Beverly Hills
tomford.com

**15 THE WEBSTER MIAMI**
1220 Collins Avenue, Miami Beach
thewebstermiami.com

## LATIN AMERICA

**16 ALBERTO GENTLEMAN**
282 Rua Visconde de Pirajá, Rio de Janeiro
albertogentleman.com

**17 RICHARDS**
43 Rua Sete de Setembro, Rio de Janeiro
richards.com.br

**18 ETIQUETA NEGRA**
2835 Andrés Arguibel, Buenos Aires
etiquetanegra.us

**19 GIESSO**
1557 Avenida Santa Fe, Buenos Aires
giesso.com.ar

**20 EL PALACIO DE HIERRO**
3 Avenida 20 de Noviembre, Mexico City
soytotalmentepalacio.com.mx

## EUROPE

**21 GEORGE CLEVERLEY**
13 the Royal Arcade, 28 Old Bond Street, London
gjcleverley.co.uk

**22 HARRODS**
87–135 Brompton Road, London
harrods.com

**23 HACKETT**
137–138 Sloane Street, London
hackett.com

**24 THOM SWEENEY**
1–2 Weighhouse Street, London
thomsweeney.co.uk (by appointment only)

**25 HENRY POOLE & CO.**
15 Savile Row, London
henrypoole.com

**26 TURNBULL & ASSER**
71–72 Jermyn Street, London
turnbullandasser.com

**27 CHARVET**
28 Place Vendôme, Paris
charvet.com

**28 HERMÈS (ORIGINAL STORE)**
24 Rue du Faubourg Saint-Honoré, Paris
hermes.com

**29 LOUIS VUITTON (ORIGINAL STORE)**
101 Avenue des Champs-Élysées, Paris
louisvuitton.com

**30 DE BIJENKORF**
Dam 1, Amsterdam
debijenkorf.nl

8, 9
7
10
11
6
1, 2, 3, 4, 5
12, 13, 14
15
20
16, 17
18, 19
31, 32, 33, 34, 35

# A CITY-BY-CITY LISTING OF THE FINEST COBBLERS, TAILORS, DRY CLEANERS, AND ALL-PURPOSE NECK SAVERS AROUND THE WORLD*

**21, 22, 23, 24, 25, 26**

**27, 28, 29**

**53**

**42, 43, 44**

**45, 46**

**47**

**50**

**48, 49**

**55**

**30**    **54**    **52**   **51**    **56**

**36, 37**    **40, 41**

**31 BRIONI**
2–4 Via Gesu, Milan
brioni.com

**32 PRADA (ORIGINAL STORE)**
63–65 Galleria Vittorio Emanuele II, Milan
prada.com

**33 AL BAZAR**
9 Via Antonio Scarpa, Milan
albazarmilano.it

**34 EXCELSIOR MILANO**
4 Galleria del Corso, Milan
excelsiormilano.com

**35 VALENTINO**
20 Via Montenapoleone, Milan
valentino.com

**36 DEPARTMENTSTORE QUARTIER 206**
71 Friedrichstrasse, Berlin
dsq206.com

**37 MIENTUS**
73 Wilmersdorfer Strasse, Berlin
mientus.com

**38 JELMOLI**
1 Seidengasse, Zurich
jelmoli.ch/en-us/home

**39 SANTA EULALIA**
93 Passeig de Grácia, Barcelona
santaeulalia.com

**40 GUM***
Red Square
Moscow
gum.ru/en
*Home to Corneliani, Etro, Louis Vuitton, and more.

**41 TSUM**
2 Petrovka, Moscow
tsum.ru

## ASIA

**42 BEAMS HOUSE ROPPONGI**
1F Tokyo Midtown Galleria, 9-7-3 Akasaka, Minato-ku, Tokyo
beams.co.jp/shops/detail/beams-house-roppongi

**43 UNITED ARROWS**
3-28-1 Jingumae, Shibuya-ku, Tokyo
united-arrows.co.jp

**44 ISETAN MEN'S**
3-14-1 Shinjuku, Shinjuku-ku, Tokyo
mens.isetan.co.jp

**45 THE BAUER COMPANY**
350 GoaBeiDian, Chaoyang District, Beijing

**46 LANE CRAWFORD**
Season's Place
2 Jinchengfang, Xicheng District, Beijing
lanecrawford.com/info/store.jsp?storeId=006

**47 PARAGON**
290 Orchard Road, Singapore
paragon.sg

**48 ALFRED DUNHILL**
House Hong Kong, Landmark Prince's 10 Chater Road, Central Hong Kong
dunhill.com/the-homes/hong-kong

**49 ASCOT CHANG**
IFC Mall, 1 Harbour View Street, Central, Hong Kong
ascotchang.com

**50 TANIKA**
300 Sukhumvit Road, Near Soi 14, Bangkok
tanikatailor.com

**51 NARENDRA KUMAR**
416 Kewal Industrial Estate, Mumbai
narendrakumar.ws

**52 THE DUBAI MALL**
Level G, Bloomingdale's Atrium, the Dubai Mall, Dubai
thedubaimall.com

**53 VAKKO**
33 Abdi Ipekçi Caddesi, Istanbul
vakko.com

## AFRICA

**54 SPAGHETTI MAFIA**
199 Loop Street, Cape Town
011 27 21 424 0696

## AUSTRALIA

**55 HARROLDS**
188 Pitt Street Level 3, at the Westfield, Sydney
harrolds.com.au

**56 DAVID JONES**
310 Bourke Street, Melbourne
davidjones.com.au

# *The* **Resources**

## *ATLANTA*

**COBBLER**
Bennie's Shoes
2625 Piedmont Road
404-262-1966
benniesshoes.com

**DRY CLEANER**
Presstine Cleaners
4455 Roswell Road
404-255-4312

**FLORIST**
Michal Evans Floral and Event Design
3200 Cains Hill Place NW
404-365-0200
michalevans.com

**LIQUOR STORE**
Tower Beer, Wine and Spirits
2161 Piedmont Road
404-881-0902
towerwinespirits.com

**TAILOR**
Guffey's of Atlanta
3340 Peachtree Road NE, #10
404-231-0044
guffeys.com

**WATCH REPAIR**
Tourneau
3393 Peachtree Road NE, Suite 3082
404-760-1883
tourneau.com

## *AUSTIN*

**ALTERATIONS TAILOR**
Ace Custom Tailors
916 West Twelfth Street
512-478-9965
acetailors.com

**BARBER**
The Good Life Barber Shop
201 East Fifth Street #100B
512-320-0010
thegoodlifebarbershop.com

**COBBLER**
Golden Slipper Modern
Boot and Shoe Repair
1903 South First Street
512-442-6334

**DRY CLEANER**
Tip Top Cleaners
1014 North Lamar Boulevard
512-478-1984

**FLORIST**
The Flower Studio
1406 West Sixth Street
512-236-0916 | 888-264-2915
cobyneal.com

**LIQUOR STORE**
Spec's
5775 Airport Boulevard
512-366-8300
specsonline.com

**WATCH REPAIR**
Ben Bridge Jewelers
Barton Creek Square
2901 South Capital of Texas Highway
512-329-9066
benbridge.com

## *BOSTON*

**DRY CLEANER**
Sturgis Cleaners
135 West Broadway
617-269-1014
sturgiscleaners.com

**FLORIST**
Winston Flowers
131 Newbury Street
617-541-1100
winstonflowers.com

**COBBLER**
Ares Shoe Repair
84 Charles Street
617-720-1583

**LIQUOR STORE**
Brix Wine Shop
1284 Washington Street
617-542-2749
brixwineshop.com

**WATCH REPAIR**
Shreve, Crump & Low
39 Newbury Street
1-800-225-7088
shrevecrumpandlow.com

**TAILOR**
Jordan the Tailor
271 Newbury Street, 2nd floor
617-536-2929
jordanthetailor.com

# CHARLOTTE

**ALTERATIONS TAILOR**
Old Dog Clothing
715 Providence Road
704-335-1964

**BARBER**
The CUT Barbershop
121 West Trade Street
704-405-0800
thecutbabershop.com

**COBBLER**
Sam's Shoe Repair
301 South Tryon Street
704-342-3385

**DRY CLEANER**
Sunrise Cleaners
The Shops at Founders Hall in the
Bank of America Corporate Center
100 North Tryon Street, No. 299
704-373-0156

**FLORIST**
Elizabeth House Flowers
1431 South Boulevard
704-342-3920
elizabethhouseflowers.com

**LIQUOR STORE**
Mecklenburg ABC Liquor Store
1609 North Graham Street
704-334-4148
meckabc.com

**WATCH REPAIR**
A. Bonnart Jewelers
4219 Providence Road
704-536-5525
abonnartjewelercharlotte.com

# CHICAGO

**REWEAVING/INVISIBLE MENDING**
Without a Trace
3344 West Bryn Mawr Avenue
800-475-4922

**ALTERATIONS**
Nikiforos Tailoring and Alterations
29 East Madison Street
Suite 1715
312-427-3110
chicagotailor.com

**DRY CLEANING**
Davis Imperial Cleaners
3325 West Bryn Mawr Avenue
773-267-4560
davisimperial.com

**COBBLER**
Brooks Shoe Service
29 East Madison Street
Suite 610
312-372-2504
brooksshoeservice.com

**MEN'S STORE**
Syd Jerome
2 North LaSalle
312-346-0333
sydjerome.com

**BARBER**
Merchant & Rhoades
Gentlemen's Barber
900 North Michigan Avenue Level Six
312-337-2525
merchantandrhoades.com

# CLEVELAND

**ALTERATIONS TAILOR**
Tower City Tailoring
50 Public Square
216-621-1112

**BARBER**
Rockefeller Barber Shop
1450 West Sixth Street
216-781-3999

**COBBLER**
Brass Tack Shoe Repair
401 Euclid Avenue
216-861-1133

**DRY CLEANER**
Kwick-N-Clean
15019 Madison Avenue
216-226-3730
drycleanercleveland.com

**FLORIST**
Plantscaping
1865 East Fortieth Street
216-367-1200
bloomscleveland.com

**WATCH REPAIR**
Dewitt's Diamond and Gold Exchange
530 Euclid Avenue
216-621-6244
dewittsjewelry.com

# DALLAS

### MEN'S STORE
Stanley Korshak
500 Crescent Court
Suite 100
214-871-3600
stanleykorshak.com

### DRY CLEANING
City Cleaners
1324 Elm Street
214-744-0330

### ALTERATIONS
Gustavo's Tailors
1222 Commerce Street
214-748-6163

### REWEAVING/INVISIBLE MENDING
Royal Reweaving Shoppe
5934 Royal Lane
Suite 210
214-265-0200

### COBBLER
Deno's of Highland Park Shoe Service
62 Highland Park Village
214-521-1070
denosshoerepair.com

### BARBER
Culwell & Son Grooming Room
6311 Hillcrest Avenue
214-522-7030
culwell.com

# DENVER

### BARBER
GQ Barber Lounge
1605 Seventeenth Street
303-991-1010
gqbarberlounge.com

### DRY CLEANER
Carousel Cleaners
4040 West Thirty-Eigth Avenue
303-477-1001

### FLORIST
The Perfect Petal
3600 West Thirty-Second Avenue
303-480-0966
theperfectpetal.com

### COBBLER
Westerfield Cobblers
1512 Larimer Street, Suite #43R
303-534-2034
westerfieldcobblers.com

### LIQUOR STORE
Argonaut Wine and Liquor
760 East Colfax Avenue
303-831-7788
argonautliquor.com

### WATCH REPAIR
Myrick's Watch and Clock Repair
910 Sixteenth Street
303-629-0898

### TAILOR
Duman's Custom Tailors
438 East Colfax Avenue
303-832-1701
dumaninc.com

# HOUSTON

### BARBER
Norris of Houston
2033 Post Oak Boulevard
713-627-0000
norrisofhouston.com

### DRY CLEANER
Bells MyOwn Cleaners
2908 Fulton Street
713-227-5461
bellsmyowncleaners.com

### FLORIST
Lexis Florist
6102 Skyline Drive
713-774-8080
lexisflorist.com

### COBBLER
Houston Shoe Hospital
5727 Westheimer Road
713-952-5178
houstonshoehospital.com

### LIQUOR STORE
Spec's
2410 Smith Street
713-526-8787
specsonline.com

### WATCH REPAIR
Watches by Paulin
1337 West Forty-Third Street
713-956-7535
watchesbypaulin.com

### TAILOR
Marcello's Alterations
5015 Westheimer Street
713-623-0338
marcellosalterations.com

## *LOS ANGELES*

### BARBER

**The Shave of Beverly Hills**
230 South Beverly Drive
Beverly Hills
310-858-8281
theshavebeverlyhills.com

### REWEAVING/INVISIBLE MENDING

**Toshi's Invisible Reweaving**
427 North Canon Drive
Suite 201
Beverly Hills
310-274-3468

### MEN'S STORE

**Ron Herman at Fred Segal**
8100 Melrose Avenue
323-651-4129
ronherman.com

### ALTERATIONS

**Wilshire Tailor**
6329 Wilshire Boulevard
323-852-0345

### DRY CLEANING

**Ritz Cleaners**
306 North Larchmont Boulevard
323-464-4860
ritzcleaners.com

### COBBLER

**Arturo's Shoe Fixx**
9643 Santa Monica Boulevard
Beverly Hills
310-278-9585
arturosshoefixx.com

## *MIAMI*

### BARBER

**Churchill's Barbershop**
12 Southeast First Street
305-379-8615
churchillsbarbershop.com

### DRY CLEANING

**Rey's Cleaners**
2619 Ponce de Leon Boulevard
Coral Gables
305-443-0839
reyscleaners.com

### COBBLER

**Gables Shoe Repair**
2619 Ponce de Leon Boulevard
Coral Gables
305-443-0839

### ALTERATIONS

**Daniele di Monte**
443 Espanola Way
Suite 302
Miami Beach
305-674-8629

### REWEAVING/INVISIBLE MENDING

**Royal Cleaners Incorporated**
2100 Northeast 123rd Street
305-893-4311

### MEN'S STORE

**Damiani**
8865 South Dixie Highway
305-661-0002
damianistores.com

## *MINNEAPOLIS–ST. PAUL*

### BARBER

**Baker Barbers**
733 Marquette Avenue, Suite 137
Minneapolis
612-338-1244

### COBBLER

**Anjolens Shoe Repair**
111 Kellogg Boulevard East
St. Paul
651-222-0668

### DRY CLEANER

**Storchak Cleaners**
857 East Seventh Street
St. Paul
651-776-1671

### LIQUOR STORE

**Lowertown Wine & Spirits**
262 East Fourth Street
St. Paul
651-222-3661

### WATCH REPAIR

**Landmark Jewelers**
402 St. Peter Street
St. Paul
651-222-2282
landmarkjewelers.net

## NASHVILLE

### ALTERATIONS TAILOR

**Stitch-It & Co.**
4101 Hillsboro Circle
615-292-3008
stitchitandco.com

### BARBER

**Trim Classic Barber &
Legendary Beauty**
2315 Twelfth Avenue South
615-269-8029
trimnashville.com

### COBBLER

**Golden Boot, Inc.**
2817 West End Avenue, Suite #119
615-320-5223

### DRY CLEANER

**Oakwood Cleaners**
73 White Bridge Road
615-620-6095
oakwoodcleaners.com

### FLORIST

**A Village of Flowers**
1712 Twenty-First Avenue South
615-369-3030
avillageofflowers.net

### LIQUOR STORE

**Midtown Wine & Spirits**
1610 Church Street
615-327-3874
midtownwineandspirits.com

### WATCH REPAIR

**Belle Meade Jewelry and Repair**
4548 Harding Pike
615-269-3288
bellemeadejewelry.com

## NEW ORLEANS

### BARBER

**Aidan Gill for Men**
550 Fulton Street
504-566-4903
aidangillformen.com

### COBBLER

**Edwards Shoe Service**
3704 Magazine Street
504-895-4993

### DRY CLEANER

**Crescent Cleaners**
701 Poydras Street, Suite #131
504-525-5754

### FLORIST

**Tommy's Flowers**
533 Saint Louis Street
504-522-6563

### LIQUOR STORE

**Vieux Carré Wine & Spirits**
422 Chartres Street
504-568-9463

### WATCH REPAIR

**The Watch & Clock Shop**
824 Gravier Street
504-525-3961
clockwatchshop.com

## NEW YORK

### DRY CLEANING

**Madame Paulette**
1255 Second Avenue
212-838-6827
madamepaulette.com

### COBBLER

**Shoe Service Plus**
15 West Fifty-Fifth Street
212-262-4823

### MEN'S STORE

**Bergdorf Goodman**
754 Fifth Avenue
212-753-7300
bergdorfgoodman.com

### REWEAVING/INVISIBLE MENDING

**Alice Zotta**
2 West Forty-Fifth Street
Room 1701
212-840-7657

### ALTERATIONS

**Hong Kong Tailor Jack**
136 Waverly Place, Suite #2
212-675-0818
hongkongtailorjack.com

### BARBER

**John Allan's**
46 East Forty-Sixth Street
212-922-0361
johnallans.com

## PHILADELPHIA

**BARBER**

The Art of Shaving

1528 Walnut Street

215-875-6702

theartofshaving.com

**COBBLER**

Superior Shoe

138 South Fifteenth Street

215-972-9680

**DRY CLEANER**

Carriage Trade Cleaners

1108 Bustleton Pike

Feasterville, Pennsylvania

215-357-3400

**FLORIST**

Flower Child

1900 Market Street, Suite 105

215-988-1212

**LIQUOR STORE**

Fine Wine and Good Spirits

1218 Chestnut Street

215-560-4381

**WATCH REPAIR**

William Schwartz

Distinctive Jewelry

1831 Chestnut Street

215-665-8115

williamschwartzjewelry.com

## PHOENIX

**ALTERATIONS TAILOR**

Brother's Tailors & Clothing Company

13843 North Tatum Blvd., #21

602-494-7736

brotherstailors.com

**BARBER**

Downtown Barber Shop

216 North Central Avenue

602-253-7474

**DRY CLEANER**

Paris Laundry & Dry Cleaning

4130 North Seventh Avenue

602-277-4893

**FLORIST**

Community Florist

550 West McDowell Road

602-266-6648

communityfloristaz.net

**LIQUOR STORE**

Sportsman's Fine Wines and Spirits

3205 East Camelback Road

602-955-9463

sportsmanswine.com

**WATCH REPAIR**

Molina Fine Jewelers

3134 East Camelback Road

602-955-2055

molinafinejewelers.com

## PITTSBURGH

**ALTERATIONS TAILOR**

Alberto & Pasquale Inc.

2025 Murray Avenue

412-421-5515

**BARBER**

Puccini Hair Design

237 Atwood Street

412-621-2087

**COBBLER**

Ullrich Shoe Repair

545 Liberty Avenue

412-391-6338

ullrichshoerepair.com

**DRY CLEANER**

Galardi's 30 Minute Cleaners

119 Forbes Avenue

412-471-7968

**FLORIST**

Hepatica Florist

1119 South Braddock Avenue

412-241-3900

hepaticapgh.com

**LIQUOR STORE**

Oxford Centre Wines & Spirits

One Oxford Centre

320 Smithfield Street

412-565-7689

**WATCH REPAIR**

Henne Jewelers

5501 Walnut Street

412-682-0226

hennejewelers.com

# PORTLAND, OREGON

### ALTERATIONS TAILOR
**Kash Ross Creations**
740 Southwest
Washington Street
503-222-5552
kashross.com

### BARBER
**Hair M**
101 Southwest Main Street
503-517-0570
hairmgrooming.com

### COBBLER
**Shoes on the Run Shoe Repair**
803 Southwest Morrison Street
503-274-2986
shoesontherunrepair.com

### DRY CLEANER
**Five Star Cleaners**
2305 Southwest Sixth Avenue
503-222-7480
pdxfivestarcleaners.com

### FLORIST
**Sammy's Flowers**
2280 Northwest Glisan Street
503-222-9759
sammysflowers.com

### LIQUOR STORE
**Pearl Specialty Market & Spirits**
900 Northwest Lovejoy Street, No. 140
503-477-8604
pearlspecialty.com

### WATCH REPAIR
**Alex and Co. Jewelers Watchworks**
711 Southwest Tenth Avenue
503-223-1368
watchworkspdx.com

# ST. LOUIS

### ALTERATIONS TAILOR
**Daniel Morgan, Tailor**
2701 South Jefferson Avenue
314-664-6366

### BARBER
**Blades on Washington**
1123 Washington Avenue
314-335-7030
bladesonwashington.com

### COBBLER
**Busy Bee Alterations and Shoe**
7921 Forsyth Boulevard
314-725-1016

### FLORIST
**Botanicals Design Studio**
3014 South Grand Boulevard
314-772-7674
botanicalsdesignstudio.com

### LIQUOR STORE
**Randall's**
1910 South Jefferson Avenue
314-865-0199
shoprandalls.com

### WATCH REPAIR
**Kessler Mroz Jewelry**
777 Olive Street, Suite #101
314-621-0822
kesslermrozjewelry.com

# SAN DIEGO

### ALTERATIONS TAILOR
**Joseph's Custom Tailoring**
555 West B Street
619-232-1753
josephscustommenswear.com

### BARBER
**The Barber Shop
at the Westgate Hotel**
1055 Second Avenue
619-234-1951

### COBBLER
**American Shoe Repair**
905 East Street
619-233-8776
americanshoerepairsd.com

### DRY CLEANER
**Alpine Cleaners**
1010 Second Avenue, No. 140A
619-338-0858

### FLORIST
**Fifth Avenue Florist**
1130 Sixth Avenue
619-233-5557
sandiegofifthavenueflorist.com

### LIQUOR STORE
**The Wine Bank**
363 Fifth Avenue
619-234-7487
sdwinebank.com

### WATCH REPAIR
**San Diego Jewelers Exchange**
861 Sixth Avenue
619-232-9191
sdjex.com

# SAN FRANCISCO

### ALTERATIONS

**Cable Car Clothiers**
110 Sutter Street, Suite #108
415-397-4740
cablecarclothiers.com

### REWEAVING/INVISIBLE MENDING

**Peninou French Laundry & Cleaners**
3707 Sacramento Street
415-751-7050
peninou.com

### BARBER

**Exchange Barber Shop**
435 Pine Street
415-781-9658

### MEN'S STORE

**Wilkes Bashford**
375 Sutter Street
415-986-4380
wilkesbashford.com

### DRY CLEANING

**Pacific Heights Cleaners**
2437 Fillmore Street
415-567-5999
pacificheightscleaners.com

### COBBLER

**Union Street Shoe Repair**
2032 Union Street
415-929-7481

# SEATTLE

### BARBER

**Fifth Avenue Barbershop**
2000 Fifth Avenue
206-448-9602

### COBBLER

**Busy Shoes Quality Shoe Repair**
701 Fifth Avenue, Suite 208
206-625-1679
mybusyshoes.com

### FLORIST

**Pike Place Flowers**
1501 First Avenue
206-682-9797
pikeplaceflowers.com

### LIQUOR STORE

**Sixth Avenue Wine Seller**
600 Pine Street, Suite #300
206-621-2669

### WATCH REPAIR

**Fox's Gem Shop**
1341 Fifth Avenue
206-623-2528
foxsgemshop.com

# WASHINGTON, D. C.

### BARBER

**IZZY Salon**
2903 M Street North West
202-342-2675
izzydc.com

### COBBLER

**Cobbler's Bench**
1801 I Street North West
202-775-1952
cobblersbenchshoerepair.com

### DRY CLEANER

**Sterling Cleaners**
1331 Connecticut Avenue North West
202-723-9535
drycleaningindc.com

### FLORIST

**Greenworks**
1145 Twenty-Third Street North West
202-223-8021
greenworksflorist.com

### LIQUOR STORE

**Calvert Woodley**
4339 Connecticut Avenue North West
202-966-4400
calvertwoodley.com

### WATCH REPAIR

**Tiny Jewel Box**
1147 Connecticut Avenue North West
202-393-2747
tinyjewelbox.com

# CANADA | LATIN AMERICA

## TORONTO

### BARBER
**Truefitt and Hill**
Brookfield Place
161 Bay Street
416-640-1210
truefittandhill.com

### DRY CLEANER
**Creeds Dry Cleaning**
390 Dupont Avenue
416-923-2500
creeds.com

### FLORIST
**Antique Rose**
123 Queen Street West
416-863-6265
antiquerosetoronto.com

### COBBLER
**Kaner's Handbags & Shoe Repair**
110 Bloor Street West
416-920-9982

### LIQUOR STORE
**LCBO**
10 Scrivener Square
416-922-0403
lcbo.ca

### WATCH REPAIR
**La Maison Birks**
55 Bloor Street West, Unit 152
416-922-2266
maisonbirks.com

### TAILOR
**Robert Jones Menswear**
Royal Bank Plaza
200 Bay Street
416-362-6837
robertjonesmenswear.com

## BUENOS AIRES

### BARBER
**Peluqueria La Epoca**
877 Guayaquil
011-54-11-4903-7799

### COBBLER
**Correa**
750 Mario Bravo
011-54-11-4861-7344
calzadoscorrea.com.ar

### DRY CLEANER
**The Laundry Company**
5537 El Salvador
011-54-11-4777-9146
laundrycompany.com.ar

### FLORIST
**La Mejor Flor**
772 Paraguay
011-54-11-4314-2424
lamejorflor.com

### WINE STORE
**0800 Vino**
Delivery only
011-54-11-4966-2500
0800-vino.com

### WATCH REPAIR
**The Watch Gallery**
1910 Alvear
011-54-11-4804-8968
watch-gallery.com

## CARACAS

### ALTERATIONS TAILOR
**Giovan Carlo**
Avenida Andrés Bello
Building San Bosco los Palos Grandes
011-58-212-635-4144
giovancarlo.com

### BARBER
**Only for Men Barbaría**
San Ignacio Mall, Level Blandin
Chacao
011-58-212-263-5885
onlyformen.com.ve

### COBBLER
**La Estacion del Cuero**
Altamira Metro Station, Store Number 7
011-58-212-473-0712

### DRY CLEANER
**Quick-Press**
Av Ppal de Macaracuay Centro Comercial
Macaracuay Plaza Nivel Mirador
011-58-212-258-0457
quickpress.com.ve

### FLORIST
**Floristeria Katy**
Avenida Luis Roche
011-58-212-261-4592

### LIQUOR STORE
**Comercial Galipan**
Avenida Luis Roche, Altamira
011-58-212-262-1583

### WATCH REPAIR
**Tecnico Relojero**
Avenida Merida
011-58-212-473-0712

# EUROPE

## *RIO DE JANEIRO*

### BARBER
Barber Shop
116  Rua Lauro Müller
011-55-21-2541-1484

### DRY CLEANER
5 á Sec
6 Rua Jangadeiros
011-55-21-2287-5555

### FLORIST
Girassol Flores
80 Rua Gilberto Cardoso
Cobal do Leblon
011-55-21-2294-4206
girassolflores.com.br

### LIQUOR STORE
Lidador
120 Rua Vinicius de Morais
011-55-21-2227-0593
lidador.com.br

### WATCH REPAIR
H. Stern
490 Rua Visconde de Pirajá
011-55-800-022-7442
hstern.com.br

### TAILOR
Casa Alberto Gentleman
300 Rua Visconde de Pirajá
011-55-21-2287-7840
albertogentleman.com

## *BERLIN*

### BARBER
Shan Rahimkhan
36 Markgrafenstrasse
011-49-30-2067890
shanrahimkhan.de

### DRY CLEANER
Bestform Textilpflege
46 Luisenstrasse
011-49-30-7061694
www.mchemd.de

### FLORIST
Marsano Blumen Berlin
75 Charlottenstrasse
011-49-30-2061473
marsano-berlin.de

### COBBLER
Jacob Böhme
5 Neue Jakobstrasse
011-49-30-2791603
jacob-bohme.de

### LIQUOR STORE
Planet Wein
30 Mohrenstrasse
011-49-30-20454118
planet-weinhandel.de

### WATCH REPAIR
Bucherer
176–179 Friedrichstrasse
011-49-30-2041049
bucherer.com

### TAILOR
Ayhan Yakici
142 Friedrichstrasse
011-49-30-20452081

## *BRUSSELS*

### ALTERATIONS TAILOR
Maison Degand
415 Avenue Louise
011-32-2-649-0073
degand.be

### COBBLER
Mister Minit
38 Galerie du 25 Août
011-32-2-219-9796
misterminit.eu

### DRY CLEANER
Pressing No. 1
58 Rue Antoine Dansaert
011-32-2-512-8622

### FLORIST
Bloemen Jettie
138 Lakensestraat
011-32-2-219-4070
jettie.be

### LIQUOR STORE
Nicolas Sablon
41 Rue Joseph Stevens
011-32-2-511-0035
nicolas.com

### WATCH REPAIR
Gilson Jewellers in the Hilton
38 Boulevard de Waterloo
011-32-2-512-8699
gilsononline.be

## FLORENCE

**ALTERATIONS TAILOR**
Sartoria Marinaro di Mario Sciales
Via de' Tornabuoni 7
011-39-055-21-5854
sartoriamarinaro.com

**BARBER**
International Studio Hair
50123 Via Panicale
011-39-055-29-3393
internationalstudio.com

**COBBLER**
Clinica della Scarpa
Borgo la Croce 14
011-39-055-24-5592

**DRY CLEANER**
Lavasecco Donatello
Piazzale Donatello 33
011-39-055-24-3650

**LIQUOR STORE**
Enoteca Pontevecchio
Corso dei Tintori 21
011-39-055-246-6848
enotecapontevecchio.com

**WATCH REPAIR**
Locman
Via de' Tornabuoni 7 6/r
011-39-055-21-1605
locman.it

## ROME

**BARBER**
Sergio Valente
107 Via del Babuino
011-39-06-6790-637
sergiovalente.it

**COBBLER**
Gatto
34 Via Salandra
011-39-06-6477-0050

**DRY CLEANER**
Bolle Blu 2
59 Via Palestro
011-39-06-446-5804

**FLORIST**
Ciaffoni Floral Design
80/82 Via Flavia
011-39-06-4844-58
ciaffoni.eu

**LIQUOR STORE**
Trimani
20 Via Goito
011-39-06-4469-661
trimani.com

**WATCH REPAIR**
Hausmann & Co.
406 Via del Corso
011-39-06-6871-501
hausmann-co.com/en

## VIENNA

**ALTERATIONS TAILOR**
Schneider u Maurer OEG
5/7 Kärntnerstrasse
011-43-1-513-9931

**BARBER**
Strassl Exklusiv
Ringstrassen-Galerien
Kärntner Ring
011-43-1-512-2344
strassl.at

**COBBLER**
Petkov
5 Mahlerstrasse
011-43-1-513-6480
petkov.at/footwear

**DRY CLEANER**
Putzerei Kaiser Rudolf
9 Krugerstrasse
011-43-1-512-4356

**FLORIST**
Saedtler
13 Opernring
011-43-1-587-4219
saedtler.at

**LIQUOR STORE**
SPAR Gourmet
2 Kärntner Ring
011-43-1-504-6382
spar.at

**WATCH REPAIR**
Juwelier Wagner
32 Kärntnerstrasse
011-43-1-512-0512
juwelier-wagner.at/en/

# ASIA

## ZURICH

### BARBER
**The Barber Shop**
23 Alfred-Escherstrasse
011-41-43-317-1131
thebarber.ch

### COBBLER
**Fritz Huwyler and Co.**
42 Stadelhoferstrasse
011-41-44-251-4695
huwyler.com

### DRY CLEANER
**Terlinden Textilpflege**
58 Asylstrasse
011-41-44-251-2569
terlinden.ch

### FLORIST
**Marsano**
28 Bahnhofstrasse
Paradeplatz
011-41-44-211-2002
marsano.ch

### LIQUOR STORE
**Glen Fahrn**
5 Oberdorfstrasse
011-41-44-520-09-87
glenfahrn.com

### WATCH REPAIR
**Bucherer**
50 Bahnhofstrasse
011-41-44-211-2635
bucherer.com

## BANGKOK

### ALTERATIONS TAILOR
**Premier Tailor**
O.P. Place Shopping Centre
30/1 Soi Charoenkrung 38, New Road
Suite 19, 2nd Floor
011-66-2-630-6396
premiertailorbangkok.com

### BARBER
**Toni & Guy**
989 Siam Discovery, Rama 1 Road
011-66-2-658-0128-9
toniandguy.co.th

### COBBLER
**Momoko**
J Avenue Mall, Thonglor Soi 15
011-66-2-714-9730
momokosite.com

### DRY CLEANER
**Dry Cleaning Service at the Mandarin Oriental Hotel**
48 Oriental Avenue Alley
011-66-2-659-9000
mandarinoriental.com/bangkok

### FLORIST
**Uraiwan Florist**
1522 New Road
011-66-2-235-2432

### LIQUOR STORE
**Wine Connection**
1 Convent Road
011-66-2-234-0388
wineconnection.co.th

### WATCH REPAIR
**Pendulum**
999 Ploenchit Road
011-66-2-656-1116-7
pendulum.co.th

## BEIJING

### BARBER
**Jin Ban Cun**
64 Di'anmen Dongdajie
Dongcheng
011-86-10-8401-6572

### COBBLER
**Sunshine Family Shoes**
Fuhua Mansion, B1
8 Chaoyangmen Nandajie
Dongcheng
011-86-10-6554-1994

### DRY CLEANER
**Fornet**
Jianwai SOHO, Building 8, 825
39 Dongsanhuan Zhonglu
Chaoyang
011-86-10-5869-0158
011-86-10-6651-6675
fornet.com.cn

### FLORIST
**Annie Flower Shop**
7 Litang Road, #2-9, Changping
011-86-10-8213-8780
chinaflower.com.cn

### TAILOR
**Jiajia Premium Alterations**
54 Lainfeng Hutong
Dongcheng
011-86-10-8403-4942

### WATCH REPAIR
**SMH Watch Service Center Co.**
1609 Scitech Plaza
22 Jianguomenwai Dajie
Chaoyang
011-86-10-6526-5806
smh.sh.cn

## DELHI

### ALTERATIONS TAILOR
Grover Tailors
47A, Khan Market
011-91-98-1002-6788
grovertailors.com

### BARBER
Silhouette Beauty Salon
at the Oberoi Hotel
Dr. Zakir Hussain Marg
011-91-11-2430-4352
oberoihotels.com

### COBBLER
John Bros.
216 Competent House,
F Block, Connaught Place, Middle Circle
011-91-98-1825-3723
johnbrothers.co.in

### DRY CLEANER
Mercury Dry Cleaners
20, Khan Market
011-91-11-2469-1352

### LIQUOR STORE
High Times
DLF Place mall, Saket, #154
ground floor
011-91-11-4140-8268

### WATCH REPAIR
Johnson Watch Co.
C-16, Connaught Place
011-91-11-4151-3121
johnsonwatch.com

## DUBAI

### ALTERATIONS TAILOR
Royal Fashion
The Dubai Mall, Lower Ground
Burj Khalifa
011-971-4-339-8484
royalfashion.biz

### BARBER
Amaya Men's Salon
Lamcy Plaza, Third Floor
Oud Metha
011-971-4-335-3282
amaya.ae

### COBBLER
Al Fareed Shoes
Mualla Road, Bur Dubai
011-971-4-359-2862

### DRY CLEANER
Butlers Dry Cleaning
and Laundry Services
The Dubai Mall, Lower Ground
Burj Khalifa
011-971-4-339-9639

### FLORIST
Covent Garden Market
The Walk at JBR
Jumeirah Beach Residence
011-971-4-317-6547

### WATCH REPAIR
Abdul Majid Mehrab Watches
Trading and Repairing
Sabkha Road, Al Futtaim Building
Shop No. 14, Ground Floor
011-971-4-228-4018

## ISTANBUL

### ALTERATIONS TAILOR
Taji Clothing
18/A Tesvikiye Caddesi, Nisantası
011-90-212-296-5073
taji.com.tr

### BARBER
Bahçecik Kuaför
in the Ritz-Carlton
15 Askerocagi Caddesi, Sisli
011-90-212-244-5954
bahcecik.com.tr/en

### COBBLER
Levent Lostra
62 Valikonaği Caddesi, Nisantası
011-90-212-219-0551

### DRY CLEANER
Dry Center
in the Cevahir Mall
22 Büyükdere Caddesi, Sisli
011-90-212-380-0566
drycenter.com

### FLORIST
Art Garden
52 Tepecik Yolu
2 Buket Apt., Etiler
011-90-212-352-7700

### LIQUOR STORE
Kav Sarap Butiği
12 Atiye Sokak, Tesvikiye
011-90-212-234-9120
kavbutik.com

### WATCH REPAIR
Konyali Alsa Saatçilik
38 Hamidiye Caddesi, Sirkeci
011-90-212-528-4487

# AUSTRALIA

## MUMBAI

### ALTERATIONS TAILOR
Sheetal
Sheetal Estate, Grant Road
011-91-22-2385-6565
sheetalindia.com

### BARBER
The Barber Shop
Trident Hotel, Nariman Point
011-91-22-6632-6543
tridenthotels.com

### COBBLER
Reboot
Plot No. 325, Garage No. 3, Siffin Apartment
B.R. Ambedkar Road, Bandra West
011-91-98-6743-5528
rebootshoelaundry.com

### DRY CLEANER
Pressto
Shop No. 16 A, Ground Floor
150 Colaba Road, Shahid Bhagat Singh Road
011-91-22-2215-1442
presstoindia.com

### FLORIST
Florista
Phoenix Mills, Ground Floor
Senapati Bapat Marg
Lower Parel
011-91-22-4344-9000
florista.in

### LIQUOR STORE
Patel Wines
GD Somani Road, Cuffe Parade
011-91-22-2218-2233
patelwine.in

### WATCH REPAIR
DiA
The Heritage Wing,
The Taj Mahal Palace & Tower Hotel
Apollo Bunder
011-91-22-2204-4400
diaprecious.com

## SHANGHAI

### BARBER
Beijing Hair Culture
Hilton Shanhai Hotel, Fourth Floor
250 Huashan Road
011-86-21-6249-7228
beijing.com.hk

### COBBLER
The Wang Hand Craft
11 Xianxia Lu
011-86-21-6229-3916

### DRY CLEANER
ClotheSpa
Pickup and delivery only
011-86-39-1812-2844
spawashchina.com

### FLORIST
Jason & Eva Flower Shop
246 Fuxing Xi Lu, near WuKang Lu
011-86-21-5466-8657

### LIQUOR STORE
Just Grapes
462 Dagu Lu
011-86-21-3311-3205
justgrapes.cn

### WATCH REPAIR
Heng Da Li Watches and Clocks
262 Nanjing Road East
011-86-21-6323-5678

## SYDNEY

### BARBER
David Jones Men's Hair Salon
65–77 Market Street
011-61-2-9266-5544
davidjones.com.au

### COBBLER
Coombs Shoe Repairs
Shop 21, Strand Arcade
011-61-2-9231-1784
coombsshoerepairs.com.au

### DRY CLEANER
20-20 of Mosman Dry Cleaners
173 AvenueRoad, Mosman
011-61-2-9969-2020
2020mosman.com

### FLORIST
Deluca's Florist
500 Oxford Street, Bondi Junction
011-61-2-9386-9796
delucasflorist.com.au

### LIQUOR STORE
Kemenys
137–147 Bondi Road, Bondi
011-61-13-881
kemenys.com.au

### TAILOR
LookSmart Alterations
36 George Street
Level 2, Shop N
011-61-2-9238-9335
looksmartalterations.com.au

### WATCH REPAIR
Antique & Modern Watch Repairs
2/2 Bridge Street, Shop 2
011-61-2-9247-5119

# INDEX

## PHOTOGRAPH AND ILLUSTRATION CREDITS.

**Page 6:** Nigel Cox; **page 8:** Alan Clarke; **page 10:** Carlos Serrao; **page 12:** conference room: Patrick Leger; Broderick: Photofest; **page 13:** Joe McKendry; **page 14:** briefcase: Studio D; illustrations: Joe McKendry; **page 15:** Bale: Lions Gate/Neal Peters Collection; illustrations: Joe McKendry; **page 16:** table setting: Joe McKendry; Wall Street: Twentieth Century Fox/Everett Collection; Office Space: Twentieth Century Fox/Neal Peters Collection; The Godfather: Paramount/Lester Glasner Collection/Neal Peters; Sweet Smell of Success: Everett Collection; **page 18:** Carlos Serrao; **page 20:** illustration: Joe McKendry; 40s: Time & Life Pictures/Getty Images; 50s: Alfred Gescheidt/Getty Images; 60s: Stephen Swintek/Getty Images; 70s: Tim Graham/Getty Images; 80s: Advertising Archives/Everett Collection; 90s: Ross Anania/Getty Images; 00s: Vittorio Zunino Celotto/Getty Images; **page 21:** Joe McKendry; **page 22:** Joe McKendry; **page 23:** Lewis: Everett Collection; **page 24:** Everett Collection/Shutterstock; illustrations: Matt Huynh; **page 25:** Clooney and Farmiga: Dreamworks/Everett Collection; illustration: Matt Huynh; **page 26:** Capri: Frederico Scotto/Getty Images; Ixtapa: Jerry Driendl/Getty Images; Buenos Aires: Christopher Groenhaut/Getty Images; Queenstown: Davis McCardle/Getty Images; **page 27:** Joe McKendry; **page 28:** illustrations: Joe McKendry; beach bag: Whitney Tressel; **page 29:** beach: Jameson Simpson; woman: Michael Dweck; shorts: Patrick Leger; **page 30:** tent: Patrick Leger; **page 31:** Whitney Tressel; **page 32:** Barnaby Roper; **page 34:** illustrations: Joe McKendry; Biel and Diddy: Associated Press; **page 35:** Onassis: Central Press/Getty Images; Hefner: Playboy Archive/Corbis; Flynn: George Hurrell/John Kobal Foundation/Getty Images; Casanova: Granger Collection; Rubirosa: Bettman/Corbis; **page 36:** Bernardini: Keystone/Getty Images; Andress: UA/Neal Peters; Welch: Twentieth Century Fox/Neal Peters; Fawcett: Bruce McBroom/MPTV; Derek: Orion/Neal Peters; Cates: Universal/Neal Peters; Anderson: Everett Collection; massage: Everett Collection; **page 37:** illustrations: Joe McKendry; Eleanor: Hulton Archive/Getty Images; Elizabeth: Bettman/Corbis; Catherine: The Art Archive/Corbis; West: Hulton Archive/Getty Images; Bancroft: Sunset Boulevard/Corbis; Sarandon: Steve Granitz/Getty Images; Moore: Jason LaVeris/Getty Images; Aquitane: Anthony Frederick Augustus Sandys/Getty Images; Antoinette: Martin II Mytens/Getty Images; Bacall: John Kobal Foundation/Getty Images; Onassis: Hulton Archive/Getty Images; Bruni: Anwar Hussein Archive/ROTA/Getty Images; **page 38:** Patrick Leger; **page 39:** Beckinsale: Carlos Alvarez/Getty Images; teddy: Creative Crop/Getty Images; candy: Joseph Clark/Getty Images; **page 40:** illustration: Patrick Leger; bag: Deb Wenof; dance: NBCU Photo Bank via Getty Images; **page 41:** Hama: Sunset Boulevard/Corbis; Nordegren: STLA/Fame Pictures; Vodianova: Stefania D'Alessandro/Getty Images; Bündchen: Jim Spellman/Getty Images; Bardot: Hulton Archive/Getty Images; illustration: Matt Huynh; **page 42:** Lendon Flanagan; **page 44:** Joe McKendry; **page 45:** Redford: Everett Collection; illustrations: Joe McKendry; **page 46:** dopp kit: Jeffrey Westbrook/Studio D; Aristotle: Imagno/Getty Images; Descartes: Leibniz: The Granger Collection;

**page 47:** illustrations: Joe McKendry; Voltaire: Kean Collection/Getty Images; Thoreau: Bettmann/Corbis; Nietzsche: Hulton Archive/Getty Images; Sartre: Keystone-France/Eyedea; Derrida: Andersen ULF/Gamma/Eyedea; Simpson: Fox/Neal Peters Collection; **page 48:** illustrations: Joe McKendry; glasses: D. Hurst/Alamy; **page 49:** Joe McKendry; **page 50:** Esquire: Studio D; Selleck: Universal TV/Neal Peters Collection; Baldwin: Orion/Neal Peters Collection; Carrell: Universal/Neal Peters Collection; **page 51:** Patrick Leger; **page 52:** food: Patrick Leger; circuit: Kagan MacLeod; **page 53:** illustration: Patrick Leger; wimp: Digital Vision/Getty Images; fists: Don Bailey/Getty Images; briefcase: Brand X Pictures/Getty Images; trainer: Jun Sato/WireImage; **page 54:** Schwarzenegger: Everett Collection; LaLanne: George Rose/Getty Images; Hulk: Universal TV/Everett Collection; Hercules: Cannon Films/Everett Collection; Bluto: Everett Collection; 1900s: Popperfoto/Getty Images; 1910s: Roger Viollet/Getty Images; 1920s: MLB Photos/Getty Images; 1930s: FPG/Getty Images; 1940s: Vic Stein/Getty Images Sport; **page 55:** illustrations: Patrick Leger; shake: Media blitz images UK/Alamy; milk: Lew Robertson/Getty Images; omelet: Scott Karcich/istockphoto; oatmeal; Dream Pictures/Getty Images; fruits: Jeffrey Coolidge/Getty Images; Gatorade: Ian Dagnall/Alamy; bacon: Rusty Hill/FoodPix/Getty Images; chips: Ilian Food & Drink/Alamy; plate: Nicholas Everleigh/Alamy; 1950s: Gamma Keystone/Getty Images; 1960s: Everett Collection; 1970s: Sven Simon/dpa/Landov; 1980s: Hulton Archive/Getty Images; 1990s: Barry King/WireImage; 2000s: Rocky Widner/NBAE/Getty Images; **page 56:** Hagen: Kirby/Topical Press Agency/Getty Images; Villegas: Greig Cowie/BPI/Corbis; Armstrong: Doug Pensinger/Getty Images; Garin: Roger Viollet/Getty Images; Federer: David Gray/Reuters/Corbis; Renaldo; Elisa Estrada/Getty Images; Pele: Agencia Estrado/AP; Lacoste: Popperfoto/Getty Images; **page 57:** F. Martin Ramin/Studio D; **Page 58:** David Prince; **page 60:** Murphy: Paramount/Everett Collection; **page 61:** illustration: Wesley Merritt; shower: Brian Hagiwara/Getty Images; **page 62:** Science Photo Library/Alamy; **page 63:** illustration: Wesley Merritt; products: Tim Bradbury; Stiller: Everett Collection; Paltrow: James Hamilton/Touchstone Pictures/The Kobal Collection; **page 64:** Bianchi: Danjaq/EON/UA/Kobal Collection; **page 65:** Taylor: Everett Collection; illustration: Patrick Leger; **page 66:** pajamas: Deb Wenof; sleep mask: Deb Wenof; illustration: Wesley Merritt; Gable: Bettman/Corbis; Stewart: Everett Collection; Sellers: Everett Collection; Hamm: AMC/Kobal Collection; Lemmon: Michael Ochs Archives/MoviePix; Murray: Mary Evans/Columbia Pictures/Ronald Grant/Everett Collection; **page 67:** sleeping: Superstock/Corbis; waking: ClassicStock/ Corbis; **page 68:** illustrations: Wesley Merritt; slippers: Deb Wenoff; blankets: Deb Wenof; platform: Shutterworks; sleigh: Elizabeth Whiting and Associates/EWA Stock; four-poster: William Abranowicz/Art + Commerce; futon: Elizabeth Felicella/Beateworks/Corbis; race car: courtesy Walmart; **page 69:** illustrations: Wesley Merritt; nightstand: Deb Wenof; Alan: Billy Farrell/BFAnyc.com; Snyder: Billy Farrell/BFAnyc.com; Spade: Marc Stamas/Stringer/Getty; Blumenthal: Getty; Esquivel: John Sciulli/Stringer/Getty; **page 70:** Joyce Lee; **page 72:**

illustration: Jason Lee; Fitzgerald: Corbis; Faulkner: Eric Shaal/Getty Images; Chandler; Bettman/Corbis; Franklin: Popperfoto/Getty Images; Roosevelt: NBC/Everett Collection; Simpson: 20th Century Fox/Everett Collection; **page 73:** corkscrews: Joe McKendry; bar: Patrick Leger; Danson: NBC/Everett Collection; Turkel: Warner Bros/Everett Collection; Szyslak: Fox/Photofest; **page 74:** Joe McKendry; **page 75:** champagne: David Muir/Getty Images; illustrations: Joe McKendry; **page 76:** dinner: The Granger Collection; Obama: Justin Sullivan/Getty Images; Bündchen: Fotonoticias/WireImage; Brady: Jim McIsaac/Getty Images; Pitt: Jim Spellman/WireImage; Timberlake: Frazer Harrison/Getty Images; Biel: Jeffrey Mayer/ WireImage; Obama: Alex Wong/Getty Images; Gandhi: Dinodia Photo Library; Jolie: Jun Sato/ WireImage; illustrations: Joe McKendry; **page 77:** map: Classic Image/Alamy; illustrations: Joe McKendry; **page 78:** Brando: Warner Bros/Neal Peters Collection; **page 79:** Caligula: Italian School/ Getty Images; Louis XIV: Charles Le Brun/Getty Images; Capote: Robin Platzer/Twin Images/Getty Images; Rubell: Tim Boxer/Getty Images; Belushi: Universal/Neal Peters; Kozlowski: Adam Rountree/ Getty Images; barbecue: Judd Pilossof/Jupiter Images; **page 80:** margarita: Brian Hagiwara/Getty Images; mint julep: Eric Anthony Johnson/Getty Images; whiskey sour: Last Resort/Getty Images; gin rickey: Bill Boch/FoodPix; red wine: beer: Getty Images; **page 81:** illustrations: Joe McKendry; beer: Randal Ford; **page 82:** Jenny Gage and Tom Betterton; **page 84:** illustrations: Matt Huynh; Sullivan and Marciano: Hulton Archive/Getty Images; **page 85:** Nolte: Rick Rowell/ABC/Getty Images; Williams: Jason Meritt/ Getty Images; Brand: Jason Meritt/ Getty Images; Hoffman: Jason Meritt/Getty Images; Goreski: Jamie McCarthy/WireImage; Marcel: Ron Tom/NBCU PhotoBank/Getty Images; Olivier: AF Archive/Alamy; Lurch: ABC Photo Archives/Getty; Gossling: Ben Glass/Warner Bros./Everett Collection; DiCaprio: Frazer Harrison/Getty Images; McConaughey: Eric Charbonneau/ WireImage; shoe: Lisa F. Young/Alamy; **page 86:** Bond: Everett Collection; Grant: Everett Collection; Dujardin: Mark Davis/WireImage; Warhol: Ron Galella/WireImage; illustrations: coat: Devon Baverman; gloves: Devon Baverman; scarf: Devon Baverman; tuxedo: Devon Baverman; illustrations: Sarah Rutherford; Bieber: Steve Granitz/WireImage; **page 87:** space: John Takai/Alamy; Hull: Everett Collection; Pacino: Everett Collection; pocket square: Renewer/Shutterstock; boutonniere: Darrin Wassman/Shutterstock; gloves: Winston Link/Alamy; cane silo: Vvoe/Shutterstock; spats: Dani Simmonds/Shutterstock; top hat: Nikodem Nijaki/Shutterstock; cape: Tatkhagata/ Shutterstock; **page 89:** Allen: United Artists/The Kobal Collection; Martin: Neal Preston/Corbis; Astaire: John Springer Collection/Corbis; Bogart: Everett Collection; Charles: Everett Collection; Brando: Everett Collection; Warhol: Bettman/ Corbis; Martin: Neal Preston/Corbis; illustrations: Joe McKendry; **page 90:** tuxedos: Whitney Tressel; Gabel: Gamma-Keystone/Getty Images; Cooper: Everett Collection; Fonda: New York Daily News/Getty Images; Bogart: Time & Life Pictures/Getty Images; Stewart: Bettman/Corbis; Barrymore: Getty Images; **page 91:** hand: Andrea Keuhn/Getty Images; illustration:

Matt Huynh; **page 92:** illustrations: Joe McKendry; **page 93:** Deb Wenof; illustration: Matt Huynh; **page 94:** Getty Images; **page 95:** illustrations: Matt Huynh; portrait: Collection Martin Parr; **page 96:** illustrations: Matt Huynh; **page 97:** Greeks: courtesy keithpitts.com; Indians: Henri Cartier- Bresson/ Magnum Photos; Jews: Everett Collection; Chinese: Stak Photographer Duo; illustrations: Matt Huynh; Sandler: New Line Cinema/Everett Collection; **page 98:** illustration: Matt Huynh; Carrell: Warner Bros/ Everett Collection; ATM: Comstock; **page 99:** illustrations: Matt Huynh; toast: Courtesy of Everett Collection; **page 100:** Blow Up; DiCaprio: Mary Evans/Dreamworks SKG/Ronald Grant/Everett Collection; measuring pants: Lambert/Getty images; pressing: Genevieve Naylor/ Corbis; stitching: Dan Kitwood/Getty Images; jacket: Moodboard/Alamy; **page 101:** F. Martin Ramin/ Studio D; **page 102:** Kent Larsson; **page 104:** David Turner/Studio D; illustration: Joe McKendry; **page 105:** illustrations: Joe McKendry; jackets: David Turner/Studio D; **pages 105-109:** bottom: Tim Bradbury; **page 108:** Sorrentino: Michael N. Todaro/ Getty Images; Windsor: Hugh Cecil/Getty Images; Guinness: Everett Collection; **page 109:** illustration: Wesley Merritt; **page 110:** tailor: Ashley Gilbertson/VII/ Corbis; illustrations: Wesley Merritt; **page 111:** Wesley Merritt; **page 112:** Windsor: Getty Images; tailor: courtesy of Cesare Attolini; illustration: Wesley Merritt; **page 113:** Roland Descombes; **page 114:** Frederik Lieberath; **page 116:** illustrations: Joe McKendry; **page 117:** illustrations: Joe McKendry; monogram: Siloto/ Alamy; **page 118:** illustrations: Joe McKendry; **page 119:** Brando: Warner Bros/Neal Peters Collection; gray crewneck: istockphoto; **page 120:** illustration: Joe McKendry; **page 121:** tailor: Philip Gendreau/ Corbis; **page 122:** Tim Bradbury; **page 123:** Joe McKendry; **page 124:** Alan Clarke; **page 126:** Courtesy of American Sheep Industry

Association; **page 127:** illustration: Joe McKendry; turtleneck: Williams + Hirakawa/Getty Images; **page 128:** illustrations: Joe McKendry; **page 129:** Dean: Everett Collection; **page 130:** illustration: Joe McKendry; Eriksson: Lake County Museum/ Corbis; Peary: Paul Thompson/Getty Images; Amundsen: Popperfoto/Getty Images; Hillary: AP Photo; North: Pathé Exchange/Neal Peters; **page 131:** Inuit: Anne Ackerman/Anne Menke/Getty Images; **page 133:** muppet: Moritz Winde/Getty Images; Bacharach: Moritz Winde/ Getty Images; illustrations: Joe McKendry; **page 134:** 1908: Hulton Archive/ Getty Images; 2012: Deb Wenof; coats: Devon Baverman; **page 136:** Waits: Joel Brodsky/Corbis; Cohen: Evening Standard/ Getty Images; Cousteau: Kobal Collection; McLaren: Luciano Viti/Getty Images; Sellers: Terry O'Neill/Getty Images; Elkann: Peter Dench/ In Pictures/Corbis; **page 137:** Vidal: Federico Garolla/Redux Pictures; clothing: F. Martin Ramin/Studio D; **page 138:** David Prince; **page 140:** illustration: Jason Lee; hangers: iStock; **page 141:** Richards: ABC/Everett Collection; illustration: Joe McKendry; Faulkner: Alfred Eriss/Time Life Pictures/Getty Images; Monk: William Gottleib/ Redferns/Getty Images; MacArthur: Carl Mydans/ Time Life Pictures/Getty Images; Baker: Bob Willoughny/Referns/Getty Images; Mastroianni: Hulton Archive/Getty Images; Dylan: Jan Persson/ Redferns/Getty Images; McQueen: Alan Band/ Getty Images; Onassis: Santi Visalli Inc/Getty Images; **Page 142:** Cruise: Kobal Collection; Gyllenhaal: Ray Tamarra/Getty Images; Armstrong: Leigh Vogel/ Getty Images; Illustrations: Joe McKendry; **page 143:** cowboy boots: Patrick Leger; socks: Joe McKendry; 3000: John Rogers/Getty Images; Hockney: Michael Childres/Corbis; Bentley: Frank Micelotta/Getty Images; Wolfe: Roger Ressmeyer/Corbis; Talese: Christopher Felver/Corbis; Ferry: Michael Ochs Archives/Getty Images; measurement: George

Cleverly; **page 145:** Joe McKendry; **page 146:** Christopher Griffith; **page 148:** illustrations: Joe McKendry; **page 149:** cobbler: Fred Morley/Getty Images; odyssey: Courtesy John Lobb; **Page 150:** shoe store, Lambert/Getty Images; brannock, refurb: Studio D; illustrations, Joe McKendry; odyssey: Courtesy John Lobb; **page 151:** shoes: David Turner/ Studio D; Bemer: Gunter Glueklich/LAIF/Redux Pictures; Vaingauz: Rachel Ceretto; **page 152:** shoes: Shakirah Tabourn; illustration: Matt Huynh; odyssey: Courtesy John Lobb; **page 153:** odyssey: Courtesy John Lobb; **page 154:** boots: Chris Eckert/ Studio D; illustrations: Joe McKendry; **page 155:** Grant: Everett Collection; illustrations: Joe McKendry; Khrushchev: Lipnitzki/Roger Viollet/ Getty Images; Goldfinger: Photofest; Presley: Driggs Collection/ Getty Images; woman in shoe: Bettman/ Corbis; shoes: David Turner/Studio D; odyssey: Courtesy John Lobb; **page 156:** Christopher Griffith; **page 158:** Delon: Artists International/Neal Peters Collection; Newman: Bettmann/Corbis; Agnelli: Time & Life Pictures/Getty Images; Aldrin: NASA; **page 160:** Adams: Everett Collection; sundial: Gianni Dagli Orti/Corbis; Caesar: Hulton Archive/Getty Images; hour glass: 19th era/Alamy; egg watch: Bettmann/ Corbis; Harrison: the Granger Collection; chronograph: Bettmann/Corbis; **page 161:** McQueen: Eyedea Presse/ GMT clock: Topical Press Agency/Getty Images; Einstein: Doreen Spooner/ Keystone Features/Getty Images; quartz rock: DEA/A. Rizzi/Getty Images; hand: Laurent Hamels/ PhotoAlto/ Corbis; astronaut: Corbis; Walken: Everett Collection; **page 162:** illustrations: Patrick Leger; **page 163:** illustrations: Patrick Leger; rubber bands, id: istockphoto; **page 166:** David Woolley/ Getty Images; **pages 168-169:** Sarah Rutherford

**Back Cover:** Joe McKendry

HEARST BOOKS
New York

An Imprint of Sterling Publishing
1166 Avenue of the Americas
New York, NY 10036

Cover Design by Ben Caruba
Interior Design by Barbara Balch

ISBN 978-1-61837-184-3


Distributed in Canada by Sterling Publishing
c/o Canadian Manda Group, 664 Annette Street
Toronto, Ontario, Canada M6S 2C8
Distributed in the United Kingdom by GMC Distribution Services
Castle Place, 166 High Street, Lewes, East Sussex, England BN7 1XU
Distributed in Australia by Capricorn Link (Australia) Pty. Ltd.
P.O. Box 704, Windsor, NSW 2756, Australia


For information about custom editions, special sales, and premium and corporate purchases,
please contact Sterling Special Sales at 800-805-5489 or specialsales@sterlingpublishing.com.

Manufactured in the United States of America

2 4 6 8 10 9 7 5 3 1

www.sterlingpublishing.com